P9-CUK-780

Date: 11/8/11

947 KOR
Kort, Michael,
A brief history of Russia /

A Brief History
of Russia

A Brief History of Russia

Michael Kort

Boston University

Facts On File

An imprint of Infobase Publishing

A Brief History of Russia

Copyright © 2008 by Michael Kort

Facts On File, Inc.
An imprint of Infobase Publishing
132 West 31st Street
New York NY 10001

Library of Congress Cataloging-in-Publication Data

Kort, Michael, 1944–
    A brief history of Russia / Michael Kort.
        p. cm.—(Brief history)
    Includes bibliographical references and index.
    ISBN-13: 978-0-8160-7112-8
    ISBN-10: 0-8160-7112-8
    1. Russia—History. 2. Soviet Union—History. I. Title.
DK40.K687 2007
947—dc22   2007032723

Facts On File books are available at special discounts when purchased in bulk quantities for businesses, associations, institutions, or sales promotions. Please call our Special Sales Department in New York at (212) 967-8800 or (800) 322-8755.

You can find Facts On File on the World Wide Web at http://www.factsonfile.com

Text design by Joan M. McEvoy
Cover design by Semadar Megged
Maps by Sholto Ainslie

Printed in the United States of America

This book is printed on acid-free paper and contains 30 percent postconsumer recycled content.

For Carol, and our first 40 years together

CONTENTS

LIST OF ILLUSTRATIONS

LIST OF MAPS

ACKNOWLEDGMENTS

I am indebted to Claudia Schaab of Facts On File for convincing me to write this book and then carrying out the multiple tasks associated with being its editor with great skill, patience, and efficiency. My friend and colleague Robert Wexelblatt, as he has done before, read and critiqued large parts of this book and was never too busy to discuss writing issues during lengthy phone conversations at any hour of the day or night. Kathleen Martin kindly critiqued the chapter on Russian literature and culture and offered valuable suggestions and insights that significantly improved it. My wonderful daughters, Eleza and Tamara, now adults, made sure their father "chilled out" a little as he intently worked to meet his deadlines. Finally and foremost, my wife, Carol, read, edited, and critiqued the entire manuscript and then again went over everything and anything connected with it at a moment's notice, regardless of other demands on her time and energy. It has become something of a cliché in acknowledgments such as these, but I really could not have written this book without her input and help.

INTRODUCTION

Russia's history is an epic saga of strength, suffering, and, ultimately, of survival. It is a tumultuous drama acted out on a vast and violent stage millions of square miles in area, where enormous casts of ordinary people were repeatedly conscripted for extraordinary historical scenes that gave credence to the claim that truth is stranger than fiction. It is a litany of extremes: extreme weather, extreme contrasts, extreme twists of fate, extreme changes of fortune, and extreme solutions for extreme problems, all of which imposed cruel sacrifices on a people who even in good times lived with hardship and in bad times endured the intolerable. And like the heavens on the shoulders of Atlas, Russia's history is a huge and heavy burden that weighs down today on a great country as it tries to overcome its past and create a society in which its people can live freely and prosper.

The Physical Setting

The Russian Federation, as Russia is known today, is the largest country in the world. Although considerably downsized from the days of the Russian Empire and the Soviet Union, when the area under czarist and subsequently Soviet control exceeded 8.5 million square miles, Russia still encompasses an area of 6.5 million square miles. That is about one-ninth of the world's total land area, including Antarctica. Extending more than 6,000 miles from west to east, from the Baltic Sea and the center of Europe across all of Asia to the shores of the Pacific Ocean, Russia is at once the largest country on two continents.

Russia is uniquely Eurasian. Two other countries, Turkey and Kazakhstan, have territory in both Europe and Asia. Yet both are culturally Asian and almost entirely Asian by geography, with only a sliver of territory in Europe. By contrast, Russia is a colossus astride both continents. Culturally and ethnically the vast majority of its people are European, but its historic and cultural ties with Asia are significant and enduring. Russia also stretches about 2,000 miles from north to south, from frozen islands in the Arctic Sea to the Caucasus Mountains and the warm shores of the Caspian Sea of southern Europe in the west and to the Altai Mountains and Lake Baikal in the physical heartland of Asia in the east. It therefore is understandable how in the mid-19th century Mikhail Pogodin, a fervent Russian nationalist and the first professor of Russian history at the University of Moscow, allowed himself to be carried away by patriotic enthusiasm when he described his native land:

> Russia! What a marvelous phenomenon on the world scene! Russia—a distance of ten thousand versts [about two-thirds of a mile] in length on a straight line from the virtually central European river, across all of Asia and the Eastern Ocean, down to the remote American lands! [At the time Russia owned Alaska.] A distance of five thousand versts in width from Persia, one of the southern Asiatic states, to the end of the inhabited world—to the North Pole. What state can equal it? Its half? How many can match its twentieth, its fiftieth part? . . . Russia—a state which contains all types of soil, from the warmest to the coldest, from the burning environs of Erivan to icy Lapland; which abounds in all the products required for the needs, comforts, and pleasures in life, in accordance with the present state of development—a whole world, self-sufficient, independent, absolute. (Riasanovsky, 1969: 3)

Most of Russia is situated on the enormous Eurasian plain, the largest such feature on the globe, an expanse that begins at the Atlantic Ocean and does not end until the uplands and mountains of Siberia deep in Asia. Once the bottom of an ancient sea, the plain is broken only by the Ural Mountains, a range of hills running due north/south for more than 1,000 miles that geographers have designated the boundary between Europe and Asia. But in a practical sense these worn, geologically ancient hills are less significant than they appear on a map and have never been a barrier to human or natural forces.

Far more impressive are the snowcapped Caucasus Mountains between the Black and Caspian Seas, which like the Urals divide Europe from Asia. The Russian Empire won control of the Caucasus region during the 19th century after decades of bitter fighting that left a deep mark on the national psyche. The long struggle inspired works by some of Russia's greatest writers, including Aleksandr Pushkin (the narrative poem "Prisoner of the Caucasus"), Mikhail Lermontov (the novel *A Hero of Our Time*), and Leo Tolstoy (the novella *Hadji Murat*). The breakup of the Soviet Union in 1991 left Russia with only the northern part of the Caucasus region, but the struggle to maintain control there grinds on as many Chechens, the same group Tolstoy wrote about more than 100 years ago in *Hadji Murat,* continue their resistance to Russian rule.

Beyond the Urals, the Eurasian plain continues eastward for about 1,000 miles as the West Siberian lowland before the land begins to rise to the Central Siberian Plateau. Farther east are a series of mountain ranges and beyond them the Bering Strait, where Asia finally ends.

The Eurasian plain has four main vegetation zones. In the far north is the tundra, a swampy region where even in summer the subsoil a few feet below the surface is permanently frozen. All that grows here are mosses, lichens, and small, stunted shrubs. Immediately to the south is the largest area of forest in the world. Most of it is an ever-green forest called the *taiga,* which means "thick forest" in Russian. A smaller, southern section, mainly west of the Urals, consists of leafy, or deciduous, forest. South of the forest is a vast prairie called the steppe, the main agricultural zone of Russia and the other countries of the Eurasian plain. The steppe resembles the North American Great Plains, but it gets less rainfall, and the rainfall decreases as one moves from west to east. Finally, in the south is desert, almost all of which is now within the borders of Kazakhstan, Uzbekistan, and Turkmenistan, three of the countries that emerged from the wreckage of the former Soviet Union.

The European part of the Eurasian plain is laced by a magnificent network of rivers that for uncounted centuries before the age of rail-roads served as the region's main highways. It was along these rivers that the East Slavs, the ancestors of today's Russians as well as of their cousins, the Ukrainians and Belarusians, first developed their civili-zation and national life. Russia's first great city, Kiev, the "mother of Russian cities," rose along the banks of the Dnieper River more than 1,200 years ago. The Dnieper, Europe's third-largest river after the Volga and the Danube, rises about 150 miles west of Moscow in a region called the Valdai Hills. It flows south into Belarus and from there into Ukraine, turning east at Kiev before taking a southwest course and end-ing its 1,400-mile journey at the Black Sea.

Many important historical events, both triumphant and tragic, have taken place along the banks of the Dnieper, beginning with the founding of Kiev. The most recent was the disastrous explosion at the Chernobyl nuclear power plant about 60 miles north of Kiev in 1986. Not far to the east is another storied river, the Don, which rises 150 miles south of Moscow and flows for more than 1,200 miles before emptying into the Sea of Azov, an inlet of the Black Sea. Along the banks of the Don in 1380, Moscow's Grand Prince Dmitry (r. 1359–89) defeated a Mongol army, the first time the Russians managed a military victory over the invaders who had conquered them in the 13th cen-

The taiga of Siberia, a forest of spruce, pine, fir, and larch, is the world's largest unbroken forest region, accounting for 19 percent of the world's total forest area. A local poet once called the taiga a "universe without an end," but today that universe is threatened by logging, coal mining, oil and gas development, and increasingly frequent forest fires. (Zastavkin, 2007. Used under license from ShutterStock, Inc.)

tury. In honor of his great victory, Dmitry's countrymen hailed him as Dmitry Donskoi (Dmitry of the Don), even though Russia's struggle for full independence lasted for another 100 years. To non-Russian readers of Russian literature, the Don is best known as the setting of Mikhail Sholokov's epic four-volume novel *The Silent Don,* which chronicles life along the river's banks from 1912 to 1920 during the last years of czarism, the Russian Revolution, and the country's civil war.

East of the Don is the mighty Volga, the longest river in Europe and the waterway Russians call their "dear little mother." The Volga rises northwest of Moscow in the Valdai Hills and then slowly winds its way for almost 2,300 miles to the Caspian Sea. The most important channel in the river network that links the Baltic, Black, and Caspian seas, the Volga has played a central role in Russian history for a millennium. It is not too much of an exaggeration to claim, as a riverboat captain supposedly once did, that "the Volga flows through the heart of every Russian."

The magnificent river certainly flows through Russian literature and art. The poet Nikolai Nekrasov (1821–77), who grew up in the town of Yaroslavl along the Volga, loved the river and sang its praises in his verses. He also expressed deep sympathy for the men, known as the

The Volga River in winter. Except in the far south, Russian rivers freeze over completely for a minimum of two months in the western part of the country to as much as eight months in northern Siberia. Along some parts of the Volga in winter the ice is six feet thick. (Kuzuma, 2007. Used under license from ShutterStock, Inc.)

Volga boatmen, who did the backbreaking work of dragging barges and ships laden with everything from wood to salt up and down the slow-moving river. Their labors, as well as their grim fortitude and common-sense wisdom, were immortalized by realist artist Ilya Repin in his huge (about 4 by 9 feet) painting *Barge Haulers on the Volga,* one of the most recognizable works of Russian art. At no time has the Volga meant more to the Russian people than between August 1942 and February 1943, when on the river's western bank the Soviet army defeated the invading forces of Nazi Germany and dealt them a crippling blow in the titanic Battle of Stalingrad. Sadly, both before and after the Battle of Stalingrad, the Soviet regime abused and mistreated Russia's "dear little mother," building dams that turned much of the river into a series of lakes, all of which have become seriously polluted by industrial and urban waste.

Although the Volga is the largest river in Europe, it is not the largest in Russia. Russia's largest rivers are in Siberia, the vast region, most of it still wilderness, that begins at the Urals and stretches to the Pacific Ocean. Siberia's endless stretches of tundra and *taiga* cover 4.8 million square miles, an area larger than Canada. Most of Siberia's great rivers—the Ob-Irtysh, the Yenisey, the Angara (a tributary of the Yenisey), and the Lena—rise in the Asian heartland and flow north into the Arctic Sea. The Angara's source is Lake Baikal, known to the native people who live near its shores as the "sacred sea" and to many others as the "pearl of Siberia." No lake on earth compares to this liquid treasure. The oldest and deepest lake in the word, fed by 336 rivers, Lake Baikal holds one-fifth of all the fresh water on the planet, as much as all of North America's Great Lakes combined. The clarity and purity of its waters are legendary: A white sheet can be seen clearly at a depth of more than 100 feet.

Today Baikal and its unique ecological system—including an estimated 1,500 plant and animal species found nowhere else—are threatened by pollution from Soviet-era factories, and the struggle to save the sacred sea has engaged not only environmentalists from Russia but concerned people from around the globe. Aside from Lake Baikal, Russia's 200,000 lakes include the two largest in Europe, Lake Ladoga and Lake Onega, both in the northwest part of the country near the Baltic Sea.

Russia's two most important cities are Moscow and St. Petersburg. From its beginnings as a village along the Moscow River, Moscow developed into a major city between the 13th and 15th centuries. It was the core of Muscovy, the principality that during the 15th and 16th centuries broke the Mongol grip on Russia and began the job of uniting all Russians into a single state for the first time. The two most familiar

Lake Baikal is surrounded by lush forests and majestic snowcapped mountains. In 1992 the entire area around the lake was declared a national park. (Tatiana Grozetskaya, 2007. Used under license from ShutterStock, Inc.)

manmade symbols of Russia—the Kremlin, the great stone fortress with its onion-domed churches, and St. Basil's Cathedral, built by Czar Ivan the Terrible to commemorate one of his military victories—stand in the middle of Moscow next to a giant plaza called Red Square. Even when it was displaced by St. Petersburg as Russia's capital for about 200 years, Moscow remained the country's cultural and economic center.

St. Petersburg, built by Peter the Great and Russia's capital from 1712 to 1918, rose as a planned city on the swampy shores of the Neva River where it flows into the Gulf of Finland. It is widely considered one of the most beautiful cities in the world. Known as Leningrad between 1924 and 1991, during World War II the city became a heroic symbol of resistance against aggression when it withstood a German siege that lasted 900 days and cost 800,000 Soviet citizens their lives. The name Leningrad, imposed on the city by the Soviet regime in 1924, was discarded in 1991, amid the collapse of the Soviet Union, by local citizens, who notwithstanding official dictates had always fondly called their city "Peter."

No introduction to the physical setting of Russia's history is complete without a discussion of the weather. Most of Russia has an extreme continental climate, with short summers and long, brutally cold winters. Over the centuries, Russians learned to manage during the winter: living behind double doors and double windows, heating even poor peasant cottages with huge stoves, and venturing outside covered by layers of clothing topped with fur coats and hats.

Many foreigners, whatever their efforts, have been less successful in coping. Thus, in the early 16th century, a German diplomat commented on "the immoderate and excessive inclemency of the atmosphere." The winter was so severe that "water thrown into the air, or saliva spit from the mouth, freezes before it reaches the ground." The diplomat added that the winter before his arrival had been even worse than the one he was experiencing. He was told how "many couriers . . . were found frozen in their carriages" and how men driving livestock, "overpowered by the excessive cold, perished together with the cattle" (Herberstein in Dmytryshyn, 1973: 205). An English diplomat in the 17th century used poetry for his report to his queen, "Loe thus I make and ende: none other news to thee. But that country is too cold, the people beastly bee" (quoted in Riazanovsky, 1969: 3). Foreigners were also amazed at how Russians had adjusted to conditions they found difficult to endure. One British visitor to St. Petersburg in the early 19th century noticed the following: "Cold to the Russians seems to be what heat is to the torpid animal, for Petersburg at this moment presents a prospect of much greater bustle and activity than during the winter months" (Robert Ker Porter in Putnam, 1952: 307).

More recently, English journalist Wright Miller lived in the Soviet Union for 25 years beginning in 1934. It appears even a quarter of a century was not enough time to adjust fully to the Russian winter:

> In the worst weather it is so cold that it seems to burn. You launch yourself out of the double doors into the street and you gasp. You narrow your shrinking nostrils to give your lungs a chance to get acclimatized, but you gasp again and go on gasping. Ears are covered against frostbite, but eyebrows and moustache grow icicles in bunches, a sweat runs from under your fur cap and freezes on your temples. Another moment, surely, and the whole nostril will freeze over; in a panic you warm your nose with your glove, but the nostrils do not freeze, and you go on warming your nose and string cheeks with your glove, and you go on gasping. Half an hour's walk gives you the exercise of an ordinary afternoon. . . . it is impossible, you think, to bear it for long, but you do. (Miller, 1961: 18)

A typical winter scene in the European part of Russia (Sobolev Andrey Alexandrovich, 2007. Used under license from ShutterStock, Inc.)

Russia's winters merit discussion because they are historically important. Aside from foreign diplomats and visitors, foreign invaders at key points have been unable to cope with the unrelenting, bitter cold. More than one foreign army has felt its numbing bite. In particular, Russians often say that their "General Winter" (along with "General Distance" and "General Mud") played a crucial role in defeating both Napoléon in 1812 and Hitler's murderous Nazi legions between 1941 and 1945.

The People

Approximately 141 million people live in Russia, about 80 percent of whom are ethnic Russians. That percentage is a dramatic change from the Russian Empire and the Soviet Union in their respective final decades, when the Russian percentage of the population was only slightly above 50 percent. That said, Russia's population has been falling since the early 1990s. The main reasons for that decline are a low birth rate and a high death rate fueled by social maladies such as rampant alcoholism and drug use and serious diseases that have spread in the wake of a broken healthcare system. While Russia has been shorn of most of its non-Russian population, there are still dozens of minority groups scattered across the vast land. Their presence is most graphically reflected by the Russian Federation's 21 official minority "republics," although in fact in several of them Russians are a majority; overall, ethnic Russians constitute almost half the population of the minority republics. Most Russians live in urban areas, the biggest of which is Moscow, home to about 8.2 million people. Russia's second-largest city is St. Petersburg, where 4.6 million people live. Next in size, and Russia's largest city in Asia, is Novosibirsk in western Siberia where the Trans-Siberian Railroad crosses the Ob River.

The Trans-Siberian is more than a railroad; it is a monument to Russian determination and ingenuity. Built between 1891 and 1915 under extraordinarily difficult conditions, with most of the work completed during the 1890s, it extends for more than 5,500 miles from Moscow to Russia's Siberian port city of Vladivostok, on the shores of the Pacific Ocean. The Trans-Siberian is considered one of the great engineering achievements of the late 19th century. During the 1970s and 1980s, the Soviet regime built a second line from central Siberia to the Pacific coast at a point about 600 miles north of Vladivostok. The extremely expensive project, known as the Baikal-Amur Mainline (BAM), is held together by more than 3,000 bridges and a series of tunnels, the largest of which, almost 10 miles long, was not completed until 2003.

The Historical Framework

Historical divisions are by definition arbitrary, but it is convenient to divide Russian history into five major eras: Kievan Russia, Muscovite Russia, Imperial Russia, Soviet Russia, and post-Soviet Russia. The Kievan era dates from the ninth century, when the first Russian state centered at Kiev emerged under a dynasty named for its semilegendary founder, Rurik, and lasted until the Mongol conquest of the 13th century. The Muscovite era dates from the Mongol conquest and its aftermath, a period when Russians were subject to foreign rule for more than two centuries. It takes its name from the principality of Muscovy (or Moscow), which during the 14th century emerged as the most powerful of the Russian principalities. More to the point, Muscovy eventually defeated the Mongols and restored Russian independence. The Muscovite period extended through the expiration of the Rurikid dynasty and the establishment of the Romanov dynasty in the 17th century.

The reign of Peter the Great marks the beginning of Russia's imperial era. It lasted from the 1690s until March 1917, when the Romanov dynasty was overthrown and the monarchy itself abolished. After eight months of disorder, during which time Russian moderates struggled to establish a democratic government, a small group of militant Marxist socialists called the Bolsheviks seized power and, after a three-year civil war, consolidated their dictatorial rule over most of the defunct Russian Empire. The Bolsheviks wanted to turn Russia into a socialist society. The state they founded, the Union of Soviet Socialist Republics (or Soviet Union), and the socialist society they built lasted until 1991. This was the Soviet era of Russia's history. Finally, after the collapse of the Soviet Union, the current era began in 1992. For lack of a better term, and because the renamed Russian Federation still operates very much under the shadow of the former regime, it generally is called the post-Soviet era.

This volume traces the wrenching changes that distinguish these five historical eras from each other and the continuities that bind them together and constitute the core of Russia's identity and fate. It is a history and fate that only the strong could survive.

1

BEFORE THE RUSSIANS, KIEVAN RUS, AND MUSCOVITE RUSSIA (TENTH CENTURY B.C.E.– 1462 C.E.)

The Eurasian plain between the Baltic and the Black seas, the approximate area where the East Slavs established their first state, offers its inhabitants many things: natural resources, room for expansion, easy travel along river routes, and good sites on which to found cities and towns. It does not offer them security. The region is not shielded by natural barriers and stands as an open invitation to potential invaders on the east or west to take this bountiful land for themselves. Once they have done so, however, these invaders must remain strong and vigilant to defend their homes against the next intruders who are sure to arrive.

Long before any of the groups involved had the ability or interest to record it, a pattern of migration, invasion, melding of populations, and displacement was established by large and small waves of humanity on the move. The pattern was already old in ancient times—almost a part of the landscape—well before the East Slavs arrived. Indeed, the competition for control over the eastern European part of the Eurasian plain, especially the southern steppe region, would continue until relatively recent times, long after the East Slavs had evolved into today's Russians, Ukrainians, and Belarusians.

The Russian Plain before the Russians

The territory that eventually became the Russian section of the Eurasian plain is divided roughly into the forest area in the north and the steppe in the south. The earliest known people of the northern forest region spoke Finnish languages. Over several centuries beginning around the sixth century B.C. they were gradually pushed farther north or assimilated by East Slavic tribes. That story was not recorded by eyewitnesses and historically is overshadowed by more dramatic events on the southern steppe.

The earliest identifiable group of people to control the steppe were the Cimmerians, who probably came to the rich, open lands north of the Black Sea from the Balkans. Little is known about them, other than what the Greek historian Herodotus (c. 484–420 B.C.) reported about their language, which indicates their geographic origins, and their ability to make iron tools. It is possible that the Cimmerians were only the ruling class in the region and that most of their subjects were other peoples who had lived there before they arrived and remained after they departed. Such a pattern probably applies to several of the groups that succeeded them. In any event, the Cimmerians asserted their control on the steppe in about 1000 B.C.E. and extended their power eastward to the Caucasus Mountains. Their stay, however, had little impact. If they left behind a legacy, it is in the name of the Black Sea's Crimean Peninsula—although even that is uncertain.

The Cimmerians were defeated and displaced around 700 B.C.E. by invaders from the east called Scythians. The new rulers came from central Asia and spoke an Iranian language, and their influence and control extended far to the east into Siberia.

The Scythians

The Scythians were nomads and, above all, highly skilled mounted warriors. Although no one knows who first domesticated the horse, the Scythians are a possible candidate for that historic achievement. They fought on horseback with bows and arrows and light swords. They used saddles and bitted bridles, which they decorated elaborately and with great care. As warriors they were famous, and feared, not only because of their martial skills but because of their gruesome custom of cutting off the heads of their defeated enemies and turning the skulls into leather-lined drinking cups, vessels they decorated with gold and proudly displayed to their guests.

The Scythians were only one of the many nomad peoples of the steppe. They did not have writing—we know about their language only from the Greeks who traded with them—and so left behind no written records of their deeds. Still, long after their disappearance the Scythians have commanded a level of interest from archaeologists and historians not extended to other steppe horsemen. This is largely because of the unusual artistic flair they expressed in magnificent works of gold.

Until relatively recently historians believed that the Scythians produced their finely crafted gold jewelry under the influence of the Greeks, who by the sixth century B.C.E. had established colonies along the Black Sea coast. Recent excavations, including those of a 2,700-year-old tomb near the Yenisey River in Siberia, just north of today's Russia-Mongolia border, tell another story. The Siberian tomb reveals that long before they came in contact with Greeks, Scythians were skilled goldsmiths with their own artistic style based on animal motifs. They created exquisite jewelry and ornaments, which they wore or used to decorate their tools, weapons, saddles, and other possessions. In later centuries, as a result of contact and trade with the cities along the Black Sea, the Greek influence became increasingly noticeable, but the original style—with its images of stags, horses, reindeer, ibex, wolves, birds of prey, and other animals—is glittering testimony to an artistic sensibility the charismatic Scythians developed on their own as they wandered across the steppe.

Some Russians have identified with the Scythians because of the historical role they once inadvertently played as a protector of the West, a role the Russians also played, equally unwittingly and unwillingly, many centuries later. The Scythians rendered that service in the late sixth century B.C.E., when they provoked the Persian king Darius the Great (c. 550–486 B.C.E.) into invading their territory. Persia was the superpower of its day, a threat to all its neighbors, including the Greek city-states just to its west. Our knowledge of what happened comes from Herodotus. Darius, the bulk of whose army was on foot, futilely pursued his mobile foe into the endless steppe north of the Black Sea. The elusive Scythians retreated, avoiding a major battle, yet frustrating the Persian king and harassing his plodding army with hit-and-run attacks and, adding insult to injury, with verbal taunts. In the end, his army unbeaten but bloodied and demoralized, Darius retreated, having accomplished nothing.

The Scythians remained masters of the steppe, but there were collateral beneficiaries of their actions to the southwest on the rocky shores of the Aegean and Mediterranean seas. While Darius was distracted chasing the Scythians, trying to catch the wind on the limitless steppe, Athens and its fellow city-states gained precious time to gather their strength for their historic confrontation with the Persians, which began two decades later with Darius still on the throne.

Centuries later the Russians, on more than one occasion and at tremendous national cost, did for western Europe what the Scythians did for the Greeks. Between the 10th and 13th centuries waves of nomad invaders from Asia, most notably the Mongols, spent most of their fury in Russia, sparing the luckier Europeans farther west. In 1812 Russia and its punishing winter destroyed Napoléon's Grand Army, in effect restoring the balance of power fundamental to the European state system. In 1914 the Russian military offensive into eastern Germany forced the Germans to send additional troops to the eastern front and thereby probably saved Paris. Finally, in World War II, Russians and other Soviet peoples played a critical role in destroying Nazi Germany and saving the Western democracies when they defeated two-thirds of the German army in battles of staggering scale and brutality. This painful national experience, and especially how generations of Russians have reacted to it, was brilliantly captured by Aleksandr Blok (1880–1921) in his darkly menacing poem "The Scythians," in which he warns western Europe that the time has come to change its condescending attitude toward his country and its people:

> You are millions, we are multitude
> And multitude and multitude.
> Come, fight! Yea, we are Scythians,
> Yea, Asians, a slant-eyed greedy brood.
>
> For you—centuries, for us—one hour.
> Like slaves, obeying and abhorred,
> We were the shield between the breeds
> Of Europe and the raging Mongol horde.
> . . .
>
> For the last time, old world, we bid you rouse.
> For the last time, the barbarous lyre sounds
> That calls you to our bright fraternal feast,
> Where labor beckons and peace abounds.

(Blok in Yarmolinsky 1964: 133, 135)

Scythian control of the steppe lasted until about 200 B.C.E., when the Sarmatians, horsemen from central Asia who had the advantage of the metal stirrup and new weapons the Scythians lacked, defeated them and drove them from the steppe. Four hundred years later, the Sarmatians were themselves displaced and consigned to historical oblivion by the Goths, a Germanic people. They in turn were driven from the steppe around 370 C.E. by the Turkic-speaking Huns, the same fierce group that 80 years later under Attila the Hun (406–453) nearly destroyed Rome. In the middle of the sixth century another Turkic people, the Avars, seized control of the steppe north of the Black Sea. By this time some East Slavic tribes were living in the region, having migrated from their likely original homeland in central Europe between the Carpathian Mountains and the Vistula River. Exactly when they arrived is uncertain; what is known is that Slavs fought in the Avar armies that attacked the Byzantine Empire in the sixth century.

The Khazars

In the seventh century a new phenomenon emerged on the eastern European part of the Eurasian plain: a relatively well-organized state, the creation of the Khazars, a Turkic-speaking people from central Asia. It eventually extended from the Volga to the Dnieper and well northward from the shores of the Black and Caspian seas and the slopes of the Caucasus Mountains. The Khazar state became wealthy through its control of key trade routes between Europe and the Middle East. Thriving trade led to the building of towns, including the Khazar capital of Itil on the Volga River near the Caspian Sea. One of the most notable features of this state, where numerous cultural groups met and intermingled, was its unusual tolerance. Under Khazar rule Christians, Jews, Muslims, and others were free to practice their religions and live according to their own customs. Khazaria, in fact, seems to have been a refuge for people fleeing persecution in other realms.

Most important historically, during the seventh and eighth centuries the Khazars fought several major wars with invading Arab armies and in the process blocked the expansion of Islam into eastern Europe. In 737, just five years after the Frankish leader Charles Martel won the battle near the banks of the Loire River in France that halted the Muslim advance into Europe in the west and pushed the invaders back into Spain, the Khazars turned back the Arabs in the east, driving them south of the Caucasus Mountains. The steadfast Khazar stand left all of eastern Europe open to Christianity, an opportunity Christian missionaries would not seriously exploit for another 200 years. In short, it changed the course of European history. As for the Khazars themselves, their ruling class converted to Judaism sometime in the eighth or ninth centuries.

The Khazar state survived as the leading power on the steppe until it was defeated by a Kievan Russian prince in 966, who thereby added to Kiev's domains territory along the lower part of the Don River near

5

the Sea of Azov and along the lower Volga. This victory turned out to be very costly for the Russians. The decline and eventual demise of the Khazar state left the invasion route from Asia open to new nomadic groups. They soon surged into the breech; with the Khazars gone the first people to fall victim to these destructive raids were the same Russians who had so recently displaced them.

The Rise of Kievan Rus

The origins of the first Russian state, which historians call Kievan Rus, are unclear and have long been a subject of historical debate. The problem, at least for patriotic Russians, is that the founders of that state probably were foreigners: warrior merchants from Scandinavia known as the Varangians. The term "Rus" most likely is a reference to the Varangians, but it is also possible that it refers to some of the East Slavs, who had been living in the region for several centuries before the Varangians arrived.

By the ninth century the East Slavs were well established on the eastern European part of the Eurasian plain. They were mainly farmers and cattle raisers, but they had also founded close to 300 towns and engaged in trade and a wide variety of crafts. Their weak point apparently was political organization, at least according to the Russians who wrote the *Primary Russian Chronicle,* a document dating from the 12th century that is the earliest known source on Russian history. The *Primary Chronicle* records that because of continual fighting among the East Slavic tribes, they turned to the Varangians with the following invitation: "Our land is great and rich, but there is no order in it. Come to rule and reign over us." (*Primary Chronicle* in Zenkovsky 1974: 49–50). Whether this request was ever made is debatable, and it is just as likely that this episode found its way into the *Primary Chronicle* to legitimize the princely dynasty that established itself among the East Slavs at the time.

In any case, it appears that in 862 a group of Varangians led by a prince named Rurik took power in Novgorod, a trading city in the northwest near the Baltic Sea. Twenty years later Rurik's successor, Oleg (d. 913), conquered the more centrally located city of Kiev, which then became the capital of Kievan Rus. Oleg brought other East Slavic tribes under his control, and Kiev became the center of a loose federation of fortified city-states ruled by princes that stretched, so it was said, "from the Varangians to the Greeks," that is, from the Baltic to the Black seas. Oleg then used his military prowess to win a favorable trade treaty from the Byzantine Empire. Dating from 911, Oleg's treaty allowed the mer-

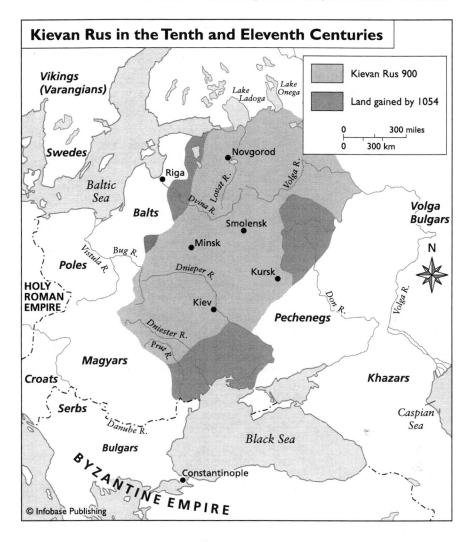

chants of Kievan Rus to do business in Constantinople, the Byzantine capital on the Black Sea and by far the largest and wealthiest city in Europe.

Along with being the most important terminus for the products of Kievan Rus, the Byzantine Empire was the most powerful cultural influence on its northern neighbor. In 944 Oleg's successor, Igor (r. 913–945), again after a military campaign secured another trade treaty with the Byzantines. His wife, Olga (regent, 945–962), further strengthened the realm as regent for a minor son; she later was designated a saint in the

Russian Orthodox Church and is Russia's first famous woman. It was Igor and Olga's son, Svyatoslav (r. 962–972), who defeated the Khazars in 966. These early rulers solidified the status of the Kievan dynasty, which took its name from Rurik and lasted until the end of the 16th century.

Kievan Rus remained a loose federation of princely city-states, with the grand prince of Kiev enjoying an often tenuous status as the leading prince. This political instability led to fragmentation and ultimately contributed to Kiev's downfall. Before that happened, however, several important developments took place that helped forge a common identity among the East Slavs that outlasted the Kievan Rus state.

In 988 Kiev's Prince Vladimir (r. 980–1015), after triumphing over his brothers in a civil war, converted to the Greek Orthodox version of Christianity, a choice that reflects Kiev's close cultural ties with the Byzantine Empire and Constantinople, the center of the Greek Orthodox faith. The conversion also gave Kievan Rus its first written language, Church Slavonic, a language closely related to the Russian spoken at the time by the East Slavs and therefore easily understood by them. Church Slavonic was written in an alphabet created by the Bulgarian Orthodox missionary Cyril (hence the Cyrillic alphabet) a century earlier. The sermons, prayer books, and other religious material that the Orthodox churchmen of Kievan Rus produced in Church Slavonic in considerable volume constituted Russia's first written literature.

These religious works complemented the much older East Slavic oral folklore, which included sagas and epic poems called *byliny*. Kievan Rus also soon produced new secular literary works. The monks who in the early 12th century wrote and compiled sagas such as the *Primary Chronicle* were churchmen, but their chronicles were in effect secular historical records. These writings constituted some of the first building blocks of Russia's secular literary tradition, alongside the epic poems that were now written down rather than memorized and works such as the 12th-century *Testament* of Grand Prince Vladimir Monomakh (r. 1113–25).

Byzantine Orthodox Christianity also brought with it what became the dominant Russian art form for 700 years: the icon, a religious image painted on wood. The first Russian icon painters learned their craft from the Byzantines, but local artists, operating within rules that dictated what was permissible, soon developed their own styles, turning icon painting into Russia's national art form. Over time Russian artists used brighter, more luminous colors than their Byzantine teachers, creating images radiating warmth and kindness. Icons not only decorated Russian churches but were found in every Russian home, including peasant huts, where they were kept in a special corner of the main living areas. Medieval Russian icon painting found its greatest master in Andrei Rublev, who was born around 1370 and died in 1430. His masterpiece, *Old Testament Trinity,* was painted for a monastery in a relatively small town; today it hangs in Moscow's famous Tretyakov Gallery along with many other cherished icons.

The conversion to Orthodoxy was a two-edged sword, however. Orthodoxy played a constructive national role in helping to unify Kievan Rus. At the same time, in the wake of the schism of 1054 that split the Christian world into a Roman Catholic West and a Greek Orthodox East, the adoption of Orthodoxy in the long run created a major barrier between the Russians and their European neighbors to the west, who followed the Roman Catholic faith.

The Halcyon Days of Kievan Rus

Kievan Rus, after another of its princely civil wars, reached the peak of its power under Yaroslav the Wise (r. 1019–54) and Vladimir Monomakh. Yaroslav gave Russia its first law code, the Russkaya Pravda, or Russian Justice. He also used Kiev's trading wealth to turn the city into a cultural and artistic center, building monuments, stone palaces, and churches, including the 19-domed Cathedral of St. Sophia, whose skillfully crafted frescoes, mosaics, and other decorations made it one of the most beautiful churches of its day. This magnificent structure still graces the city, as does Yaroslav's impressive Golden Gate, one of the fortifications he built for Kiev.

Vladimir Monomakh, a skilled military commander and highly capable ruler, was the best educated of Kiev's grand princes; he encouraged learning and the writing and preservation of chronicles. His military achievements included a string of victories over steppe nomads, as well as successful campaigns against enemies to the west. He is respected above all for his *Testament,* which urged his successors to educate themselves so they could govern as peaceful and moral rulers. By Vladimir's reign in the early 12th century, Kiev was an impressive urban center with as many as 50,000 people—including merchants, clergymen, skilled artisans, and the governing elite—and hundreds of churches. Its wealth derived from production as well as trade. Kiev's craftsmen produced fine gold and silver jewelry, bricks and other materials for building its impressive churches, and weapons.

Novgorod, about half the size of Kiev, was a flourishing trading center with strong ties to European cities to the west. Its own Cathedral of St. Sophia, smaller than Kiev's, still stands, its interior decorated by 12th-

St. Sophia Cathedral in Kiev was built in the 11th century by Yaroslav the Wise. It became the spiritual and cultural center of Kievan Rus and remains one of the most important and beautiful monuments of Eastern Slavic civilization. (Poznukhov Yuriy, 2007. Used under license from ShutterStock, Inc.)

century frescoes and its eastern portal graced by 12th-century bronze doors made in Germany. In contrast to Kiev's cathedral, Novgorod's elongated onion domes and other architectural features reflect an evolving Russian architectural style that over time became distinct from the style copied and learned from the Byzantines.

An impressive number of other towns such as Rostov, Smolensk, Suzdal, and Ryazan, each with its own churches and craftsmen, were scattered across the length and breadth of Kievan Rus. Meanwhile, several individual Kievan principalities were strong enough to extend their borders at the expense of non-Russian neighbors. Novgorod, for example, expanded toward the west and north during the 11th century. During the 12th century the northeastern principality of Suzdal pushed its borders toward the north and east.

In later eras, as Russia suffered through centuries of political absolutism and poverty, the Kievan period acquired something of an aura as a bygone golden age. This, of course, was far from the case. Kievan Rus had its fair share of problems and faults. Still, it did have two significant qualities that would be missing in later periods of Russian history.

First, Kievan Rus was a relatively free society, especially by the European standards of the time. Its princes, even within their individual principalities, did not have anything like the absolute power Russia's later czars would wield. Princely authority was limited by the power of aristocrats called boyars, who met in councils called dumas. In the cities elected bodies called *veches* exercised considerable power. The power of these institutions varied from city to city and region to region, leaving some princes with significantly more power than others. The *veche* achieved its greatest power in Novgorod. By the 12th century the city was called "Lord Novgorod the Great" and had essentially evolved into a republic. Novgorod even had a special bell it used to call its *veche* into session, a bell that became a symbol both for the city and for its proud tradition of self-government.

The boyars formed the upper class of Kievan society. Beneath them was a significant middle class, collectively called the *liudi* (the word today means "people" in Russian), whose existence testifies to the large number of towns in Kievan Rus and their extensive commercial and

St. Sophia Cathedral in Novgorod dates from the 11th century and is a monument to that city's golden era as a trading power that began during the Kievan period and lasted until the 15th century. (Sergey Khachatryan, 2007. Used under license from ShutterStock, Inc.)

productive activity. The great majority of the population were free peasant farmers called *smerdy,* although there also were various groups of unfree peasants and some slaves. Kievan citizens did not have the legal corporate guarantees that protected townspeople in Western Europe, but the countervailing centers of power that existed in Kievan Rus left the population far better off than most of their descendants would be under the czars who later would rule Muscovite and Imperial Russia.

Second, Kievan Rus was a prosperous society by the European standards of the time. The rich black soil of the steppe produced bountiful harvests. The river roads that connected the Baltic Sea and the European lands to the west with Constantinople to the south and Asian lands to the east facilitated trade that added to the relative prosperity of Kievan Rus and its people.

Both of these qualities proved to be ephemeral. By the middle of the 12th century Kievan Rus was in decline. The endless wars among its princes were taking their toll on the daily life of the people and in Kiev's ability to defend itself against nomadic invaders from Asia. At the same time Kiev's prosperity was undermined when the Crusades that began in the late 11th century opened up a more direct trade route between Western Europe and Constantinople via the Mediterranean Sea.

Almost as if by premonition, in the late 12th century an anonymous poet of Kievan Rus produced a warning for his people in a poem that became a national classic, *The Tale of the Host of Igor.* The poem tells of a military campaign in 1185 by a Russian prince against a tribe of nomads on the steppe that ended in disaster. Its main point, from which the poet often digresses, is a call for unity among the Russian princes, as disunity had brought yet another disaster upon the Russian land and people.

The call went unheeded. A series of succession struggles followed Vladimir Monomakh's death. One of them ended in 1169 with the sack of Kiev, not by steppe nomads, as one might have expected, but by a Russian prince, Andrei Bogolyubsky. After a period of relative peace that lasted from the mid-1170s to the mid-1190s, continued princely rivalries bred more disorder. In 1203 Russian soldiers again sacked Kiev, by now gravely weakened after a large part of its population fled the disorder on the steppe and moved either farther west or to the more secure principalities in the northeast. As they fought each other, the princes of Kievan Rus paid no attention to foreign threats. In effect Kievan Russ had fragmented into about a dozen small principalities constantly at odds or fighting with each other at the worst possible time: Far to the east on the distant Siberian steppe in today's Mongolia a new threat was rising, one that would bring misery to Russia on an unimaginable scale.

The Mongol Conquest

Until the middle of the 12th century the Mongols were nomad tribes numbering perhaps a million and a half people who roamed the steppe grassland north of China. Superb horsemen and mounted warriors, they were fearsome opponents but probably spent as much time fighting each other as they did raiding the farms and towns of settled people who lived on the southern edge of their pasture homeland. Their mobility and formidable fighting skills made them a constant danger to isolated or small settlements, and they could be a painful nuisance to the Chinese, who had built their famous Great Wall centuries earlier to keep nomads like the Mongols from disturbing their empire. Despite their proximity north of the Great Wall the Mongols were not yet a threat to China itself, nor to other powerful civilizations to the west, such as the Muslim states in Persia, Iraq, and elsewhere in the Middle East.

For centuries Kievan Rus had been forced to devote considerable resources to fending off steppe nomads, but that had never included the Mongol clans and tribes living deep in Siberia within the orbit of China. Then, at the dawn of the 13th century, a tribal chieftain named Temüjin, later known to a terrified world as Genghis Khan (c. 1162– 1227), united the Mongol tribes and everything changed. In the space of a few decades the Mongols would shake the Eurasian world, conquering empires, destroying cities and entire cultures, and spreading terror and destruction from the Pacific shore to the center of Europe. Many peoples did not survive the Mongol onslaught. Of those that did, none suffered more than the people of Russia.

It is not easy to explain how the Mongols, known in Russian history as the Tatars, defeated and conquered advanced societies with populations far larger than their own. For example, in the 13th century China probably had a population of more than 100 million, while Russia had about 10 million. Some of the Mongols' success can be attributed to the great speed and mobility of their mounted units, their superb tactics and extraordinary coordination between battle units, and their advanced weaponry, the main exception to their generally primitive technology. The Mongol warriors used a short bow of compound materials with a longer range than even the famous and far larger English longbow. Unlike the English bow, the Mongol version was small enough to be used by a mounted warrior; Mongol horsemen could shoot arrows quickly and accurately from their saddles while moving at a gallop. The Mongols even thought of defense: Each warrior wore a silk shirt next to his skin that stretched when hit by an arrow, allowing the arrow to be more easily removed without doing more damage to the wounded man.

Subject to brutal discipline, Mongol horsemen seemed to be fearless in battle. Their massive and indiscriminate use of terror—destroying entire cities and murdering entire populations as examples to the next target—undermined the will and ability of opposing armies and populations to resist. As they swept irresistibly forward, they added to their ranks by incorporating fighting men from their defeated enemies, including experts in siege warfare able to build weapons that could overcome the walls of any city. Finally, in Genghis Khan they found a leader of military genius and pathological cruelty who forged them into the world's best fighting force; after his death in 1227, they found leaders, albeit lesser ones, whose military skills made them hardly less formidable than he had been. The result of their collective effort, in an astonishing short period of time, was the greatest land empire in history.

The first Mongol assault on Russia was a reconnaissance foray in 1223 into the region controlled at the time by Turkic nomads called the Polovtsy (or Cumans). The Polovtsy had a long history of conflict with the Russians—they had defeated Prince Igor in 1185—but since the last decade of the 12th century the old foes had been living relatively peacefully side by side. As the new menace intruded into their territory, the Polovtsy sent a prophetic plea to the Russian princes: "Today they have taken our land; tomorrow they will take yours" (Quoted in Vernadsky 1961: 44). Several prominent Russian princes, who by then rarely cooperated with each other, actually responded. Their intervention ended in disaster. The Mongols crushed the poorly coordinated Russian-Polovtsian forces in a battle on the Kalka River near the Sea of Azov and brutally executed many of their prisoners. Then they withdrew back into inner Asia and did not return for more than a decade.

The full-scale Mongol invasion of Kievan Rus began in 1237 with an assault against the eastern principality of Ryazan. The Mongol force probably numbered about 170,000 fighters: about 50,000 Mongol horsemen, the core of the army, and some 120,000 warriors from other groups of Turkic nomads the Mongols had already defeated. It is very unlikely that even a unified Russia could have stopped the Mongols, but the Kievan princes, locked in their petty quarrels, did not seriously try to mount a unified defense. The first Mongol target was Ryazan;

THE DESTRUCTION OF RYAZAN

The Mongol destruction of Ryazan was a harbinger of the terrible things to come. The city's fate was recorded in many manuscripts. *The Tale of the Destruction of Ryazan* is a composite account in which fact is embellished by fiction. Still, it conveys the essential truth about the nature and destructiveness of the Mongol conquest.

> *And they took the city of Riazan on the 21st day of December. . . .*
> *They burned to death the bishops and the priests and put the*
> *torch to the holy church. And the Tatars cut down many people,*
> *including women and children. . . . And they burned the holy city*
> *with all its beauty and wealth . . . And not one man remained*
> *alive in the city. All were dead. All had drunk the same bitter cup*
> *. . . And there was not even anyone to mourn the dead. Neither*
> *father nor mother could mourn their dead children, nor the chil-*
> *dren their fathers or mothers. Nor could a brother mourn the*
> *death of his brother, nor relatives their relatives. All were dead.*
> *And this happened for our sins. (Tale of the Destruction of Riazan*
> *in Zenkovsky 1974: 202)*

its prince was ignored when he pleaded to his peers for help, and the Mongols totally destroyed the city.

As for the rest of Kievan Rus, the actual conquest and attendant slaughter lasted five years. In 1238 the Mongols took the city of Vladimir, home of Russia's grand prince. The citizens who took refuge in the city's main church were burned alive; the Mongols hacked to pieces those who tried to flee from the fires. Scenes like this were repeated in other cities. Shortly after Vladimir fell, its Grand Prince Yury II (1189–1238) and his army were crushed in a battle on a minor stream called the Sit River. The grand prince himself was killed. Kiev fell in December of 1240 after a long, heroic defense. That resistance had its price. The destruction at Kiev was so total that six years later a visitor from Europe found only 200 houses standing in that formerly stately city. The only major Russian town the Mongols did not attack and sack was Novgorod, protected from the Mongol cavalry by the dense forests and swamps of the far northwest. In 1241 and 1242 the Mongols overran Russia's western principalities and pressed onward into Poland and Hungary, where they crushed the mounted knights of those countries, the most important battle taking place in 1241. The same dreadful scenario was repeated in the Balkans. The Mongols did not stop until news arrived in 1242 that their leader, the great khan in Mongolia, had died. Their commanding general, Batu (d. 1255), then moved his main army back to the Volga River, while he himself focused on the succession struggle in Mongolia.

The only bright spot in this pitch-black night of defeat and destruction was Novgorod. Spared from attack by the Mongols from the east, it was able to make a stand against Swedish and German invaders from the west. The victory over the Swedes took place on the Neva River at the Gulf of Finland. In honor of this victory, Novgorod's Prince Aleksandr, who had led his city's forces, became known as Aleksandr Nevsky ("of the Neva," 1220–63). Two years later Nevsky defeated the invading Teutonic Knights on the ice of Lake Peipus, a large, kidney-shaped body of water about 120 miles west of Novgorod that today stands astride much of the current border between Russia and Estonia.

The Mongol Yoke

The Russians call the following 250 years the "Mongol Yoke." In the immediate aftermath of the conquest, as much as 10 percent of the surviving population may have been enslaved, and many of the country's best craftsmen and artisans were deported to the east to serve the dreaded great khan. The Mongols established a huge state known as the Golden Horde, itself a part of the larger Mongol empire. It extended from the steppe west of the Black Sea deep into Siberia, with its capital at the new city of Sarai, on the Volga just north of the Caspian Sea. From there the Golden Horde controlled some of the Russian steppe region directly while ruling most of the country indirectly through local princes. These princes had to travel to the Mongol capital to be confirmed as rulers of their individual principalities through a debasing ceremony in which they had to bow before the Mongol khan; a long stay was often required. The khan chose the Russian grand prince in the same manner. Competing Russian princes used a variety of methods to secure their positions, including the coveted post of grand prince. Bribery and promises to deliver more tribute than their rivals were standard procedure.

As long as they did not defy the khan and collaborated with him, the Russian princes could enjoy their positions as rulers over the local population. Life was much more difficult for the common people. They were subject to heavy taxes, initially collected directly by Mongol agents, and, beginning in the 14th century, by the Russian princes themselves They could be conscripted into the Mongol army and be enslaved if they did not pay their taxes. Meanwhile, the *veches* lost their power of self-government. These facts explain why revolts led by princes were rare, while urban revolts during the 13th and 14th centuries were far more common.

The Mongol conquest set in motion several important long-term developments. In the wake of the conquest's destruction itself and the generations of economic exploitation that followed, the Russian economy stagnated and increasingly lagged behind the economies of states farther west. Trade declined and economic life became increasingly agrarian and local. Compounding matters, agricultural yields in the north, to which the Russians were confined, were poorer than on the southern steppe, which had become the domain of Mongol horsemen and herders. As a result, since the 13th century Russia has been burdened with a legacy of economic backwardness compared to western Europe.

The Mongol conquest also cut many of Russia's ties with the Byzantine Empire and, more significantly, with western Europe. In the centuries to come, while western European culture was enriched by Humanism and the Renaissance, Russian cultural development was stunted and brutalized by poverty and political oppression. Another important development was the threefold division of the East Slavs. The Great Russians, about 70 percent of the East Slavs, emerged from the principalities of the northeast that paid tribute to the Mongols. Farther west, the East Slavs who became subjects to the rising powers of Poland and Lithuania emerged as today's Belarusians, or White Russians, and Ukrainians, or Little Russians, the latter group being about five times as numerous as the former. Notwithstanding the considerable historical and cultural legacy that once united the three groups, there were enough differences so that after 1991 centrifugal forces led to a parting of ways and the creation of three independent countries.

Perhaps most important, the Mongol conquest had a major influence on the development of the Russian state. The Kievan inheritance was a complex one. Kievan princes had exercised a great deal of power, especially those in the northeast. Kievan Rus also had learned the Byzantine concept of caesaropapism—the idea that the monarch should have both temporal and spiritual powers. Yet princely power in Kievan Rus had been balanced by the power of the nobles and the activities and prerogatives of the *veches*. This is what was destroyed by several centuries of Mongol rule. The Mongol khan was an absolute sovereign. All of his subjects were obligated to serve the state. He was the sole owner of all the land; all others held it on condition of service to the state. The Mongol khan, to be sure, ruled most of Russia indirectly through the princes, but he was their model, and they were his agents as tax collectors and enforcers of the law. The khan's power over all of his subjects bolstered the power of the princes over the Russian people. Mongol rule in Russia gravely weakened the power of the boyar nobility and virtually eliminated the *veches,* pushing Russia down the road to autocratic rule. That tendency was strengthened as one principality—Muscovy—gradually gained power at the expense of the others. Eventually the Mongols were driven out of Russia, but they left behind an oppressive political legacy that over time evolved into Russian autocracy.

The Rise of Moscow

The collapse of Kievan Rus was followed by the rise of Moscow. A small village during Kievan times, not even mentioned in Russian chronicles until 1147, Moscow was part of the principality of Vladimir at the time of the Mongol invasion. Moscow was one of the first towns the Mongols pillaged when they invaded Russia in 1237. The town recovered, as it was forced to many times in its history, and slowly began to grow. It did not become a separate principality with its own ruling house until 1301. In the grim oppressiveness of Mongol rule, Moscow—or Muscovy, as the principality was called—enjoyed several advantages. Its population gradually swelled as people from the exposed steppe sought safety in the northern forests. Its location on the broad Moscow River—a tributary of the Oka, which in turn flows into the Volga— placed it on important trade routes and aided its economic growth.

Moreover, once it became a principality Moscow was blessed with a line of princes who were long-lived, intelligent, ruthless, and—not inconsequentially—lucky, an attribute in short supply in Russia but desperately needed while the Mongols ruled. Moscow's princes proved uniquely skilled at navigating the treacherous rapids of dealing with their Mongol overlords. They consistently outmaneuvered their rivals from other principalities, using strategic marriages, wars, and other methods to add territory to their domains until Moscow became the most powerful of all the Russian states.

The Muscovite ruling house belonged to the branch of the Rurikid dynasty that descended from Alexander Nevsky. It took its first major step up the ladder of power when Prince Yury (r. 1303–25) married a sister of the Golden Horde khan and won appointment from his new brother-in-law as Russia's grand prince. Yury's successor, his younger brother Ivan (r. 1325–41), built brilliantly and ruthlessly on the foundation he inherited. Technically known as Ivan I, he is best known by his unofficial title "*Kalita,*" or "Moneybags." When Ivan became prince of Moscow, the title of grand prince had recently

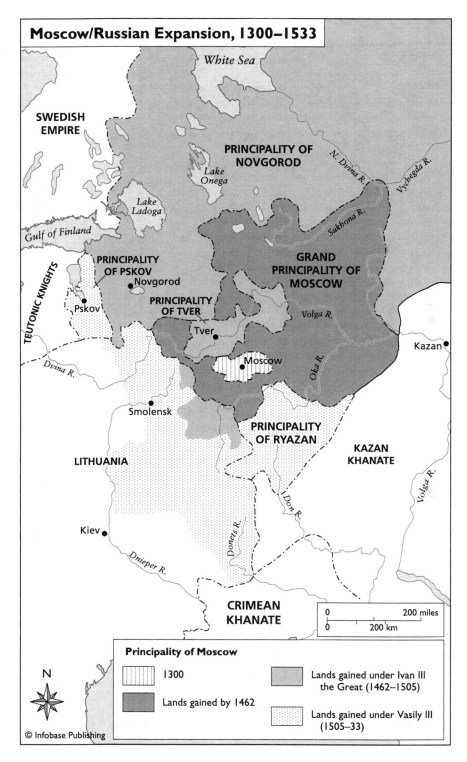

Moscow/Russian Expansion, 1300–1533

White Sea

SWEDISH
EMPIRE

PRINCIPALITY OF
NOVGOROD

Lake
Onega

N. Dvina R.

Vychegda R.

Lake
Ladoga

Sukhona R.

Gulf of Finland

TEUTONIC KNIGHTS

PRINCIPALITY
OF PSKOV

Novgorod

GRAND
PRINCIPALITY OF
MOSCOW

Pskov

PRINCIPALITY
OF TVER

Volga R.

Kazan

Dvina R.

Tver

Moscow

Oka R.

Smolensk

PRINCIPALITY
OF RYAZAN

KAZAN
KHANATE

LITHUANIA

Volga R.

Kiev

Donets R.

Don R.

Dnieper R.

CRIMEAN
KHANATE

| 0 | 200 miles |
| 0 | 200 km |

N

Principality of Moscow

1300

Lands gained under Ivan III
the Great (1462–1505)

Lands gained by 1462

Lands gained under Vasily III
(1505–33)

© Infobase Publishing

Moscow's Kremlin stands as a symbol of Russia and serves as the center of its govern-
ment. The original Kremlin was a wooden structure built in the mid-12th century; the red-
brick walls that surround the Kremlin today date from the reign of Ivan the Great. (Denis
Babenko, 2007. Used under license from ShutterStock, Inc.)

been transferred to the ruler of the neighboring principality of Tver. Ivan got
it back by collaborating with the Mongols in a devastating military campaign
against Tver, which had made the grave error of rebelling against Russia's
overlords. The campaign left Tver in ruins, a result that did not bother
Ivan at all. His skills at collecting taxes, the source of his moniker "Kalita,"
convinced the khan to grant Ivan the job of collecting Mongol tribute from
all the Russian princes. Ivan further augmented his principality's position
among Russians wherever they lived when he convinced the metropolitan of
the Russian Orthodox Church to relocate the church's headquarters from the
town of Vladimir to Moscow. With the church came revenues from all over
Russia, and with them Moscow's ability to build its first stone churches as it
staked its claim as the country's spiritual center.

Moscow's next outstanding ruler was Dmitry Donskoi (r. 1359–89).
Dmitry more than doubled Moscow's size by annexing major hunks of
territory to the northeast. He survived several dangerous conflicts early
in his reign, including a confrontation with Lithuania, a powerful non-
Russian state that had expanded from its original base near the Baltic
coast eastward into Russia and southward all the way to the Black Sea, in
the process wresting Kiev and much of today's Ukraine from the Golden

Horde. To shore up his defenses, Dmitry built stone walls around the Kremlin in Moscow and fortified several other towns in his principality.

In 1371 Dmitry took advantage of the Golden Horde's weakness to win a reduction in tribute and then stopped paying entirely in 1375. Trouble started when the khan demanded payment—at the level that had been in force before 1371. When Dmitry refused, the khan, Mamai, moved north with a 200,000-man army. Dmitry met the menace at Kulikovo field on the shores of the Don and shocked everyone by routing the hated Tatars. It mattered little that two years later the same Tatars, under a new khan, attacked and burned Moscow or that Tatar rule would last for another 100 years. The Mongols finally had been beaten, their aura of invincibility destroyed, their grip on Russia weakened. Russia's dignity, trampled under Mongol hoofs for a century and a half, had been at least partially restored. For that achievement on the banks of the river Don, Moscow's Prince Dmitry became Russia's Dmitry Donskoi and a national hero to a nation that desperately needed one.

DMITRY DONSKOI AND THE BATTLE OF KULIKOVO

The Battle of Kulikovo on September 8, 1380, was a heroic moment in Russian history that united Russians in a feeling of enormous joy and pride. It did not begin that way. When Moscow's Prince Dmitry called on his fellow princes to support him against the country's Mongol oppressors, their response was hardly unanimous. There was little confidence that Dmitry could defeat the Mongols, even though he had beaten them in a relatively small battle on the Vozha River in 1378. Most princes and towns did send troops, but key powers such as Novgorod, Pskov, and Tver did not. The prince of Ryazan originally sided with the Mongols. Dmitry nonetheless assembled a formidable army, perhaps as large as 150,000 men, and marched south from Moscow to meet the massive Mongol force of about 200,000.

The site Dmitry chose for the battle, Kulikovo "field," belies its name in a way that favored the Russians. It actually is a hilly area cut by streams, a terrain that prevented the Mongol cavalry from exploiting its mobility. When the fighting started, the Mongols found they had to charge Russian positions directly rather than flank and envelop them.

(continues)

21

DMITRY DONSKOI (continued)

The battle was ferocious—according to one report, after being knocked unconscious Dmitry ultimately was found under a pile of corpses—but a final Russian ambush from troops hidden in the forest brought the Russians victory and gave them an inspiring moment in their history.

Here is how one Russian chronicler, Sofony of Ryazan, described what happened, in an epic poem known as the *Zadonshchina,* which means "Tale of Events Beyond the Don":

> Great Prince Dmitri Ivanovich sets in the golden stirrup
> and takes his sword in his right hand.
> The sun shines brightly from the east,
> showing him the road (to victory)....
>
> The earth became black from horse hooves.
> The field became strewn with Tatar bones.
> Much blood was spilled upon the field
> Strong regiments came together and clashed,
> and they trampled the hills and the meadows....
>
> The storm clouds began to gather
> and from them shone the lightning,
> and thunder roared mightily.
> It was the clash of the sons of Russia
> with the Tatar infidels, for they seek revenge for Tatar offenses.
> The gilt armor of the Russian princes gleamed.
> Their steel swords rained upon the Tatar helmets....
>
> Indeed, the tide turned, and the Russian
> regiments began to cut the Tatars to pieces.
> And despair seized the infidels.
> Princes fell from their mounts,
> and Tatar corpses began to cover the field.
> And blood flowed in a stream.
> The infidels began fleeing on all sides....
>
> And then Prince Dmitry Ivanovich addressed the dead:
> Fellow princes, boyars, and sons of boyars,
> you have found peace everlasting here, between
> the Don and the Dnieper, on the prairie of Kulikovo....
>
> (Safony of Ryazan, Zadonshchina, in Zenkovsky 1974: 216–223)

Moscow's strength, especially relative to other Russian principalities, continued to grow. The principality gained new territory under Dmitry Donskoi's immediate successors, Vasily I (r. 1389–1425) and Vasily II (r. 1425–62), notwithstanding a long and damaging civil war during Vasily II's reign. Vasily I even showed some appreciation of art and culture; he commissioned Andrei Rublev (c. 1360–1430), generally recognized as the greatest of all Russian icon painters, to decorate the Assumption Cathedral in Vladimir with his frescoes.

One victim of Moscow's new strength was Novgorod. In stark contrast to authoritarian Moscow, whose prince had become increasingly powerful, Novgorod essentially was an aristocratic republic controlled by its *veche,* which selected the city's prince. The *veche* normally was dominated by the city's leading commercial families, who reinforced their control through a council of notables. Novgorod's wealth, which set it apart from the rest of Russia, came from trade and its control of a vast swath of territory in Russia's northeast, a forest region that was its source of valuable furs, honey, and other raw materials. Along with its vast forests, Novgorod's territory also included almost 20 towns. Unfortunately, it was caught in a vise between Lithuania and Moscow, and it was badly weakened after a defeat by Moscow in 1456. By the time Vasily II died and was succeeded by Ivan III (r. 1462–1505), the stage had been set for Moscow to unify Russia under its control. Although that remained a formidable task, Ivan III and his successors proved equal to the challenge.

2

INDEPENDENCE AND UNIFICATION: THE LAST RURIKIDS TO THE FIRST ROMANOVS (1462–1694)

Ivan III became grand prince of Moscow in 1462 and ruled until 1505, a reign that became a watershed in Russian history. During this era Russia's centuries-long disunity came to an end, as Ivan annexed most of the other Russian principalities, quadrupling Moscow's territory in the process. So did the centuries of painful and humiliating subservience to the Mongols when, in 1480, Ivan officially declared Russia independent of the Golden Horde. Despite serious setbacks, Ivan skillfully managed Moscow's relations with the powerful non-Russian states of the region, including Tatar polities other than the Golden Horde and Lithuania and Sweden, powerful European monarchies to the west. Ivan relentlessly increased his powers as grand prince within his domains at the expense of other princes and noble families. He broke new symbolic ground by calling himself "czar" (Caesar) of all Russia. For his success in promoting Russia's unity, Ivan III earned the unofficial designation "gatherer of the Russian lands." For his achievements as a whole, however ruthlessly he went about realizing them, with considerable justification he is called Ivan the Great.

Gathering the Russian Lands

Before he could gather Russian lands beyond Moscow's borders, Ivan had to secure the domains of his father, Vasily II, who had followed the prevailing custom of dividing his realm among his five sons into appanages. Ivan understood quite well that one principality with five princes, each with local authority, was a formula for instability and weakness, even if he was the ruling grand prince. He used a combination of force, diplomacy, fortuitous deaths, and chance opportunities to push his brothers aside and consolidate exclusive control over Muscovy. Luck was an important part of the process, especially when two of Ivan's brothers died without heirs and their territories reverted to him. Still, the process of internal consolidation took three decades to complete, leaving Ivan to juggle several priorities simultaneously under difficult conditions.

Meanwhile, Ivan was busy "gathering" externally. Two principalities, Yaroslavl and Rostov, both of whose territories were almost surrounded by Moscow, were easily swallowed when Ivan bought off their grand princes. The principality of Tver, once Moscow's main rival, fell to a direct invasion in 1485. Ivan also tightened Moscow's noose around a few other principalities that were not formally annexed until after his death.

Above all, Ivan did not let Novgorod, his prime objective, escape his grasp. Its conquest was Ivan's most notable success, as the city controlled a vast forested hinterland rich in natural resources stretching far to the northeast. Apart from advancing the goal of territorial unity, this campaign, which lasted for most of the 1470s with a few sequels in the 1480s, also served Ivan's effort to destroy all rival sources of internal political power as he built his absolutist state. By this time Novgorod was already in trouble. Caught between Moscow and Lithuania, the city was divided between factions favoring one powerful neighbor or the other. Novgorod had been forced by Vasily II to sign a treaty tying it closely to Moscow. When it began to tilt toward the west and Lithuania, Ivan used that as an excuse in 1471 to attack the principality. He took as his victory prize some territory and a promise of allegiance, but for the moment he left Novgorod's system of government intact.

In 1478 Ivan once again invaded and seized the city. This time the bell tolled with undeniable finality for Novgorod and its political system. Ivan carried out extensive executions. He deported thousands of the city's boyars and merchants, giving their land to Muscovites who held it on condition of service to him. Finally, Ivan abolished Novgorod's *veche* and its elected offices and annexed the city and its enormous hinterland. That acquisition alone almost doubled Moscow's size. Adding insult to injury, Ivan seized Novgorod's famous bell, the proud symbol of its republican way of life, and removed it to Moscow, declaring, "A *veche* bell in my patrimony, in Novgorod, shall not be . . . I will rule the entire state" (Riazanovsky 1969: 115). Just to make sure that statement would not be challenged and that no opposition survived, Ivan conducted further purges of the city's elite during the 1480s, deporting 9,000 boyars, smaller landholders, and merchants in 1489 alone and replacing them with loyalists from Moscow.

Novgorod's fall left representative government in Russia on life support, tenuously alive only in Pskov, the so-called younger brother of Novgorod on Russia's western fringe. Ivan satisfied himself with tightening the noose around Pskov, leaving the final task of strangling it completely and annexing it to Moscow to Vasily III, his son and successor, who dutifully completed the job in 1510.

While he was gathering Russian principalities, Ivan expanded Moscow's borders at the expense of non-Russian states. His targets included the Kazan khanate, one of the Tatar states that had emerged from the crumbling Golden Horde before Ivan became grand prince. He waged a series of military campaigns against Kazan over a 25-year period to secure Moscow's eastern frontier, and ultimately reduced Kazan to a vassal state. Meanwhile, in 1480, 240 years after the fall of Kiev, Ivan formally restored Russian independence by renouncing all allegiance to the remnant of the once-mighty Golden Horde. He backed up that declaration by sending an army to intercept a Tatar force sent by the khan to assert his authority. The two armies encountered each other on opposite sides of a tributary to the Oka River, but they did not fight a major battle. Rather, after a failed Tatar attempt to cross the river, a standoff occurred, after which the Tatars retreated. It was an anticlimactic end to more than two centuries of national trauma. Within a generation, the Golden Horde itself, battered by Moscow and rival Tatar states, was totally destroyed.

Ivan also expanded Russia's borders westward at the expense of Lithuania. He began with a drawn-out series of skirmishes in the late 1480s and early 1490s, and concluded with a full-scale war from 1500 to 1503. His quarrel with Lithuania was motivated, aside from the usual issues of power and expansion, by a heavy dose of national pride and historical memory. In the course of its expansion, Lithuania had conquered a huge swath of territory that formerly belonged to Kievan Rus, including Kiev itself. As far as Ivan was concerned, Moscow was the legitimate heir to all these territories, not non-Russian, Catholic Lithuania, and he was determined to enforce that right.

Ivan used diplomacy as well as military force against the powerful Lithuanians, especially an alliance with the Crimean Tatars, another of the successor states to the defunct Golden Horde. By 1503 he had won from the Lithuanians considerable territory that had once belonged to Kievan Rus east of the Dnieper River. However, the city of Smolensk, Ivan's main target, remained beyond his reach; it was left to his son

Vasily III finally to take Smolensk in 1514. All this was only the beginning. For approximately half the century following Ivan III's initial attacks on Lithuania, Russia would be at war against one or another of its western neighbors and rivals.

The Czar and the Third Rome: Ivan and Autocracy

Ivan III meant what he said about ruling the "entire state" alone. To that end he enlisted every force he could muster, including historical prestige and religious authority. He drew on both of these in the wake of the destruction of the Byzantine Empire, seat of the Greek Orthodox Church, which took place less than a decade before he became grand prince. By the early 15th century the Byzantines were reeling under repeated blows from the Muslim Ottoman Turks, whose conquests in Europe already extended well into the Balkan Peninsula. Desperate for military support from Roman Catholics to the west, their longtime bitter rivals but also fellow Christians, Constantinople's Greek Orthodox leaders in 1439 agreed to reunification under the authority of the pope. That measure was rejected by Russia's leading prelates, who denounced what they considered capitulation to the "Latin heresy." These prelates then established the Russian Orthodox Church under a native Russian metropolitan. This step toward theological independence was confirmed in 1453 when the Turks stormed Constantinople and put an end to the Byzantine Empire.

All this added to Moscow's prestige—it was now the seat of the new Russian Orthodox Church. Ivan built on that foundation when, in 1472, he married Sophia Paleologue, the niece of the last Byzantine emperor. Elaborate Byzantine court ceremonies now were replicated in Moscow, and Ivan added the fallen empire's two-headed eagle to his family seal: It became and remained a symbol of Russian czars until the fall of the monarchy in 1917. But much more than symbolism was involved. Ivan and his predecessors had been expanding the powers of the grand prince, gradually but inexorably turning the Muscovite state into an autocracy. The Byzantine ceremonies and symbols in effect claimed for Moscow's grand prince the powers of the Byzantine emperor, who had ruled in Constantinople as an absolute monarch over both his empire and the church.

During the 1480s Ivan began referring to himself with the Russian word *czar*, which means Caesar, thus further enlisting Roman as well as Byzantine precedent in the project to build absolutism in Russia. He also used the Russian word for "autocrat." In 1493 Ivan added the title

"Sovereign of All Russia." His claims were enthusiastically endorsed by the Russian Orthodox Church, which strongly supported the evolution of absolutism in Moscow. The church benefited from Moscow's standing as an entity of international, and indeed historic, importance. Within a few years of Ivan's death the doctrine of the Third Rome emerged. As expounded by a leading churchman in a letter to Vasily III in 1510, the original Rome fell because of heresy; Constantinople, the "second" Rome, fell to infidels; and their legitimate, and permanent, successor was Moscow, the home of the Russian Orthodox Church and therefore the "third" Rome.

The main barrier to building an absolute state in Moscow was its aristocratic landowning class, the boyars. A key to their status and power was the right to own hereditary estates—which were called *votchina*—without any obligations to the grand prince. In addition, the boyars continued to meet in a council called the boyar duma. Although the duma lacked specific powers, by virtue of tradition it acted as a break on the authority of the grand prince. Ivan did not directly attack the boyars' economic and political powers; rather, he chipped away at them. He established a new class of nobles by granting estates called *pomestie* on a conditional basis, primarily in exchange for military service. Land for this purpose often came from newly conquered territory.

This strategy accomplished several objectives. Ivan was trying to build up a new centralized army to support his ambitious foreign policy; the old system of relying on personal troops from his court and assistance from princes and boyars in times of crisis clearly would no longer suffice. Doling out *pomestie* estates in return for military service gave him the officers who would form the core of the new army and relieved his treasury of the burden of paying them, as these officers were compensated by income from their new estates. At the same time, the *pomestie* system created a new class of nobles to counterbalance the venerable boyars.

Ivan's annexation of rival principalities reinforced this effort. He deported thousands of boyars from those territories, giving their estates to newly designated *pomestie* nobles, whose loyalty was to Moscow and Ivan, while resettling the deportees on new estates with conditional *pomestie* tenure. Meanwhile Ivan did what he could to undermine the boyars who remained on their *votchina,* mainly by legal maneuvers that incrementally blurred the distinction between the two forms of tenure, to the disadvantage of the *votchina* estates.

In 1497 Ivan issued a new law code called the *Sudebnik.* Designed to standardize procedures in courts throughout the realm, the *Sudebnik* had several noteworthy provisions. One article mandated the death penalty for rebellion and sedition. This was a harsher penalty than specified in the earlier Russkaya Pravda (although Moscow's princes in the 14th and 15th centuries had used the death penalty against people they deemed traitors), and in effect testified to the growing power of Moscow's grand prince. So did Ivan's use of the death penalty and other severe sentences against people of princely rank.

Another article in the *Sudebnik* regulated the right of peasants to leave the estates of their landlords and migrate to other places. As in the past, peasants were still technically free to move, but the *Sudebnik* limited when they could move to two weeks in the late fall, after the harvest had been collected. They also had to pay an exit fee to their landlords, which in almost all cases was a difficult obligation to meet and therefore a serious obstacle to departure. This directly promoted the interests of Ivan's *pomestie* nobles, who could serve in Ivan's army and fight his wars only if they could count on peasant laborers to farm their estates. During the 16th century the right of peasants to move would be further restricted until, by the middle of the 17th century, when another law code was issued, Russia's peasants were reduced to serfdom. Thus Ivan accomplished two things: one by intention—building an autocratic state; and one unintentionally—laying the foundations for serfdom. Together these institutions would have a defining—and deleterious— influence on Russia's development for centuries to come.

Finally, Ivan III was a great builder. As he saw it, the city of Moscow, the capital of his realm, needed impressive stone buildings to match the grandeur of the state. To that end he imported prominent Italian architects, as his own country's architects and builders did not have the skills necessary to build the grand structures he wanted. Some of those skills, such as solid-bond masonry, had been known in Russia prior to the Mongol invasion but had been largely forgotten. Others, including many of the modern technologies and methods used to build western Europe's Renaissance churches, had never reached Russia as it stag- nated during the centuries of Mongol rule.

Ivan's most notable project by far was the rebuilding of the Kremlin, a decadeslong effort that produced the red brick walls—65 feet high and as thick as 20 feet—that run for more than 7,000 feet around the huge compound. They were designed to withstand the latest European artillery. Ivan's other projects included the grandiose Assumption Cathedral, the largest in the Kremlin—he ordered the famous Italian architect and engineer Aristotle Fieravanti to build the greatest cathe- dral Russia had ever seen—graced with five golden domes and four

The Bell Tower of Ivan the Great, begun by Ivan the Great and raised to its current height by Boris Godunov. Until the late 19th century it was forbidden to build a taller structure in Moscow. (Vova Pomortzeff, 2007. Used under license from ShutterStock, Inc.)

gables. The czars would use that cathedral for coronations until the end of the monarchy. The smaller Annunciation Cathedral was built by native craftsmen from Pskov and subsequently used by the czars for baptisms and weddings.

Ivan also built secular structures in the Kremlin. His Palace of the Facets, a striking example of Renaissance architecture with a majestic facade of white stone on the western edge of the Kremlin's central square, served to receive foreign dignitaries. In 1505, the year he died, Ivan started an ambitious bell tower. Completed in 1508 and raised to its current height of 263 feet in 1600, the Ivan the Great Bell Tower is the tallest structure in the Kremlin and was the tallest in Moscow until the late 19th century. Imposing and dramatic, it was aptly named.

Vasily III

Vasily III (r. 1505–33) was a worthy successor to his father and ruled Muscovy for the considerable period of 28 years. From the point of view of historical stature, it was Vasily's misfortune to have his reign sandwiched between the tenures of Russia's two mighty, charismatic

Ivans. The watershed accomplishments of Ivan the Great and the fire and brimstone of Ivan the Terrible have tended to obscure the substantial but unspectacular achievements of Vasily III. This somewhat unfair development is perhaps best illustrated by his lack of an unofficial sobriquet after his name; perhaps "Vasily the Consolidator" or "Vasily the Stabilizer" might have been suitable.

In any event, Vasily continued ably to implement his father's policies. He completed the annexation of the principalities of Pskov and Ryazan, deporting their leading boyars in the ruthless manner of his father. He took Smolensk from Lithuania and held it. He expanded the powers of the grand prince without pushing too hard against the boyars, and continued building a centralized army directly under his control. If Vasily suffered military defeats, so did his father and predecessor; if he was unable to stop a Tatar army from reaching Moscow, neither could his son and successor, Ivan the Terrible. Vasily's worst failing, and he is blameless on this count, was that he died suddenly in 1533 when his eldest son, Ivan, the heir to the throne, was only three years old. A decade of unstable regency followed. Then the teenage Ivan IV grasped the levers of power. What ensued was a reign that began well enough and produced needed reforms, given the standards of that place and time, but ultimately became a time of upheaval and madness that left Russia badly scarred and on the verge of chaos.

Ivan IV

The Early Years

Ivan IV (r. 1533–84) still casts his shadow over the land. The awe and dread he evoked during his reign resonate so strongly that it seems strange to write that he has been dead for more than 400 years. Ivan was highly intelligent, possibly brilliant. He also, it seems fair to say, was possessed. Ivan went through periods of deep religious devotion. He was driven by a messianic commitment to Russia's greatness and what he considered its God-given mission to lead humanity, a calling he believed he had to serve at any cost. He also was haunted by personal demons—some known to historians, others known only to Ivan, and still others that he himself could probably not identify—that made him erratic, paranoid, ruthless, and capable of acts of extreme cruelty, including mass murder.

In the remarkable pantheon of Russia's rulers, Ivan's intense qualities are not unique: Vladimir Monomakh shared his religious devotion and, like him, was highly literate and well read; Peter the Great matched, and Stalin exceeded, his cruelty, and Stalin shared his paranoia; Lenin shared his twisted messianic idealism and was equally capable of mass murder (although no Russian ruler comes close to Stalin in that category); Peter the Great had his charisma and could be terribly cruel; Peter III and Paul I, although not quite insane, were severely unbalanced. But the boiling, flammable blend of religiosity, cruelty, messianic fanaticism, personal charisma, brilliance, and violent insanity is uniquely Ivan's. Some Russian linguists have argued that the word "*grozny*," used to describe Ivan, is correctly translated not as "terrible" but as "dread" (in the sense that people dreaded him) and that therefore English speakers know him by an incorrect name. Not all dictionaries agree—but given the whole of Ivan's tyrannical rule, what may be a mistranslation is not a misnomer.

Historians agree that Ivan's difficult childhood deeply influenced his later actions. The country's leading boyar families took advantage of the regency and the absence of a strong monarch to reassert their privileges, especially after the death of Ivan's mother, possibly by poisoning, when the boy was eight years old. Aside from looting the state treasury and grabbing land, the boyars and princes also viciously attacked each other. Murders, arbitrary arrests, torture, and an assortment of other crimes were common, with some of the worst violence taking place in the presence of Ivan himself.

Although Ivan personally was never threatened or hurt and was treated with respect in public, in private the boyars and princes at the royal court often insulted and neglected him, so with good reason he feared for his life. Ivan learned their methods well: When he was only 13 he had a prince executed, according to one report by being thrown to a pack of dogs and torn limb from limb. By the time Ivan was 17 and ready to assert his rule, he fiercely hated the boyars. He had concluded that they were a danger to the Russian state and that their power had to be shattered once and for all.

Ivan's coronation in 1547 signaled that times were about to change. In a ceremony modeled on the Byzantine example, Ivan eschewed the old title of grand prince of Muscovy and instead had himself crowned czar of all the Russias. What Ivan III had suggested and set as a goal, Ivan IV now explicitly proclaimed: Russia's ruler was vested with unbridled autocratic power, and he would use it to the fullest. In addition, by proclaiming himself czar of all the Russias and invoking the authority of the Orthodox Church and the legacy of the Byzantine Empire, Ivan was staking a claim for Russia as a great power that all other states must respect and, indeed, accept as their superior.

The year 1547 witnessed two other major events. First, the czar took a wife, Anastasiya Romanova, from a prominent boyar family. It

was a good match and a happy
marriage with a sad ending. Her
death in 1560—Ivan believed she
was murdered—devastated him,
and while the mental changes
that led Ivan to launch a reign of
terror at that time clearly ante-
dated Anastasiya's death, that loss
and the deep personal distress it
caused him must have contributed in some way to the dreadful
events that soon took place. The
other major event of 1547 was
the great fire that destroyed most
of Moscow. The riots that followed unnerved Ivan and pushed
him to reform how his realm was
governed.

Ivan the Terrible, the first Russian ruler to officially take the title czar (Library of Congress)

It is crucial to understand that
Ivan's reforms during the first and so-called good part of his reign were
designed to provide more efficient government and strengthen the state
in the service of autocratic rule. They had nothing to do with sharing
power; in fact, they were intended to achieve precisely the opposite.
Ivan worked with a small group of able advisers called the Chosen
Council, which he pointedly staffed with men from various classes,
including churchmen, to limit the influence of the boyars.

One early innovation was an appointed assembly called the *zemsky
sobor,* assembly of the land, which included members from all social
classes except the peasantry. Its formal job was to help Ivan's officials
run the country, but its actual purpose seems to have been to win
the czar public support. It met for the first time in 1549 or 1550 and
then sporadically thereafter, accomplishing little. Ivan also established
elected units of government called zemstvos, but again, local zemstvo
officials were elected not to represent the people but to serve the government by collecting taxes and maintaining order. Ivan's new law code,
the *Sudebnik* of 1550, likewise was designed to improve government
efficiency in areas like judicial procedure and tax collection. Ivan also
created a new military force, the *streltsy* (shooters). Essentially a palace
guard, the *streltsy* were paid by the government and directly under its
control and constituted the first permanent troops in the Russian army.

St. Basil's Cathedral was built by Ivan the Terrible and remains one of the most identifiable and beautiful symbols of Russia. (Dmitry Kosterev, 2007. Used under license from ShutterStock, Inc.)

In 1556 Ivan issued a decree regulating the property rights and military obligations of the *pomestie* landlords. They gained full hereditary rights to their estates, but at the same time their military obligations became permanent. Of course, land without labor to work it was worth little, so in his 1550 law code Ivan affirmed the restrictions on peasant movement imposed by his grandfather 53 years earlier. These and other burdens, mainly high taxes and the demands of military service, caused many peasants to ignore the law and flee, especially toward the east and south, where in the mid-1550s Ivan's conquests had opened up new land. Later in his reign, after totally disrupting the life of the country, the czar responded by significantly increasing landlord control over the peasantry. He moved the peasants further along the road to serfdom by establishing the so-called forbidden years when peasants could not leave their current estates under any circumstances. The first forbidden year seems to have been 1581; it would be followed by many more until the peasants were permanently bonded as serfs to the estates on which they were born. During the 1580s Ivan also ended taxes on the landlords' lands and shifted the burden to the peasants.

Ivan's early efforts in foreign affairs generally went well. In 1552 he sent his army eastward toward the Volga River and the khanate of Kazan. Kazan was a target not only because of Ivan's expansionist goals but because of the khanate's raids against Russian territory in which tens of thousands of people were carried off and then sold into slavery. After hard fighting, Ivan's troops took the city of Kazan and Russia annexed the khanate. The victory made Ivan extremely popular, a worthy successor in Russian eyes to Aleksandr Nevsky and Dmitry Donskoi. Back in Moscow, he celebrated his victory by building the extraordinary St. Basil's Cathedral. Built in brick in the style of Russia's traditional wooden churches, with a golden dome topping each of nine churches (a tenth church and dome were added shortly after Ivan's death), St. Basil's has been a Moscow landmark since its completion in 1560, as recognizable as the Kremlin and as symbolic of Moscow as the Eiffel Tower is of Paris or the Empire State Building is of New York City.

The conquest of Kazan was followed by the conquest of Astrakhan to the southeast. Together these victories opened up the lower Volga steppe region to Russian settlement for the first time. It also for the first time brought a large non-Russian population under Moscow's control, thereby marking the start of Russia's transformation into an empire. Soon Russian fur traders and Cossacks—warlike descendants of runaway peasants from Muscovy, Poland, and Lithuania who beginning in the 16th century had established independent communities along the middle and lower Dnieper and Don rivers—crossed the Urals and established Moscow's claim to western Siberia, initiating a process that within a century would lead to Russia's expansion to the Pacific.

The Kazan Kremlin dates from the Tatar era. Ivan the Terrible rebuilt much of it after he conquered the khanate of Kazan in 1552. (Khafizov Ivan Harisovich, 2007. Used under license from ShutterStock, Inc.)

Ivan's attempt to expand westward was unsuccessful, despite early gains in the late 1550s and early 1560s in the opening phase of what is called the Livonian War. The war began against German Livonian knights in an attempt to seize territory along the Baltic coast, but eventually Poland and Sweden became involved against Russia. By the early 1580s, a quarter century of war and hardship had resulted in defeat and no territorial gain. More successful was the establishment of trade relations with England, which occurred after an English explorer, seeking a northern route to China, sailed into the frigid White Sea in 1553 and made landfall in Russia.

Ivan the Terrible: The Later Years

It is said that when St. Basil's was finished in 1560 Ivan had its architect blinded so that he could never again build anything so beautiful. The story may be apocryphal but the fact that so many people then and now believe it to be true says something about Ivan. It also says something about the year 1560. That date marks the approximate start of the second part of Ivan's reign, the years in which the czar brought terror and misery to his people on a shocking scale.

It is impossible to know what set Ivan off. His youthful hatred of the boyars intensified in 1553 when he became deathly ill and many of the leading boyars refused to swear allegiance to his infant son Dmitry as heir to the throne. In 1560 Ivan abolished his Chosen Council and things went downhill from there. A series of arrests and executions followed. In 1564 the boyar Prince Andrei Kurbsky, one of his most trusted officials and one of the top commanders in the storming of Kazan, defected in protest to Lithuania. He was joined by other boyars who had come to fear for their lives in the wake of Ivan's increasingly erratic and vicious behavior. Ivan and Kurbsky later exchanged a famous series of mutually recriminating letters. Ivan, in response to Kurbsky's accusation that he was a tyrant, spelled out his belief in the legitimacy of autocratic rule: Simply put, the powers of Russia's autocrat came from God, and therefore he had the right to act as he saw fit, responsible only to God. That did not convince Kurbsky or many other boyars, and Ivan knew it, but he had no intention of letting their objections stand in his way.

In December 1564 the czar left Moscow, paused to pray at a monastery, and stopped in a small town about 60 miles from the capital. He announced his wish to abdicate, and sent two letters to Moscow: One denounced the boyars and the second called on the common people to support him. In January 1565 he returned to Moscow with a vengeance, establishing the so-called *oprichnina.* The term had two meanings. First, it referred to a special administrative subdivision of the realm. Ivan divided Russia into two parts: the *oprichnina,* the czar's personal domain, which

IVAN IV DEFENDS AUTOCRACY

After Prince Kurbsky, one of his leading boyars, defected to Lithuania and denounced Ivan as a tyrant, the czar wrote a defense of autocratic rule in a letter he sent to the defector.

> . . . And we praise [God] for his great mercy bestowed upon us. . . . as we were born to rule, so have we grown up and ascended the throne by the bidding of God. . . . [From the ruler] of this Orthodox true Christian autocracy, which has the power over many dominions, a command [should be sent to you]; but this is our Christian and humble answer to him who was formerly boyar and advisor . . . of our autocratic state and of the true Christian Orthodox faith, but who is now the perjurer of the holy and life-giving Cross of the Lord and destroyer of Christianity . . .
>
> . . . But as for the Russian autocracy, they themselves [i.e., the autocrats] from the beginning have ruled all their dominions, and not the boyars and not the grandees . . .
>
> . . . Many other things too will you find in the reigns of the tsars. They have restored the kingdom in its times of trouble and they have frustrated the thoughts and ill deeds of the wicked. And [therefore] it is always fitting for tsars to be perspicacious, now most gentle, now fierce; mercy and gentleness for the good; for the evil—fierceness and torment. If a tsar does not possess this quality, then he is no tsar . . .
>
> Behold then [this] and consider what sort of government was [lit. is] formed in the various powers and governments, when in them their tsars listen to eparchs and counselors, and to what destruction they came. Is this what you advise for us, namely to come to such destruction? . . . How excellent and how befitting! It is one thing to save one's own soul, but another to be responsible for many souls and bodies. . . . And is it befitting for a tsar: when he is struck on the cheek, for him to turn the other cheek? Is this then the supreme commandment? For how can a tsar govern his kingdom if he himself be without honor? . . . (Fennell 1955: 15, 27, 41, 57, 59)

he would administer any way he wanted; and the rest of the country, which would be run in the usual way by the formal government. Second, and much more important, the term referred to the corps of men who ran that personal domain—the *oprichniki*—who eventually numbered 6,000 and whose job was to destroy all opposition to the czar.

Dressed in black cloaks, mounted on black horses, and carrying with them an emblem of a dog's head and a broom that signified how they would sweep away all traitors, the *oprichniki* did their appointed job with great zeal and effectiveness through a reign of terror, complete with mass arrests and murders and horribly gory, sadistic executions. Thousands of boyars lost their lands and their lives. Many ordinary people died as well, especially in towns Ivan suspected might shelter lingering opposition to his rule. In Novgorod alone, in just five weeks in 1570, the *oprichniki* killed an estimated 40,000 people. They killed 9,000 in Tver and thousands more elsewhere. The czar rewarded them well for their work: often *oprichniki*, many of whom came from the lower classes, ended up as the new owners of the confiscated estates.

IVAN THE TERRIBLE COMMITS MASS MURDER

The following is a contemporary account of how Ivan dealt with the city of Novgorod in 1570 during the era of the *oprichnina*:

> . . . The Tsar commanded that the powerful boyars, the important merchants, the administrative officials, and the citizens of every rank be brought before him, together with their wives and children. The Tsar ordered that they be tortured in his presence in various spiteful, horrible, and inhuman ways. After many various unspeakable and bitter tortures, the tsar ordered that their bodies be tormented and roasted with fire in refined ways. He ordered that each man be tied to a sled, be dragged to the Volkhov bridge behind fast-moving sleds, and be thrown into the Volkhov river from the bridge. The Tsar ordered that their wives and children be brought to the Volkhov bridge where a high platform had been erected. He commanded that they be chained on the arms and legs and that the children be tied to the mothers and then be thrown from the platform into the waters of the Volkhov River. Meanwhile, the Tsar's men, nobles and soldiers, moved about in small boats on the Volkhov River, armed with spears, lances, hooks and axes. When the people, men and women of all ages, surfaced, they were stabbed by the soldiers with hooks, lances, and spears, or they were struck with axes. In a horrible manner they were submerged without mercy in the depths of the river, and abandoned to a terrible and bitter death. (Dmytryshyn 1973: 238)

Not surprisingly, Ivan's reign of terror disrupted life in Russia at every level, including the army's ability to defend the country. Thus in 1571, as the *oprichniki* were running wild, a Tatar army from the Crimea invaded Russia, burned the outskirts of Moscow, and seized thousands of captives. It did not help that during the crisis Ivan executed the commander of his army. When the Russian army later defeated the Crimean Tatars, Ivan again executed his commanding general, a prince whose popularity the czar considered a threat. Ivan finally abolished the *oprichnina* in 1572—characteristically, he began by executing many of it leaders—having gravely weakened, though not destroyed, the boyars and his other opponents.

But the killing did not entirely stop. In 1581 an enraged Ivan struck and killed his eldest son, namesake, and heir to the throne, a scene immortalized by the great 19th-century artist Ilya Repin in his painting *Ivan the Terrible and the Death of His Son*. The czar himself lived for three more years. When he died, he left behind a sickly, feeble heir; an exhausted, demoralized, and destabilized population; aristocratic survivors of his terror determined to take back their old privileges; and powerful foreign enemies ready to take advantage of Russia's weakness. It was a formula for chaos.

The Time of Troubles

A decade and a half of relative calm prevailed before the storm. Fyodor II, Ivan's eldest surviving son and successor, lacked both the intellect and the interest to govern Russia. That job therefore fell to a group of advisers led by the young czar's brother-in-law, the largely illiterate but highly intelligent, crafty, and ambitious Boris Godunov. Under Godunov's direction the country recovered economically and continued its expansion into Siberia. At the same time the most important underlying problems, especially peasant discontent, remained unresolved. The most important event of Fyodor's reign was probably the unexplained death of his brother Dmitry, heir to the throne and the ruling dynasty's last male member. Many people suspected foul play and pointed to Godunov as the suspect, an unlikely scenario according to most historians. In any case Fyodor died childless, and a meeting of the *zemsky sobor* chose Boris Godunov as czar.

Godunov knew how to govern, but he had many enemies among the boyar families, and his luck was running out. A drought in 1601 led to a severe two-year famine. Armed bands desperate for food scoured the countryside looting anything they came across. In 1604 someone (possibly a former monk) claiming to be Fyodor's brother Dmitry, who had miraculously escaped the murder plot, invaded Russia with several thousand Polish troops. His forces augmented by hungry peasants, the first False Dmitry, as he was known, advanced toward Moscow. Just then Czar Boris suddenly died and his young son and heir was murdered. What followed is aptly known as the Time of Troubles.

The Time of Troubles began with the brief, chaotic rule of the first False Dmitry. Having alienated most Russians by relying on Polish supporters and converting to Catholicism, Dmitry was murdered by a mob in 1606. A group of boyars then proclaimed one of their own, Vasily Shuisky, as czar. He managed to hang on to the throne for four years despite a series of upheavals, starting with uprisings by various boyar rivals. Shuisky also survived a widespread rebellion of peasants, serfs, slaves, and other dispossessed groups led by the Cossack Ivan Bolotnikov, which aimed to overthrow the entire social order and lasted until 1607.

Meanwhile, a second False Dmitry crossed the frontier with Polish backing. When Shuisky turned to Sweden for help—giving up Russia's claim to disputed territory in return—Poland, a rival of both Sweden and Russia, entered the war directly. Amid this swirling, destructive confusion, Shuisky was driven from the throne in 1610 and a small group of boyars took control in Moscow.

Russia then hit bottom. That summer, besieged by two armies, one Polish and the other a Russian force loyal to the second False Dmitry, a hastily convened group of boyars in Moscow elected the son of the Polish king to be Russia's czar; in return the Poles quickly disposed of the second False Dmitry. But a Catholic Polish czar was anathema to most Russians, and under the instigation of the Orthodox Church a rebellion soon broke out.

The anti-Polish Russian forces found able leaders in the butcher Kuzma Minin and the nobleman Dmitry Pozharsky. By the end of 1612 the Poles had been driven from Moscow, and in 1613 a *zemsky sobor* chose Michael Romanov as czar. Czar Michael came from the boyar family that had given Ivan the Terrible his beloved wife, Anastasiya. The dynasty he founded would rule Russia for more than 300 years.

The First Romanovs

The Romanov dynasty took root, and Russia gradually recovered from the Time of Troubles under the new dynasty's first two czars, Michael (r. 1613–45) and Alexis (r. 1645–76), and during the short, relatively uneventful reign of feeble third Romanov, Fyodor III (r. 1676–82). These three reigns form a seven-decade transition period between the Muscovite era that ended in the 16th century, when Russia still existed on the fringe of European life and remained relatively untouched by contact with the West, and the imperial era that begins in the 18th century, when Russia became a major player in European affairs and was greatly affected by a wide range of Western intellectual, cultural, and economic influences. Compared to the decades that preceded it, the early Romanov era was relatively stable, but it was still a difficult time. The government treasury was consistently stretched beyond its limits, and efforts to squeeze more resources out of the common people with extra taxes added to their already considerable burdens.

There are three key facts about the reign of Michael Romanov. First, none of its problems ever spun out of control, and at Michael's death the crown passed in an orderly fashion to his son Alexis. Second, the powers of the autocracy remained uncompromised. True, the *zemsky sobor* was often convened, but it met for short periods, was very loosely organized, and did nothing to limit the czar's power. Michael's main adviser, the man who actually made the decisions until his death in 1633, was his father, Philaret, who as patriarch, a post dating from 1589, also headed the Russian Orthodox Church. Third, Russia was largely at peace during Michael's reign. A treaty with Sweden in 1617 left Russia in control of Novgorod but excluded from the Baltic coast. A 1618 truce with Poland lasted until 1632; after two years of fighting, a peace treaty was signed in 1634 (misnamed the "eternal peace").

The reign of Alexis saw several significant developments. The most important by far was the new law code of 1649. Its provisions confirmed serfdom as the condition of virtually all peasants, who accounted for 90 percent of the czar's subjects. The 1649 code gave the landlords control of virtually every aspect of the serfs' lives, left the serfs with almost no redress against their masters, and in fact reduced them to a status having more in common with conventional slavery than with serfdom as that institution had existed in Europe during the Middle Ages. Another significant development of this reign was the split (*raskol*) in the Russian Orthodox Church. It occurred because the reigning patriarch introduced reforms in church liturgy to correct errors that had been made over time in translating Greek texts into Russian. The opponents of reform became known as Old Believers, a small but significant sect within the Orthodox tradition to this day.

Meanwhile, the oppressive conditions under which the peasantry lived led to a massive rebellion in 1670–71 led by the Cossack Stepan

THE RUSSIAN AUTOCRACY COMPARED WITH EUROPEAN MONARCHIES

Although the European monarchies of the early modern era were absolutist and offered their subjects few of the protections taken for granted in modern democracies, European travelers to Russia were struck by the absolute and arbitrary nature of the czar's powers compared with what they were accustomed to at home. They also noted that Russia lacked political or social estates with recognized rights to limit the monarch's actions. Baron Sigismund von Herberstein, an ambassador in the service of the Holy Roman Emperor, visited Muscovy in 1517 and 1526 during the reign of Vasily III and described what he saw:

> In the sway which he [the Russian autocrat] holds over his people, he surpasses all the monarchs of the whole world. . . . He uses his power as much over ecclesiastics as laymen, and holds unlimited control over the lives and property of all his subjects. . . .

Adam Olaerius was part of a diplomatic mission to Russia from one of the many German rulers during the 1630s, when Michael Romanov was czar. His impressions were similar to those of von Herberstein:

> The politik Government of Muscovy is Monarchical and despotical. . . . No Master hath more power over his slaves, than the Great Duke hath over his subjects, what condition or quality soever they be of. (Szamuely 1974: 6–7)

(Stenka) Razin. The rebellion surged through the Volga region until it finally was suppressed and its leader executed. Razin, however, was more than a mere rebel leader; his charisma turned him into a folk legend. He remains the most celebrated of the four leaders of the major peasant rebellions of the 17th and 18th centuries (the others are Bolotnikov, Kondraty Bulavin in 1707–08, and Yemelyan Pugachev in 1773–74). Revered by ordinary people and the subject of countless songs and legends, he was also lionized by Aleksandr Pushkin, Russia's greatest poet. The following verse from one popular ballad, whose lyrics expressed faith in the fallen rebel's resurrection, is typical of how generations of Russian peasants viewed Razin:

43

Rise, oh rise, beautiful sun,
Warm us the poor folk,
Sturdy lads, fugitives:
We are not thieves, nor brigands,
We are comrades of Stenka Razin.

(Lozonova 1935: 53)

In the Volga region, ravines, burial grounds, and other rural spots were named for him. It was also said that near Saratov, a town on the Volga, is a hill one can climb at night to learn Razin's secret. That secret is class war, and its impact on Russia and its people, when its devotees in the 20th century got their chance to wage it as Razin in the 17th century could not, would be shattering.

On the foreign front, a massive Cossack-led uprising in the Ukraine against Poland that began in 1648 opened a window of opportunity for Moscow to take over that region. In 1654 Moscow reached an agreement with the Cossack leadership that called for a union in which the Cossacks would continue to exercise self-government. The alliance led to renewed war with Poland. After 13 years of fighting the Treaty of Andusovo (1667) divided the Ukraine between the two powers at the Dnieper River. Russian control stopped at the river's eastern bank with the exception of Kiev, which stands west of the river but ended up in Russian hands.

Two Czars on the Throne

The long reign of Alexis was followed by the short reign of his sickly teenage son, Fyodor III. At the latter's death in 1682 a struggle for power emerged between the families of Alexis's two wives (he remarried after his first wife died in 1669), each of which offered a male contender for the throne. Both candidates were minors, opening the door for the ambitious princess Sophia, one of Alexis's daughters by his first wife. She and her supporters staged a bloody coup that established her as regent for her two younger brothers, who were eyewitnesses to the killing of some of their relatives. The scheme put two czars on the throne: Sophia's sickly and mentally limited 15-year-old full brother Ivan (as "first" czar) and her highly energetic and intelligent 10-year-old half brother Peter (as "second" czar). In 1689 Sophia's unsuccessful effort to remove her brothers and become ruler in her own right failed, and she was exiled to a convent, in effect prisoner for life. Peter's supporters now controlled the government, although he himself, still a teenager, busied himself with other interests. He began to govern directly in 1694 upon the death of his mother and was rid of his co-czar when Ivan died in 1696. A new era in Russia's history had begun.

3

IMPERIAL RUSSIA: THE ERAS OF PETER THE GREAT AND CATHERINE THE GREAT (1694–1801)

When the 18th century began Russia was still known to Europeans as Muscovy, a distant, backward, partially Asiatic, and largely alien realm that few people visited and even fewer viewed positively. By the century's end Russia was recognized as a major European power, one with lingering unattractive features—especially its despotic government and the institution of serfdom—but an accepted participant in the European state system and a country whose educated elites at various levels were engaged in European life.

The growth of European influence on Russia, a process known today as Westernization, continued on throughout the century. However, two rulers at its opposite ends, Peter the Great (r. 1682–1725) and Catherine the Great (r. 1762–96), are with good reason the most associated with that process. The two monarchs had much in common beyond the sobriquet "the Great." Each of their reigns was an era of internal reform based on European models, and each saw expansion abroad. Each featured the new capital of St. Petersburg as its showpiece: Peter founded the city and made it Russia's capital, and Catherine lavished attention on it. And each failed Russia utterly by reinforcing the grip of serfdom on the peasantry and of autocracy on the nation as a whole.

Yet, there is at least one major difference between the two reigns. The reign of Peter, whatever its shortcomings, was one of substance, involving serious changes in important institutions. Peter created the modern Russian state. Before him there was no distinction between the czar's person and the government. Peter made that distinction, in effect establishing the concept of the state with the czar as its first servant.

He also expanded the government's activities into most areas of national life. Among other things Peter founded the modern Russian army, built Russia's first major industrial base, and forced the country's elite to adopt certain Western customs and habits.

Catherine's reign, whatever the czarina's pretensions, was one of style. She beautified St. Petersburg with new buildings, promoted the arts, corresponded with leading thinkers of Europe's Enlightenment such as the French philosophers Voltaire and Diderot, and expanded Russia's borders. But these and similar activities were window dressing; they did not involve structural change to any important institutions.

The Education and Early Career of Peter the Great

The ruler who would go down in history as Peter the Great was a self-made man, notwithstanding his royal birth. His formal schooling was limited: The tutor assigned to educate him when Peter was five was a hopeless drunkard. Even that instruction ended in 1682, when a coup by his half-sister Sophia crowned the 10-year-old boy as the official "second czar" while in reality pushing him and his mother out of the Kremlin to a village outside Moscow.

Peter was extremely intelligent, intellectually curious (at least regarding matters of technology and military science), physically vigorous, incredibly strong-willed, and utterly ruthless in enforcing that will. He stood at least six feet seven inches tall, towering over his contemporaries physically as he ultimately did figuratively over the country he strove with all his might to change. He was and remains both admired and hated, praised for what he did and condemned for how he did it, extolled for modernizing his country and excoriated for putting crushing burdens on its people, respected as a statesman and reviled as a tyrant. It is, of course, not surprising that Peter the Great has elicited such disparate evaluations. What is interesting about those diametrically opposed assessments is that they are often made by the same commentator, depending on the subject.

It is normally the job of monarchs to prepare their heirs to succeed them. Peter received no such assistance. He prepared himself to rule, and even his detractors would have to admit that he did a good if not excellent job. He turned his exile from the Kremlin into an opportunity. Free from Sophia's supervision, Peter set off on his own to look for the kind of teachers he wanted among the European technocrats and military experts who lived in a section of Moscow set aside for foreign residents, the so-called German quarter.

Peter's potpourri of unofficial instructors included a Dutch merchant, who first taught him the use of the astrolabe and then, at Peter's request, became his instructor in mathematics and a variety of technical military subjects; an English officer hired by Alexis in the 1660s; and a Swiss adventurer who, among other things, taught the young czar about the attractions of raucous living and drunken orgies. Peter did not allow his marriage in 1689, arranged by his mother for political reasons, to interrupt his active and varied social life; he eventually ended the marriage in 1699 by forcing his wife to enter a convent.

Tapping the knowledge of numerous foreign specialists, the young czar, who had already mastered carpentry, stone masonry, and other crafts, learned a variety of practical skills, especially those with military applications, such as how to build and sail boats and how to fire artillery. His boyhood playmates, like his teachers, were a motley crew from all classes and stations in Russian society, far from what one would have expected for someone of Peter's royal rank. Most prominent among them was an illiterate but intelligent and ambitious youth named Aleksandr Menshikov, whose career probably started as a peddler on the streets of Moscow. Menshikov moved up from there to become the czar's closest friend and one of Russia's top officials. Young Peter used the military specialists he knew and whatever funds were made available to him by his half sister's court, which did not take him seriously, to train his friends into his own small private army. These so-called toy regiments were crucial to Peter's survival in his successful struggle against Sophia and her supporters in 1689, which ended with her exile to a convent. Subsequently they became the core building blocks of a new and modern Russian army. All this Peter did while still in his teens.

Peter was 22 years old when, in 1694, he began his direct role in governing Russia, by which time he had acquired a wide range of military skills. He quickly put them to use. His first major initiative was an offensive against the Ottoman Empire with two aims: seizing territory for a Russian harbor on the Black Sea and ending Crimean Tatar raids into Russia. The operation became a painful but valuable learning experience.

In 1695 Russian forces attacked the fortress of Azov on the Don, which controlled the northern access to the Sea of Azov. The attack, made against the advice of his best foreign general, a Scotsman named Patrick Gordon, failed with heavy losses. Peter then retreated and spent the winter building a fleet of galleys to blockade Azov and keep the Turks from resupplying the fortress by sea. The czar himself supervised the work. In the summer of 1696 the Russians took Azov. Peter was relieved but hardly satisfied.

The campaign above all had revealed to him the extent of Russia's military backwardness. Understanding full well that the most technologically and militarily advanced countries were in western Europe, Peter decided to send selected Russians there to learn the necessary technology and techniques. Characteristically, he decided he had to be among them.

The result was his "grand embassy," a remarkable 18-month tour whose impact would resonate throughout the rest of Peter's reign. The grand embassy numbered about 250 people when it left Moscow in early 1697, with Peter traveling incognito as the bombardier Peter Mikhailov, a ruse that from the start was an open secret. Peter's concerns actually went beyond European military technology. He was interested in European customs as well, as these had obviously contributed to the West's success. He also hoped to form an alliance of Christian countries against the Muslim Turks, a plan that ran aground on the rock of bitter rivalries among those countries.

Above all, however, Peter was there to see and learn, especially about shipbuilding and other naval matters. He visited several European countries, but his most important destinations were Holland and England. In Holland he visited the scientific institutes of Amsterdam and worked in the city's shipyards. In England, according to one shipwright who saw Peter in the shipyards, "the tsar of Muscovy worked with his own hands as hard as any man in the yard" (editors of *Horizon Magazine* 1970: 154).

While in London Peter also visited an arsenal, a museum, and, among other government institutions, the mint. He met members of Britain's Royal Society and questioned them about science and scientific instruments, such as the microscope. Significantly, Peter showed no interest in Parliament or British political theory. Before returning home he recruited about 750 engineers, seamen, and other naval specialists, mainly Dutchmen but also some Englishmen, Scots, Italians, Greeks, and others, to work in Russia. He would hire many more during his reign. Peter also bought huge quantities of arms and equipment. It took 10 ships to transport everything and everyone back to Russia.

Most important, as he surveyed the thriving countries of the West and compared them to his homeland, Peter became more convinced than ever that Russia had to learn from Europe if it was to become a modern, powerful state able to hold its own and protect its interests in the international arena. That meant sending more Russians to Europe to study, bringing European experts to Russia to work and teach, and making reforms at home to promote economic development, technical education, efficient government, and even changes in how people behaved.

The grand embassy was cut short when Peter received news of a revolt by the *streltsy* aimed at restoring Sophia to power. The actual revolt had already been suppressed by the time Peter got the news, but upon arriving in Moscow the czar took a direct role in investigating its origins and punishing the rebels. He personally participated in the torture and execution of prisoners. About 1,000 were executed; their bodies, bearing telltale signs of the brutal treatment they had endured, were left on public display for months as an unmistakable warning to others.

Reform and War

Even before he disposed of the *streltsy,* Peter made it clear he was going to change how things were done in Russia. In the late 17th century Russian men still wore long beards, unlike the men Peter had met in western Europe. In what became a famous and symbolic scene, shortly after arriving in Moscow the czar personally cut off the beards of a group of nobles. Henceforth, anyone around the czar was expected to look and dress like a modern European.

In 1700 Peter took an overdue step and reformed the Russian calendar, which at the time reckoned years from the presumed creation of the world. Unfortunately, at least for students of Russian history, Peter adopted the Julian calendar rather than the newer and more accurate Gregorian calendar. Because the Julian calendar already trailed the Gregorian calendar by 11 days and was losing an additional day each century, the study of Russian history through the first months of the Soviet era has since been littered by two dates for each historic event— the date used by Russians and the date used by outsiders. Not until March 1918 did Russia finally adopt the Gregorian calendar. That is why the "February" revolution that brought down the czar in fact took place in March 1917, while the "October" revolution of the Bolsheviks that led to the founding of the Soviet Union actually took place in November of that year.

As he initiated his reform, Peter simultaneously prepared his army for war. His plans for an alliance against the Ottoman Empire having fallen through, the new target was Sweden, master of the Baltic coast. Peter was determined to secure new ports for Russia, whose only port at the time was Arkhangelsk on the White Sea, at once too out of the way and also frozen and useless for half the year. So began the Great Northern War, destined to last for more than two decades. It began disastrously for Russia. Sweden's new king, Charles XII, was a daring and skilled general who led a well-trained army equipped with modern weapons. In November 1700 the Swedish army, although badly out-numbered, routed the Russians at the town of Narva, about 10 miles from the coast of the Gulf of Finland (an inlet of the Baltic Sea).

PETER THE GREAT SUPERVISES HIS WORKFORCE

John Perry, an Englishman who served as both a naval officer and a hydraulic engineer before coming to Russia, lived and worked there for 14 years. He had good reason to complain about his treat-ment at the hands of Czar Peter, including lack of payment for his services and threats to his life, but that did not prevent him from appreciating the czar's talents and dedication to his work, as the fol-lowing extract indicates:

> As the Czar has taken a particular regard to have his own sub-jects qualfy'd to serve him on all these occasions, he has spared no pains for it, but continually busies himself amongst these men, in ordering and giving his directions in every thing that relates to his army and his navy, and delights in it, so that it may be said of him, that he is from drummer to the general, a compleat soldier; besides his being engineer, cannoneer, fire-worker, ship-builder, turner, boatswain, gun-founder, blacksmith, etc. All which he fre-quently works with his own hands, and will himself see that every thing be carried on and perform'd to his own mind, as well in these minutest things, as in the greater disposition of affairs.
>
> After the loss of said battle [Narva], the Czar spent the great-est part of his time in the effectually giving his order for the rais-ing of recruits, and in the placing his officers, seeing his regiments exercised, and providing all things whatsoever were necessary for his army. . . .
>
> And though afterwards, during the course of the war, he spent most of his time with the army, yet all the while he neither neglected the preparation of his fleet . . . nor the carrying on his resolution of reforming his people and government
>
> One more thing I will mention. The places where his naval prepa-rations are made and where his armies are disposed, being very far distant sometimes from one another, which requires him very often to undertake long and tedious journeys from place to place. He has, I believe . . . travell'd twenty times more than ever any prince in the world did before him . . . (Perry, in Putnam 1952: 50)

The defeat drove home to Peter more than ever the direct relationship between technological and economic modernization and military strength. He was fortunate that the mercurial Charles decided to focus his attention on Poland instead of delivering a knockout blow against Russia. Peter used his time well. The army was entirely retrained, employing European advisers and methods. New ironworks, powder mills, and other factories were built to enable Russia to produce its own weapons, everything from flintlocks with bayonets to artillery. The seven ironworks built in the Urals between 1701 and 1704 was the start of that region's development into a center of heavy industry and the first major step in the industrialization of Russia. As early as 1703, while Charles was busying himself in Poland, Peter returned to the Baltic and seized a section of the coastline. A year later he took Narva.

The czar never stopped improving his army. Later reforms created a national conscription that applied to all classes from serfs to noblemen. The latter provided the army's officers and were trained in newly established military schools. The country's armaments industry continued to be built up until it was capable of producing a wide array of weapons, from muskets to bayonets to artillery, that were the equal of European equipment. After a decade of effort the army reached a strength of 200,000 men on permanent duty, second in size in Europe only to the French army. Peter also created Russia's shipbuilding industry and from scratch built its first navy—28,000 men, four dozen major ships, and hundreds of smaller craft. It was a quality force, good enough to win a major victory over the well-regarded Swedish navy in 1714 and to worry Britain, the strongest naval power in the world. Peter's military reforms in turn drove other economic and administrative reforms, all designed so that Russia could maintain the forces he had built.

All of this was dreadfully expensive. By 1711 the military was consuming 90 percent of the state budget; in 1725, the year Peter died, the figure was 75 percent. This was unavoidable given that war was the common denominator of Peter's reign. Virtually every year was spent in military conflict with one rival or another.

Peter's greatest single triumph took place in the Ukraine at a town southeast of Kiev called Poltava, where the czar got his revenge against Charles XII by routing the invading Swedish army. After that victory in 1709—and in the wake of a Cossack revolt in 1707–08—Peter tightened the central government's controls on the Ukraine by seriously limiting although not entirely eliminating Cossack autonomy, which had been guaranteed in 1654. Peace with Sweden did not come until 1721, however, three years after Charles XII was killed while fighting in

Norway. The Treaty of Nystadt confirmed Russia's annexation of former Swedish territory along the Baltic coast. After that treaty was signed Peter formally took the titles Peter the Great and Emperor, in effect marking the beginning of Russia's imperial era.

The low point of Peter's military career came in 1711 along the Pruth River northwest of the Black Sea, in a war against Turkey that was a direct result of the Poltava victory. In 1710 the Turks, egged on by Charles XII and France, which feared Russia's growing power, declared war. Peter reacted by leading an army toward the Black Sea via the Balkans. Russia's Orthodox czar expected support from the Balkan Orthodox Christian population, which had been suffering under brutal Muslim Turkish rule for centuries. But with minor and inadequate exceptions that help did not come, and Peter and his troops found themselves surrounded by a vastly superior Turkish force. That misadventure cost Russia Azov and the rest of the spoils from Peter's earlier

The Bronze Horseman in St. Petersburg. This imposing statue of Peter the Great by the French sculptor Falconet was commissioned by Catherine the Great and completed in 1782. Aleksandr Pushkin's magnificent poem of the same name has made it by far the best-known statue in Russia and one of the most famous statues in the world. (Liudmila Gridina, 2007. Used under license from ShutterStock, Inc.)

victory over the Turks; given the dire military situation the czar was in when the agreement was negotiated, he got away cheaply. A war against Persia in 1722 and 1723 brought Russia territory along the western shore of the Caspian Sea, but almost all of that narrow, indefensible strip of land was returned to Persia a decade after Peter's death.

St. Petersburg

Most great reform efforts have a showpiece or symbol. Peter's was an entire city, appropriately named St. Petersburg after his patron saint. The czar wanted a new capital city that would both symbolize and promote his effort to modernize Russia and be what he called Russia's "window on the west." The site he chose for his grand new edifice, where the Neva River forms its delta before flowing into the Gulf of Finland, was not promising: a desolate, dreary, northern marshland subject to constant flooding. The climate—bitterly cold in winter, uncomfortably hot in summer—was as uninviting as the landscape. Peter officially founded his new city in 1703. He spent a great deal of time there as it was being built and therefore knew firsthand the enormous problems involved. They did not deter him in the least. After one of the innumerable floods that disrupted construction and life in general, he wrote to a close adviser:

> The day before yesterday, the wind from the southwest blew up such waters as, they say, have never been seen before. In my house, the water rose up twenty-one inches above the floor; and in the garden and on the other side along the streets people went about freely in boats. However, the waters did not remain long—less than three hours, Here it was entertaining to watch how the people, not only the peasants but their women, too, stay on the roofs and trees during the flood. Although the waters rose to a great height, they did not cause bad damage. (Massie 1980: 363)

Many of the czar's subjects did not share his enthusiasm for the city he called his "paradise." Hundreds of thousands of forced laborers toiled under dreadful conditions that included several attacks by Swedish forces attempting to retake the region. Canals had to be dug and the land around them raised, work that often had to be done quite literally by hand since the requisite picks and shovels were not available. At least 30,000 workers died; to them and to countless others Peter's "paradise" was the "city built on bones." Nor did the nobles Peter compelled to move to St. Petersburg share his enthusiasm for the project or vision for its future. One member of the royal family expressed a widely held view when she said she hoped the city would "remain a desert" (Massie 1980: 365).

In the end, as in so many other contests of will, Peter triumphed. During his reign the czar brought outstanding craftsmen from Europe to create elegant and graceful stone buildings. No detail escaped his attention. Trees are important to any city, and Peter beautified his city with 5,000 lime trees from Holland and other varieties such as chestnuts, oaks, and maples. To supplement the government's efforts, he ordered residents to plant maples on their streets. The city grew, officially becoming Russia's capital in 1712, and by the end of Peter's reign had a population of 100,000. By the late 18th century, after Catherine the Great had made her contributions, St. Petersburg was a large and impressive city laced with hundreds of canals that its admirers called the "Venice of the North." In the early 19th century Aleksandr Pushkin spoke for many of Russia's increasingly Europeanized elite in "The Bronze Horseman" when he compared Moscow and its inward-looking, old-fashioned ways to the ultramodern, westward-looking St. Petersburg:

> To that young capital is drooping
> The crest of Moscow on the ground,
> A dowager in purple, stooping
> Before an empress, newly crowned.

> (Pushkin, "The Bronze Horseman," in Yarmolinsky 1964: 96)

Administrative and Economic Reforms

At various points during his reign Peter introduced administrative reforms in an effort to improve Russia's government. None of his measures worked particularly well. In 1708, to correct the evils of overcentralization, he divided the country into eight provinces, subsequently increasing the number to 11. Eventually Peter decreed further subdivisions. Later, copying the Swedish system, he established nine central departments, called colleges, with responsibilities for specific areas such as foreign affairs, state revenue, the army, the navy, and so on. None of this worked, as Russia lacked trained officials to staff its bureaucracy and local initiative to help that bureaucracy do its job. Peter also ended the independence of the Russian Orthodox Church by silencing that institution's opposition to his policies and better controlling its land and other wealth. This was achieved in several steps between 1700 and 1721, the last of which was to abolish the position of patriarch and establish a state agency called the Holy Governing Synod to run the church.

Peter's most important administrative reforms were financial, all designed to squeeze more resources from the Russian people to feed his growing war machine. Here Peter was undeniably successful. As early as 1701 his government was collecting more than twice the revenue collected in 1681, and by 1724 the figure had nearly tripled from 1701. There was nothing complicated about Peter's methods. He taxed everything he could, from beards, beehives, and Old Believers to chimney stacks, ice blocks, watermelons, and non-Orthodox marriages. Ranging beyond direct taxation, having taken control of Orthodox monasteries early in his reign, Peter used some of their income to fund his military.

Sometimes, as in the case of beards, the tax was designed to change behavior and encourage the adoption of European customs as well as to raise revenue. That dual motive also seems to have applied to the decision to legalize and tax the "ungodly herb" tobacco, whose use spread rapidly and provided the state with considerable revenue. Tobacco was sold at a tidy profit through a state monopoly, as were salt, liquor, furs, fish oil, caviar, coffins, and other items.

The needs of the state also governed economic policy. In the service of the military, Peter established Russia's first industrial base and did more than anyone else before the late 19th century to develop the nation's industry. As a result of his efforts by 1725 Russia had about 200 large industrial enterprises. The main concentration, almost 70 enterprises, was in metallurgy, but there also were major producers of lumber, gunpowder, textiles, glass, sailcloth, leather, and other commodities. In 1700 Russia had been producing only one-fifth as much pig iron as England; by 1725 its production exceeded England's. The center of Russia's metallurgical industry was in the Urals, where both state-controlled and private enterprises worked to supply Russia's military needs. In other words, the state was both the main promoter and the chief consumer of industrial goods and as such often interfered in the activities of private producers. When combined with the lack of purchasing power on the part of Russia's poverty-stricken masses, government interference often got in the way of economic development.

The Growing Social Divide

One revenue enhancer towered over all the others—the poll, or "soul," tax Interestingly, it was not a new idea but dated from the regency of the despised Sophia. Before Peter's reign Russian peasants were taxed on a household basis. Each household paid a certain amount, regardless of how many members it had. The flaw here from the state's point of view was obvious: Peasants avoided the tax by squeezing as many bodies as possible into a single household, which in turn decreased the total number of households and with it the state's revenue. One common technique was for sons to crowd with their families under their father's roof. In 1718 the household tax was replaced by the poll tax on every adult male "soul," regardless of where he lived. To make sure every soul was paying up, between 1718 and 1722 a careful census was taken. Revenues soared, and by 1724 the poll tax was providing more than half the government's total revenue.

The poll tax revenue was crucial to Peter, who despite unprecedented levels of government expenditure managed to generate enough revenues to keep Russia out of debt. However, the historical importance of the poll tax lies not in its role as a revenue producer but in its social impact, something far beyond Peter's concerns. It was the final major step in the development of serfdom. It erased the last surviving distinctions between different groups of peasants, who under Peter's military reforms had also become equally exposed to recruitment for the army.

Peter finished the job of reducing all Russian peasants to bondage in yet one more way. Even with the poll tax some peasants had escaped serfdom, including people who for one reason or another did not live on land owned by nobles; in most cases they lived on state-owned land. Between 1719 and 1724 Peter introduced a series of taxes and obligations that reduced these people to a status similar to that of serfs. Instead of serving noble landlords, these peasants would serve the state. Peter gave this group a name in 1724 when he referred to them as state peasants.

In addition to having to bear the poll tax, serfs carried other heavy burdens. They owed labor and dues to their landlords, which increased steadily during the 18th century. Furthermore, landlords had the power to interfere in almost every aspect of their serfs' lives and to administer harsh punishments for even the smallest infractions. State peasants, who were not subject to private landlords, were generally better off, even though they had a labor obligation to the state. There was one important exception: state peasants could be conscripted to work in Russia's new factories and mines, where working conditions were terrible and punishments brutal, even by the standards to which serfs were accustomed. This dreaded fate sometimes befell entire villages. Furthermore, state peasants could be turned into serfs by several methods, most notably when czars awarded the land they lived on to favored noblemen, a common practice during the 18th century.

These were bitter pills to swallow, whether for serfs or for state peasants. Other than rebelling, all they could do to help themselves was to escape to the frontier lands of the south and east, something many of them tried despite severe punishment if they were caught.

The solidification of serfdom guaranteed noble landlords control over the peasants who lived on their estates. In return Peter demanded that the nobles serve the state. Those who did not serve in the military were expected to serve in a civilian capacity and staff the government bureaucracy. To regularize the overall system, in 1722 Peter established a Table of Ranks, a hierarchy of 14 grades with parallel ranks in civilian and military service. Members of the nobility had to start at the bottom and work their way up on the basis of merit, a requirement that typified Peter's approach. Also typical for Peter was that free commoners could climb the Table of Ranks ladder. If they rose to a certain rank they could themselves attain noble status.

Peter understood very well that a modern, technologically advanced country had to be an educated one. To that end in 1701 he established Russia's first secular school, the School of Mathematics and Navigation; it was run by one of Peter's foreign experts, a Scottish mathematician. Other schools followed, all specializing in technical, scientific, and practical subjects, as did a requirement that the sons of noblemen receive a primary education.

Peter also directed that Russia establish an Academy of Sciences to promote learning, an idea that emerged from his conversations in 1711 and 1712 with the German philosopher Gottfried Leibniz. The academy was set up shortly after Peter's death, with his personal library at its core. It eventually fulfilled its mission with great distinction. Its first members were 17 scholars imported from Germany. The czar also encouraged the printing of books, including translations of foreign scholarly works. Almost twice as many books were published in the final quarter century of his reign than in the entire 17th century, although all this activity took place on printing presses controlled by the state or the church. The contrast in scholarly books is much greater: almost 400 volumes versus 19. The unwieldy Russian alphabet was simplified, and Arabic numerals were introduced to facilitate work in mathematics and science. Peter's avid interest in geography led to several expeditions into remote parts of eastern Asia, including one that discovered the Bering Strait, which separates Siberia in Asia from Alaska in North America.

These advances were designed for the elite who served the state, while the peasants remained untouched. The long-term implications for Russia were enormous. While the country's elite became more literate and Europeanized, its masses remained mired in illiteracy and attached to their ancient traditions. Increasingly the two unequal groups differed in forms of speech, manner of dress, and overall outlook. Even before Peter's reign an ominous social fault line had emerged in Russian society between the elite and the general population. Peter's policies deepened that fissure and added to it a yawning cultural gap. That gap would grow over time until Russia in effect had two separate cultures. Their mutual opposition and lack of comprehension constituted a divisive and dangerous national problem.

Peter's Legacy

Whether the subject is economics, politics, foreign affairs, religion and social life, or education, one point is central to understanding Peter and his place in Russian history: Whatever his innovations, he was a product of the Russian political tradition and therefore had only one master, the autocratic Russian state. In his view autocracy alone could establish and guarantee the power and greatness of Russia. That is why he insisted that the nobility serve the state and that the people as a whole accept without question any of the state's demands or any restrictions it wished to impose—including serfdom.

In case anyone dared to disagree with him or his methods, Peter established a special bureau called the Preobrazhensky Prikaz to serve as a ruthless political police. He and Ivan the Terrible thus stand as the founders of Russia's political police tradition, which darkened Russian political life under all succeeding czars and took on an even more monstrous form under their successors, the Communist Party leaders who ruled Russia for most of the 20th century.

For all his efforts to organize Russia, Peter did a poor job of preparing for his succession. Several years after banishing his wife to a convent, Peter remarried. His bride, who as his mistress had already borne him two daughters, was an attractive non-Russian peasant. Prior to the marriage she had converted to Orthodoxy and taken the name Catherine. She proved to be the ideal consort for the czar, and Peter had her crowned empress in 1724. Unfortunately for Peter, his sons by Catherine had died in childhood. Alexis, his son by his first wife, who opposed Peter's policies, had died under torture in 1718, during Peter's investigation of his alleged plans to undo his reforms.

The problem Peter faced was that Alexis had a young son who was still alive. The child had a strong, though not exclusive, claim to the throne, and Peter feared that as emperor his grandson would do what Alexis had not lived to accomplish. In 1722 Peter therefore issued a decree that he would appoint his successor. But he hesitated to make a choice, allowing chance to intervene. While sailing in December 1724, the emperor of Russia jumped out of his boat into icy waters to help victims of a nearby shipwreck. He caught pneumonia and his health quickly deteriorated. Peter died in early 1725, having failed to name his successor. It was the only important decision of his reign that Peter the Great left for others to make.

From Peter the Great to Catherine the Great

Five rulers sat on the Russian throne between the country's two "Great" 18th-century rulers. Peter's wife, with the support of Menshikov and Peter's elite guards regiments, succeeded her husband as Catherine I, but she lived and ruled for only two years. At her death in 1727, the late emperor's 11-year-old grandson, the son of Alexis, became Russia's ruler as Peter II. In the court intrigue that followed, Menshikov was

The Winter Palace, built during the reigns of Elizabeth and Catherine the Great, became the home of the royal family until the monarchy was overthrown in March 1917. It was then the headquarters of the short-lived Provisional Government. The Winter Palace is one of the four buildings that today house the Hermitage Museum. (Dainis Derics, 2007. Used under license from ShutterStock, Inc.)

pushed aside and exiled to Siberia, but before much else could happen Peter II, the last male Romanov, died of smallpox in 1730. Russia's king-makers had reached the bottom of the Romanov barrel.

They first came up with Peter's niece, Anna of Courland, the daughter of his half-brother Ivan V and the widow of the Duke of Courland (a Baltic duchy formerly run by German knights but at that time part of Poland). Anna's strange reign—she was fascinated by the grotesque—lasted 10 years. It was marked mainly by intrigue between her German advisers and the Russian nobility and by laws that strengthened even further the nobility's control over the serfs. Next from the depths of the royal barrel came the infant Ivan VI (r. 1740–41), a great-grandson of Ivan V, before a coup by the guards regiments gave the throne to Elizabeth (r. 1741–62), one of Peter the Great's daughters by his beloved Catherine.

Elizabeth was a competent adult, a significant step up from both Anna and Ivan VI, but that was the extent of her qualifications. Her main skill seems to have been the ability to spend funds from the state treasury on a lavish scale. To her credit she hired the architect Bartolomeo Rastrelli, who designed and built, among other projects, two elegant palaces in villages close to St. Petersburg and, between 1754 and 1762, the grand, Baroque/Rococo Winter Palace in the capital itself. Not completed until Catherine the Great was on the throne, the building now forms the core of the famous Hermitage Museum.

Major government decisions under Elizabeth were often left to the empress's various favorites. New legislation continued to favor the nobility at the expense of the serfs, including a law granting nobles the right to exile their serfs to Siberia. In foreign affairs Russia took the side of Austria and France against Prussia in the Seven Years' War, a struggle that saw Prussia driven to the brink of total defeat by 1762, the year Elizabeth died.

The most notable domestic achievement of Elizabeth's reign was the founding of the University of Moscow, the initiative of one of her advisers, the polymath Mikhail Lomonosov. Born the son of a fisherman in Arkhangelsk, Lomonosov managed to get a good education through effort and deception—he falsely claimed to be a nobleman. After studying at an elite academy in Moscow, he attended universities in Germany for five years. Lomonosov became a brilliant scientist who did pioneering work in chemistry, physics, and other fields. Russia's first outstanding world-class scientist and intellect, well ahead of his time in many of his insights and discoveries, Lomonosov was also an outstanding literary scholar and poet.

Elizabeth's successor requires a reader of royal minds to explain properly. He was her nephew Peter of Holstein-Gottorp, the son of her older sister and thus the grandson of Peter the Great. He was born, as his name indicates, in Germany. He was a Lutheran with pretensions to the throne of Sweden. He did not come to Russia until the age of 14 and never dropped his admiration for his native Germany or his thorough dislike for Russia. He had limited mental abilities and was given to fits of violence. Whatever her reasons, Elizabeth chose him to inherit the Russian throne, which he did as Peter III.

The new czar made two major decisions in his short reign. First, he excused the nobility from compulsory state service. Henceforth, while nobles enjoyed their privileges (including exemption from paying taxes), their estates, and their serfs, all protected by the Russian state, they would have no obligation to give anything in return. Second, with Prussia and its king Frederick the Great on the verge of defeat in the Seven Years' War, Peter took Russia out of the war, saving Prussia from disaster and depriving Russia of significant gains. This understandably made Peter many enemies among the Russian governing elite, as did a series of other missteps, such as making obvious his distaste for the Russian Orthodox Church.

Fortunately for Peter's enemies, another German-born candidate for the throne was at the Russian court, Peter's wife, Catherine. She had begun life as the undistinguished daughter of a minor German prince before being married off to the heir to the Russian throne in 1745. Unlike her husband, whom she despised, Catherine was intelligent and politically astute. The result was a coup in the summer of 1762. Peter III was deposed and murdered, and the former princess Sophia Augusta Frederica of Anhalt-Zerbst became the Empress Catherine II of Russia.

Catherine II as Reformer and Wartime Leader

Catherine II began her reign with two distinct disadvantages: She was a foreigner dependent on court intriguers who had put her on the throne, and she was a woman in a man's world involved with plotters who had deposed and murdered the man who was at once Russia's czar and her husband. But Catherine had significant advantages too: She was highly intelligent, possessed keen political skills and timing, could be as ruthless as any man and yet when necessary exercise self-control, and knew how to manipulate people and how to take advice. She also was willing to work hard.

Catherine the Great, empress of Russia from 1762 to 1796 (Library of Congress)

Catherine's enormous vanity and ambition, as well as her lifestyle, which included more than 20 lovers, added drama, hypocrisy, and irony to her long and successful reign. Several of those lovers, notably the extremely capable Prince Gregory Potemkin, were also key advisers.

Potemkin is notable not just for his role in helping Catherine run Russia but for what one of his exploits reveals about his monarch's character. He was the creator of the famous "Potemkin villages," fake communities that really were nothing but life-size wooden stage scenery and well-dressed peasant actors, that he showed to Catherine, from a suitable distance, to demonstrate the prosperity of the Crimea when she toured the region in 1787. The empress, always on the hunt for achievements to satisfy her vanity and traveling with two European monarchs she was trying to impress, was only too glad to be fooled.

Catherine came to the throne after having evolved into a staunch Russian patriot, and she was determined to strengthen the Russian state and expand Russia's power. She was also a student of the European Enlightenment. She had read Voltaire, Montesquieu, and other kindred thinkers, and aspired to be an enlightened despot, a fashionable concept among some Enlightenment thinkers of the time. She hoped to introduce reforms and improvements in Russia that would win her acclaim not only at home but in Europe as well.

One of Catherine's first acts was to finish a job Peter the Great had begun by confiscating all lands belonging to Orthodox monasteries and churches. It was a twofold gain for the new empress: The government could immediately collect the dues of 1 million adult peasants living on those lands, and Catherine in the future could use those lands to reward nobles for service they might render the state.

In 1766 Catherine undertook what she hoped would be a major Enlightenment initiative when she issued her *Nakaz* (Instruction) calling for reform of Russia's law code. The *Nakaz* was said to be based on the writings of Montesquieu, but the claim was propaganda rather than fact. A core Montesquieu principle is the division of powers among the executive, legislative, and judicial branches of government. Catherine, a firm believer that Russia required autocratic rule, left that principle out of her *Nakaz*. Nor did she deal seriously with serfdom, an institution condemned by the Enlightenment. The empress gave the job of spinning her *Nakaz* into a code of laws to a Legislative Commission made up of elected deputies—nobles, townspeople, and others but, significantly, not serfs. Called in 1767, it met for over a year but had not produced anything when it was disbanded in 1768 at the outbreak of war with Turkey.

The war with Turkey brought Catherine into the realm of foreign affairs. There she did not have to pretend to act according to any principles other than Russian national interests as defined by her. In that realm she enjoyed her most impressive successes.

The czars had long sought to reach the Black Sea and to reestablish Russian rule on the fertile southern steppe for the first time since that area had been lost to nomad invaders from Asia during the Kievan era. The 1770s was a good time to strike, an act the Turks facilitated by declaring war. The Ottoman Empire, whose armies had once threatened the very heart of Europe, had weakened during the 18th century. In the 19th century it would decline further still, turning into what statesmen of the day called the "sick man of Europe." However, Turkey was not yet decrepit in Catherine's day, which meant Russia faced hard fighting on both land and sea before winning a decisive victory.

By the Treaty of Kuchuk Kainardji in 1774, Russia added a wide swath of steppe north of the Black Sea in what today is Ukraine and won the independence of the Crimea, which it annexed in 1783. Russian ships were allowed on the Black Sea and permitted to pass through the straits leading to the Mediterranean. The Ottomans also recognized Russia as the protector of their empire's Christian subjects in the Balkans. In addition, while the war with Turkey was being won, in 1772 Russia joined with Prussia and Austria for the first partition of Poland, a former power in central Europe now in an advanced state of decay. Russia's share was a nice slice of territory in what today is Belarus.

These two gains, coming only two years apart from each other, constituted a significant step in reversing painful losses Russia had suffered centuries earlier but had never forgotten. They also constituted a major advance in Russian power and prestige in Europe and a highly satisfying triumph for Catherine. And there was more to come: Two subsequent partitions (1793 and 1795) extended Russia's borders west of Warsaw as they wiped Poland from the map, while a second war with Turkey between 1787 and 1791 confirmed Russia's earlier gains and added still more territories along the Black Sea coast. When everything was completed, in addition to Lithuania and other Baltic coast territories, Russia had won control of all of what today is Belarus and Ukraine, thereby reuniting all Russians, Belarusians, and Ukrainians under a single rule—a state of affairs destined to last for almost two centuries.

Not everyone was pleased with this development. Russia's territorial expansion under Catherine brought millions of non-Russians into the empire. These non-Russians included not only various Baltic nationalities, Poles, Jews, and other groups that had no cultural or historical links with Russia, but also Ukrainians, who by the 19th century increasingly saw themselves as distinct from Russians. The growing multinational nature of the Russian Empire concerned Catherine, who worried that

CATHERINE THE GREAT INSPECTS THE CRIMEA

Prince Charles de Ligne accompanied Catherine on her tour of the Crimea in 1787. An admirer of the empress, de Ligne dismisses as "ridiculous" the story he has heard about Potemkin villages, information that turned out to be quite accurate. Interestingly, further on in his letter he provides evidence that Catherine indeed was being misled by Potemkin as she inspected various parts of her realm.

> . . . They have already spread about the ridiculous story that cardboard villages were set up along the line of our route for hundreds of miles; that the vessels and cannons were painted images, the cavalry horseless, and so forth. . . .
> I know very well what is trickery; for example, the empress, who cannot rush about on foot as we do, is made to believe that certain towns for which she has given money are finished; whereas they are often towns without streets, streets without houses, and houses without roofs, doors, or windows. Nothing is shown to the empress but shops that are well-built of stone, colonnades of the palaces of the governors general, to forty-two of which she has presented silver services of a hundred covers. . . .
> (Cross 1971: 233–234)

it posed a threat to the country's unity. Her response was an oppressive policy that came to be called "Russification." Under Catherine it mainly took the form of destroying local institutions that minority nationalities had previously used to run their affairs. The first target was the Ukraine and its various Cossack communities, whose remaining autonomy and native institutions were abolished. Similar polices then were applied to the Baltic provinces, Polish-inhabited territories, and the region north of the Caucasus Mountains.

The Pugachev Revolt

While Catherine was dealing successfully with Turkey and Poland, she was neglecting urgent and complex problems at home. Simply put, the government's oppression of its people was driving them once again, as in the days of Razin, Bolotnikov, and Bulavin, to the breaking point. The burdens of serfdom on the country's peasants were growing heavier. In the late 1760s there had been rumors of impending emancipation; instead, as Russia conquered new lands, serfdom was extended to them and they ceased to be havens for escaped serfs from the older parts of the country. East of the Volga near the Urals, thousands of serfs toiling in mines and factories worked under horrible conditions. Cossacks living along the Don and near the Urals bitterly resented the government's relentless assault on their traditional autonomy. Resentful Old Believers, desperate fugitive serfs, and an assortment of other groups victimized in one way or another by the Russian government added to the social tinder throughout the land.

The Russians have a saying that a single spark can ignite a prairie fire. In 1773 the Cossack Yemelyan Pugachev, an army deserter, came to the Urals and created that spark. The rebellion he ignited, initially of Cossacks, quickly won broad support and became the largest peasant uprising in Russia's history, surpassing even the great upheaval of Stepan Razin. The rebellion spread from the Urals to the Volga region, rallying tens of thousands of serfs to the cause, as rebel troops killed several thousand landlords, government officials, and other supporters of the regime. At its peak Pugachev's army numbered between 20,000 and 30,000 men. Pugachev claimed to be Peter III, who had managed to escape death at the time of his overthrow and now had returned to reclaim his throne He promised a social revolution that included liberation of the serfs (and hanging their landlords), religious freedom for Old Believers, and restoration of Cossack autonomy.

From the summer of 1773 through the fall of 1774, Pugachev's armies won a series of victories, seriously frightening Catherine. In the end, however, his poorly organized and largely untrained troops could not stand up to well-led regular army troops. These became available, along with several key generals, in the summer of 1774 after Russia and Turkey signed a peace treaty. By late 1774 Pugachev was defeated. He was then betrayed by some of his followers, taken to Moscow in a cage, and, in most unenlightened fashion, brutally tortured and executed. The savage reprisals carried out against thousands of peasants who had followed Pugachev were also not consistent with Catherine's presumed commitment to Enlightenment principles.

Reforming Autocratic Rule

The Pugachev rebellion demonstrated two things: The burden on Russia's peasants was excessive, and the government apparatus outside the country's main cities, which collapsed in many areas during the revolt, was inefficient and weak. Catherine and her advisers ignored the first lesson, perhaps inevitably given her needs and values, but did respond to the second.

Aside from the military budget that any czar had to meet, Catherine was a profligate spender on things that interested her: building and remodeling palaces and public buildings, providing generously for her favorites, patronizing the arts, and maintaining her lavish court. She was also completely sympathetic to the efforts of her nobles to maintain a standard of living consistent with the style of the imperial court. That required more income, which meant both increasing the labor peasants had to do in the landlords' fields (often five or even six days per week) and increasing the dues they paid their landlords. That in turn required reinforcing the landlords' control over their serfs. But that could happen only if local government was improved and strengthened—and this imperative Catherine took to heart.

Her chief vehicle for improving local government was the provincial reform of 1775, which relied on decentralization to achieve greater efficiency. The reform abolished the huge provinces inherited from former czars and divided Russia into 41 (later 50) smaller provinces, each headed by an appointed governor. Each province was further divided into 10 districts. Within each province specialized agencies handled specific areas of responsibility, staffed by centrally appointed officials; however, at the district level, local nobles filled key administrative posts. One notable feature of the reform gave each province a special agency for social welfare; among other things, it was to provide hospitals and schools. The actual impact was minimal. These reforms at the local level were riddled with problems but nonetheless lasted until after serfdom was abolished. Catherine followed up in 1785 with a reform of town government, which, however, gave only limited local powers to wealthy town dwellers.

Far more significant than these administrative reforms was the Charter of the Nobility, issued in 1785. It codified and thereby solidified the nobility's privileges, including exemption from taxation and absolute control over their estates, while at the same time confirming their relief from all obligations to perform state service. The charter completed the job of turning Russia's gentry into a parasitic class, living off the forced labor of the serfs while contributing virtually nothing to the well-being of the state.

Catherine meanwhile both strengthened and extended serfdom, with the latter being more important because the landlords already had virtually total control of their serfs. She routinely rewarded those who had served her interests with huge grants of state lands, complete with the peasants who lived on them. These policies turned well over a million people into serfs, brought serfdom to the newly conquered lands in Belarus and the Ukraine, and raised the institution to the peak of its development in the Russian Empire as a whole. To put it mildly, these policies were out of place for a monarch who once had said she would rely on the Enlightenment concept of natural law to improve the lives of the Russian people.

On the positive side of the ledger, Catherine did promote economic development by eliminating many government monopolies and allowing more classes of people to open industrial enterprises. With Potemkin in charge, the government promoted colonization and development in the southern territory taken from the Turks, a region Catherine called "New Russia." This led to the founding of Odessa, which during the 19th century grew into a cosmopolitan city and, as the embarkation point for the export of Ukrainian grain, Russia's second-most-important port after St. Petersburg.

Enlightenment and Repression

Catherine the Great considered herself an intellectual proponent of the Enlightenment. She corresponded in French with Voltaire, Diderot, and other philosophes and helped several of them financially, especially Diderot. Perhaps that is why after visiting her in 1773 the publisher of the *Encyclopédie* gushed that Catherine combined "the soul of Brutus with the charms of Cleopatra" (Quoted in Florinsky, vol. 1, 506).

The empress wrote plays, built a theater (at the Winter Palace), and published her own literary magazine, to which she was the main contributor. She sent agents to scour Europe for art, buying entire collections and eventually accumulating a private collection of 4,000 paintings and 10,000 drawings that became the basis of the magnificent Russian state collection visitors can see today at the Hermitage Museum. She also beautified St. Petersburg and its suburbs with her construction projects, including additions to the Winter Palace and the construction of the Tauride Palace, a neoclassical structure considered the masterpiece of the distinguished Russian architect I. E. Starov.

Catherine established schools, including a teacher's college and a school for noble girls ("well-born young ladies") called the Smolny Institute, which in 1917 became the headquarters from which the Bolshevik Party planned its seizure of power. Late in her reign the government established a network of high schools in 26 provincial capitals and built nearly 170 elementary schools for children of merchants and other nonnoble classes (excluding serfs).

In her early years as empress Catherine made a great show of encouraging not only literature and the arts but journalism and the free exchange of ideas. After the Pugachev revolt and even more so after the start of the French Revolution in 1789, however, she behaved above all as an intolerant Russian autocrat. This can be seen in the fates of the two outstanding social critics of her reign, both noblemen: Nikolai Novikov and Aleksandr Radishchev.

A Freemason and his country's leading journalist, Novikov did more than any contemporary to promote Enlightenment ideas in Russia through his own writings, a journal that had a variety of contributors, a publishing house, and philanthropy. His activities began to be restricted in the mid-1780s. Catherine's fear of the French Revolution and its ideas did the rest: In 1791 the government suppressed his publishing activities, and in 1792 he was arrested. By the time he was released and pardoned by Catherine's successor, her son Paul I, Novikov was a broken man. Radishchev holds an even more prominent place in Russian history as the author of *Journey from St. Petersburg to Moscow,* the first critique of serfdom ever published in Russia. His devastating book, published in 1790, infuriated Catherine, who denounced him as "a rebel worse than Pugachev." For daring to tell the truth about serfdom, he was exiled to Siberia, where he remained until Paul I allowed him to return to his estates. In 1801, in despair over the lack of change in his country, Radishchev committed suicide.

Catherine the Great died in 1796, having put on a great show. The philosophes loved her, as did the Russian nobility. Russian patriots were thrilled by the territorial gains she won for the empire, and European visitors were impressed by what she had done to enhance the grandeur of St. Petersburg and the Russian court. But Catherine's administrative reforms had achieved little: Russia was still badly governed by a corrupt bureaucracy. Her wars and various projects at home had been expensive, and the burden of paying for them fell more heavily than ever on the serfs. Furthermore, no matter how much the people paid, it was never enough to keep Russia from falling deeply into debt.

As for serfdom, under Catherine it was extended and made more onerous. The nobility became more parasitic than ever, and by permitting the nobles to avoid state service she in effect undid the historical justification for serfdom. Finally, the gap between the educated elite, increasingly Europeanized, and the masses, mired in poverty and tradition, was wider and deeper than ever. It was matched only by the gap between Catherine's Enlightenment pretensions and what she actually achieved in Russia.

The Reign of Paul I

Catherine was succeeded by her son Paul (r. 1796–1801). Assuming Paul was the son of Peter III, which some historians doubt, he is proof of the cliché "like father like son." In any event, he was certainly not much like his mother. His behavior was erratic, and he made powerful enemies, especially when he revoked some key features of the Charter of the Nobility, including the section that made nobles immune from corporal punishment, and when he forced the army to introduce Prussian uniforms and drill practices. The slightest offense or error by people of any rank could lead to arrest or exile to Siberia.

Russia's leaders were appalled when he abandoned the coalition fighting Napoléon, and flabbergasted when he sent an expedition of Cossacks to invade India, a distant realm separated from Russia by towering mountains and in a region of the world where it had no conceivable interests. With some justification many people around the court became convinced the czar was mad. In 1801 he was overthrown and murdered in a palace coup. His son and successor, Alexander I, was involved in the coup but apparently did not expect it to end in the murder of his father. His remorse and guilt for that may have played a role in his own strange behavior at several points in the reign to come.

4

THE NINETEENTH-CENTURY CRISIS: THE MYSTIC AND THE KNOUT (1801–1855)

The first half of the 19th century brought new challenges for the Russian Empire, some overtly threatening but ultimately of a short-term nature and others more subtle but also more dangerous to the established order in the long run. The most serious immediate threat was the struggle with Napoléon, which lasted for over a decade and reached its peak in 1812 when the French emperor invaded Russia and reached Moscow. Russia successfully met that challenge. It refused to give in to Napoléon, and in 1814 its armies played a key role in defeating him, reaching Paris itself. Not even the Soviet victory over Nazi Germany in World War II brought Russian forces so deep into western Europe.

The long-term threat was far more complex, requiring much more than dogged resistance and a determined military response. It grew out of the changes generated in Europe by the Industrial and French revolutions. Between the 1780s and the mid-19th century Britain became the world's first industrial power, and other countries on the Continent such as France were following in its wake. Industrialization gave the modernized armies of Europe an increasing technological edge over their Russian counterpart. At the same time, the democratic ideals of the French Revolution were spreading across Europe. As political reform broadened the social base on which western European governments rested, in Russia the opposite happened. In the absence of reform, educated Russians attracted to Western political ideas increasingly came to oppose the autocratic system under which they lived. It was this multipronged threat—economic, technological, social, and political in nature—to which Russia was unable to respond.

The two men who successively sat on the throne, the brothers Alexander I (r. 1801–25) and Nicholas I (r. 1825–53), were very different from each other. Alexander was, at least for a while, open to discussing—as opposed to actually implementing—new ideas; he was also conflicted, guilt-ridden, and even mystical. Among the epithets applied to him are the "enigmatic czar" and the "crowned Hamlet." Younger brother Nicholas was reactionary, close-minded, brutal, and direct. Far from being enigmatic, he was predictable almost to a fault; indeed, predictability was among his few virtues. In the end Alexander I and Nicholas I shared a commitment to total autocratic rule and a corresponding inability to confront Russia's fundamental problems. With them in charge Russia did nothing to deal with these problems and in effect wasted the first half of the 19th century. There was a high price to pay for such neglect and dereliction of duty, as Russia found out between 1853 and 1856 during the Crimean War.

Alexander I: Talking about, and Tinkering with, the System

Alexander was in his early twenties when he became czar, only a few years removed from an education supervised by a Swiss tutor devoted to the Enlightenment and republican ideals. As a youth Alexander had read Descartes, Locke, and Rousseau. On the other hand, he had received military training from Count Aleksei A. Arakcheyev, a reactionary and thoroughly unenlightened nobleman who would later be the architect of Alexander's notorious project to beef up the size of the Russian army by creating so-called military colonies.

Alexander moved in two divergent directions during his first year on the throne. Having announced that he would rule as his grandmother Catherine had, he restored to their positions thousands of people Paul had dismissed or imprisoned and returned to the nobility the privileges Paul had withdrawn. Alexander did not just undo his father's transgressions; he also ended restrictions his grandmother had imposed on publishing houses and on the printing of foreign books. At the same time, as soon as he became comfortable on his throne Alexander pushed aside some of the liberal-minded noblemen and court figures who had played central roles in bringing him to power. In foreign policy the new czar moved Russia back into the pro-British camp in its struggle with France and Napoléon.

Alexander did not chase away all reform-minded advisers. Shortly after becoming czar he formed a Committee of Friends, some of whose members held liberal views, to discuss reform. Although many conservatives feared the committee might compromise the power of the autocracy, they need not have worried. Its chief recommendation was strictly administrative: to replace Peter the Great's system of colleges (departments)—only three of which actually were functioning—with eight ministries based on contemporary western European models. The Senate, which also originated with Peter, received new administrative and judicial powers. It was also given the power to issue decrees subject to the czar's veto; however, Alexander made emphatically clear that his autocratic powers would remain unchallenged and unquestioned.

That reaffirmation of unfettered autocracy did not preclude some positive steps. The government made a strong new commitment to education. Aside from gathering educational activities under the roof of a new ministry of education, it drastically increased overall spending, founded more than 40 secondary schools, and established several universities.

The czar even tinkered ever so slightly with serfdom. A decree in 1803 on "free agriculturalists" permitted landlords to free their serfs, but only with land. Given the proclivities of the nobility, the decree's effect was minimal: In the following half century, fewer than 400 landlords liberated about 115,000 male serfs with their families. Later decrees limited the authority of landlords in the Baltic region over their serfs. But that was as far as reform went. Serfdom as an institution remained largely untouched, and Alexander continued the practice of his grandmother and father of enserfing state peasants by turning them over to private landlords. Thus, even in his early reformist days Alexander did much more for the landlords than for the serfs.

Alexander's so-called early reform period was interrupted between 1805 and 1807 by war against Napoléon. When he returned to thoughts of reform it was under the influence of a new and remarkable adviser, Mikhail Speransky, a brilliant official whose talent had carried him from his modest origins as the son of a village priest to the top of the imperial bureaucracy. Speransky authored a comprehensive administrative reorganization plan designed, he said, to end centuries of arbitrary autocratic government and to base the Russian state on the rule of law.

The country would be divided into four administrative levels, from township to the national government. Each would have separate administrative, judicial, and elected legislative institutions. However, only the lowest-level assembly would be elected directly by the people; each of the higher assemblies would be chosen by the one directly below it. More important, despite the elaborate separation of *functions,* all *power* would remain with the czar.

The great question, then and now, is whether Speransky intended for his grand restructuring of Russia's government to be the first tentative, cautious step toward a genuine constitutional regime, with the czar's power in practice limited by a legislature with genuine power of its own. All the debates regarding that question have always been rather moot, as Alexander showed no interest in most of Speransky's program. He implemented only the parts designed to improve the efficiency of the bureaucracy. The brilliant bureaucrat antagonized most nobles and top-level bureaucrats with his cautious ideas about judiciaries and elected legislatures, and he soon found himself out of favor. Alexander

MIKHAIL SPERANSKY ON RUSSIA'S CONDITION AT THE START OF THE 19TH CENTURY

More than any of his colleagues in the Russian government, Mikhail Speransky understood the anachronistic and corroded foundations upon which the Russian Empire stood. He expressed his concerns in a memorandum written in 1802, which included a devastating comment on the Russian social system based on autocracy and serfdom:

> The outward impression is that we have everything, and yet nothing has any real foundation. . . .
> I should like someone to point out the difference between the dependence of the peasants on the landlords and the dependence of the landlords on the sovereign; I should like someone to discover whether in fact the sovereign does not have the same right over the landlords as the landlords have over the peasants. Thus, instead of all the splendid divisions of a free Russian people into the very free classes of nobility, merchants, and the rest, I find in Russia two classes: the slaves of the sovereign and the slaves of the landlords. The first are free only in relation to the second, but there are no truly free persons in Russia, except beggars and philosophers. . . . The nobles, having no sort of political existence, must base the freedom of their life . . . on the enslavement of the peasants. The peasants, in the condition of slavery which oppresses them, look up to the throne, as the single counterforce, which is able to moderate the power of the landlords. (Seton-Watson 1967: 103)

dismissed him in 1812 and thereafter dabbled only briefly in the dangerous area of political reform.

Russia and Alexander at War

Although Alexander brought Russia back into the British camp in 1801, he managed to remain at peace with France for the next four years. Maintaining good relations with France and Napoléon was not easy. Along with following a national policy favoring Britain and Austria over France, Alexander had personally concluded that Napoléon was a threat to Russia no less than to Britain. Therefore, when war in Europe resumed in 1805, Russia joined Britain, Austria, and other countries in the so-called Third Coalition, which turned into the Fourth Coalition in 1806 after Austria was knocked out of the war and Prussia came in on the anti-French side. The Russians lost two major battles against Napoléon, at Austerlitz in 1806 and at Friedland in 1807, but they bled the French in the process and did not collapse.

Both sides were ready for an agreement. Napoléon had not won the decisive victory he sought, while the Russians were exhausted and, by 1807, also at war with Persia and Turkey. The result was the Peace of Tilsit, which brought Russia into an uneasy alliance with France. The Tilsit agreement also reduced Prussia to a second-rate power, thereby leaving Russia as the dominant power in eastern Europe.

Over the next several years Russia successfully fought three other wars. A short war with Sweden gave the empire control of Finland. The other two yielded new territory south of the Caucasus at the expense of Persia and a region on the northwestern coast of the Black Sea called Bessarabia at the expense of Turkey.

Soon Russia was in a much bigger and tougher war, as economic and strategic tensions and suspicions between the two erstwhile Tilsit allies undermined that agreement. In June 1812 Napoléon invaded Russia at the head of an army that eventually numbered 600,000 men, slightly fewer than half of them French. Unable to stop the French directly, the Russians retreated, thus keeping their army intact and lengthening French supply lines.

When the French approached within 75 miles of Moscow, the Russians turned and met them at the savage Battle of Borodino. More than 100,000 of the 250,000 men who fought on both sides became casualties, 58,000 on the Russian side and 50,000 on the French side. Battered but not broken, the Russians retreated, leaving the road open for Napoléon to take Moscow in mid-September. It did him little good.

Alexander refused to negotiate, and fires soon broke out in the largely deserted city. Unable to sustain his army so far from its supply bases in Europe, Napoléon was forced to retreat. Now Russia's merciless "General Winter" entered the fray. Brutal cold took a terrible toll on the retreating French troops, who also had to defend themselves against constant harassment from Russian forces. Napoléon made it out of Russia in mid-December with fewer than 30,000 men. For Russia it was a national and patriotic triumph, retold and embellished most notably in Tolstoy's *War and Peace* but also by countless other Russian historians, writers, and poets.

Napoléon was down but not out. The war against him lasted for two more years. Prussia and Austria rejoined the coalition against the French emperor, and in October 1813 a combined army of Russian, Prussian, and Austrian units defeated him in the "Battle of the Nations" at Leipzig in eastern Germany. In rapid succession the Russians and Prussians reached Paris in March 1814, Napoléon abdicated and left for the island of Elba in April, the Treaty of Paris restored peace with France, and the Congress of Vienna, tasked with establishing a durable peace by settling affairs in the rest of Europe, began meeting in September.

With the Bourbon monarchy restored in Paris and the French threat to dominate Europe apparently ended, Britain and Austria now worried about the menace posed by another power: Russia. The specific issue around which that fear crystallized was Poland, which according to Alexander's plan officially was to be restored as a separate kingdom—but with the Russian czar as its king. Both Britain and Austria opposed this dangerous expansion of Russian power and maneuvered to block it. In January 1815 Britain, Austria, and France signed a treaty and went to the brink of war to force Russia to accept a significantly smaller Poland, and with it a correspondingly reduced influence in central Europe. Meanwhile, with the Congress of Vienna still in session, Napoléon returned from Elba in March 1815 and hostilities resumed. The fighting continued until his decisive defeat at the hands of the British and Prussians at Waterloo in mid-July, 10 days after the Congress concluded. With Russian troops in Paris and participating in the occupation of France, Alexander I and his empire stood at the height of their international power and prestige.

Alexander I: Reaction and Mysticism

The final decade of Alexander's reign was a peculiar brew of reaction and religious mysticism mixed with a few largely meaningless doses of change—primarily one stillborn political project and one inadequate social reform. The political project was a draft constitution Alexander at first supported in 1819 but then decided to ignore. The social reform was the abolition of serfdom in the empire's Baltic provinces between 1816 and 1819, which freed the peasants without land and thereby left them destitute and still dependent on their former landlords for economic survival.

Alexander meanwhile was drifting into a curious form of mysticism that drew from Catholic and Protestant as well as Russian Orthodox traditions. He became convinced that religion had to be the basis of government and that he, Alexander, had been chosen by God to redeem humankind. The first concrete manifestation of these beliefs was the 1815 agreement with Prussia and Austria for a Holy Alliance, which called for nations to conduct international affairs according to precepts of Christian morality.

The Holy Alliance had no impact on international affairs, but that was not true of some of Alexander's religiously inspired projects at home. In 1817 the Ministry of Education became the Ministry of Education and Public Worship. That name change signaled the start of a campaign to purge universities of professors and textbooks deemed anti-Christian, as defined by the obscurantist official who headed the ministry, and a more expansive effort to infuse Christian values—as understood by certain government bureaucrats—into Russia's secular education system as a whole. For several years one school, the University of Kazan, quite literally came to resemble a monastery. After 1820 censorship in general was intensified.

The most important initiative of this period, and its symbol, was the project to establish military colonies. This enterprise is associated most closely with its director, Count Aleksei A. Arakcheyev, Alexander's old military tutor, although the czar himself had thought up the idea in 1810. The goal was to lower the cost of maintaining a huge standing army, which Russia's leaders insisted had to equal the combined forces of Austria and Prussia. A new class of soldier-farmers would support themselves and their families as agriculturalists, freeing the state from that expensive obligation, while also training and maintaining their military readiness. Several districts were set aside primarily for this enterprise. Regular army soldiers were settled on the land and freed from their tax and labor obligations to the state. Peasants already living in these regions involuntarily became part of the experiment. The government helped the settlements to improve agricultural techniques and provided money for schools and other social services.

Whatever the virtues of this plan in theory, in practice it was extremely unpopular and ultimately a failure. Russian serfs and state peasants had hard lives, but at least they had leisure time to enjoy. That disappeared in the military colonies, where the colonists' lives were minutely regulated according to strict military discipline. Just as in the army, bugle calls announced when colonists should rise, work, eat, and sleep. Marriage required official permission. Making matters worse, when all the expenses for social services and the loss in tax revenue were figured in, the military colonies were expensive. By 1825 there were about 750,000 men, women, and children in the military colonies whose daily routine combined many of the worst features of serfdom and military barracks life. There was widespread discontent and one major mutiny, but Alexander refused to dismantle the colonies. They would remain, the czar emphatically stated, "whatever the cost," even if he had to "line the road from Petersburg to Chudovo [a distance of about 66 miles] with corpses" (McConnell 1970: 142).

Alexander I died unexpectedly in December 1825 while on a visit to the Sea of Azov. He was only 48 years old and childless, his two daughters by his wife having died in infancy (Alexander also had several children by a longtime mistress). These circumstances created a pall of uncertainty throughout the country. Some people refused to believe Alexander was dead, and rumors persisted for years that he was still alive living as a holy man in Siberia.

Adding to the confusion, while it was generally assumed that Alexander's brother Constantine, next in line for the throne according to age, would be the next czar, the royal family had worked out an arrangement in 1823 in which Constantine had given up his claim to the throne in favor of his younger brother Nicholas. Nicholas, unlike either of his older brothers, had a son, which meant that designating him as heir stabilized the succession for another generation. The problem was that this dynastic arrangement had been treated as a family affair and worked out in secret; nearly a month passed between Alexander's death and the proclamation of Nicholas as emperor.

Meanwhile a group of army officers and civilians committed to Enlightenment values and despairing of change under Alexander had been conspiring for several years to overthrow him. Although surprised by the czar's death and unprepared to act, they decided to seize what looked like a golden opportunity and launched their coup in the closing days of December. The reign of Nicholas I thus got off to a bloody start.

The Decembrist Revolt

The December 1825 revolt against the monarchy takes it name from the month in which it took place. It was badly organized and failed completely, but it is still historically significant because it left an important legacy. Unlike the violent but essentially aimless peasant rebellions of the 17th and 18th centuries and the various palace coups that preceded it, the Decembrist Revolt was a revolutionary upheaval carried out by educated members of the Russian elite intent on implementing modern programs of political and social change. Most of the Decembrists were army officers with aristocratic backgrounds—many of the leaders served in elite guards regiments. They had fought in Europe during the Napoléonic Wars and in the process learned about Western political ideas and social conditions, both of which they found superior to what prevailed in Russia. The contrast between what they saw in Europe, along with what they believed they had done there as soldiers for the Europeans, and the situation they found in their homeland evoked a sense of irony and anger that strengthened their desire for change. As one of them wrote from prison after the failure of their project:

> Did we free Europe in order to be put in chains ourselves? Did we grant France a constitution in order that we dare not talk about it, and did we buy at the price of our blood preeminence among nations in order that we might be humiliated at home? (Crankshaw 1976: 56)

In holding these views the Decembrists represented a trend in Russian society larger and more durable than themselves, even though they as individuals ended up on the scaffold or in Siberian exile and had no personal role in future developments. Among their sympathizers, even in 1825, were some of Russia's leading literary figures, including Aleksandr Pushkin and the dramatist Aleksandr Griboyedov. Both men had ties with revolutionary circles prior to 1825. Griboyedov, who came from a prominent gentry family, was investigated after the revolt before being cleared of complicity and allowed to continue his career as a diplomat. Pushkin may have been saved due to his exile from St. Petersburg five years earlier for expressing what were considered seditious views, which kept him from taking part in the conspiracy. That tendency to support radical change, which became more pronounced with each passing decade, explains why the Decembrist Revolt, which ended so quickly, ultimately was the start of an enduring political movement.

The Decembrists were not a single organization with a common program. They were divided into several organizations that over time evolved into two groups: the Northern Society based in St. Petersburg and the Southern Society based in Tulchin, a town in the southern part of the country that housed a large army base. The two had markedly different agendas.

The Northern Society, made up mostly of wealthy nobles, was moderate and favored a constitutional monarchy. Its leader, Nikita Muraviev, a guards officer from a leading noble family who had fought with distinction against Napoléon and been among the Russian troops that entered Paris, even drew up a constitution. It provided for a constitutional monarchy, a bicameral legislature, a federal structure with 13 states and two provinces, freedom of expression, and the abolition of serfdom. This program, which included legalized clear and unequal distinctions between various groups of citizens depending on wealth, was not nearly radical enough for the Southern Society and its most dynamic member, Pavel Pestel, who labeled the constitution "legalized aristocracy."

Pestel, a colonel and the son of the governor-general of Siberia, was a militant Jacobin, a type that later would become a permanent part of the Russian revolutionary tradition. He advocated what amounted to a centralized revolutionary police state, which he described in a treatise he called *Russian Justice*. All citizens were to be equal; they would also be equally under the absolute control of the state. Any teaching that strayed from what Pestel called the "laws and rules of pure morality" would be "absolutely prohibited," as would all "private societies established with some specific object." To make sure that these injunctions were carried out, Pestel devoted a great deal of attention to how Russia's new police force would be organized.

Although not a socialist—he advocated free enterprise—Pestel infused some socialist principles into his program such as dividing half of Russia's farmland equally among the peasants and keeping the rest for larger national purposes. Pestel had no tolerance for any national group within the empire other than the Great Russians; all would have to assimilate, other than the Jews, whom the anti-Semitic Pestel planned to deport.

Despite their differences, the Northern and Southern Societies kept in contact and maintained a commitment to work together. Then Alexander died. Hoping to take advantage of the confusion regarding Constantine and Nicholas, the Northern Society leaders hastily put together a plan. It called for officers to rally the soldiers in their regiments to refuse to take the oath of loyalty to Nicholas in a ceremony scheduled for December 26. Instead the soldiers were to demand that Constantine become czar and be required to grant Russia a constitution.

The rebellion started badly when several key units refused to join, but about 3,000 troops did rally to the Decembrist colors and march to Senate Square in the center of St. Petersburg. Some were shouting "Constantine and Constitution," a slogan that some of the less educated troops apparently believed referred not to Constantine and a fundamental political document but to Constantine and his wife. The government massed 9,000 troops in the square, and the two sides faced each other without acting for several hours. Nicholas himself was at the scene, eventually placing himself at the head of a guards unit where he could easily have been shot by one of the rebels. To his credit Nicholas tried to end the rebellion without bloodshed, but in the end he ordered a battery of four cannon to fire on the crowd. The rebels scattered, about 60 people were killed, and the rebellion in the north collapsed. It never really got started in the south, where Pestel and other leaders were quickly arrested. One member of the Southern Society did manage to escape and briefly rally a regiment to the cause, but he and his troops were quickly captured. The Decembrist Revolt was over.

Nicholas himself took charge of the investigation that followed. He was shocked that so many officers from leading noble families had been part of the rebellion, and that realization and the serious threat it posed colored his entire reign. The investigation was thorough, touching about 600 people. Eventually 121 conspirators were tried by a special court. Five were hanged, including Pestel and the militant poet Kondraty Ryleyev, 31 were sentenced to hard labor for life in Siberia, and 85 men received shorter terms. Those sentenced to Siberia were allowed to bring their wives and families with them. Over time many of these sentences were partially commuted. At the coronation of Alexander II in 1856, the 29 Decembrists still in Siberia were allowed to return home, subject only to a ban on living in St. Petersburg or Moscow.

The Decembrist Revolt and its failure had two long-term repercussions that worked against each other, in the irony typical of Russian history. First, for more than a generation the government's effort to stamp out dissent crippled beyond repair any advocacy of gradual, liberal reform or the establishment of a constitutional regime. Second, given the times and the impact of European ideas, the defeat of the Decembrists could not put the genie back in the bottle. Their quixotic revolt marked the beginning of organized revolutionary resistance to the czarist regime. That resistance would take many forms and experience many failures in the century to come, but it did not end until the monarchy finally collapsed in 1917.

Nicholas I : Shoring Up the System

Nicholas I, the "iron czar," was and has remained the object of contempt and even outright hatred. His countrymen called him the
"knout." His fellow army officers—Nicholas served in the military
from 1814 until the end of his brother's reign and eventually commanded a division of the elite guards—disliked him intensely, in part
because of his obsessive enforcement of even the most trivial element of military discipline, a liability that may explain his hesitation
to claim the throne in 1825. One prominent contemporary writer
described his reign as "desert landscape with a gaol [jail] in the middle," while another wrote how it was a time when a thinking person

Monument to Nicholas I, Russia's czar from 1825 to 1855, in St. Petersburg (Library of
Congress)

had to be "permanently afraid: this was the basic rule of life" (quoted in Szamuely 1974: 134).

A month after Nicholas died a professor at the University of Moscow confided to his diary that a "long and . . . joyless page in the history of the Russian empire has been written out to the last word" (quoted in Seton-Watson 1967: 279). Even staunch supporters of the regime despaired of him, including one prominent official who lamented that "the main failing of the reign of Nicholas Pavlovich was that it was all a mistake" (quoted in Crankshaw 1976: 30).

Nor was Nicholas popular with foreigners. During a state visit to Britain a young Queen Victoria was unnerved both by his demeanor and by his thinking. She commented that "the expression in his eyes is terrible. I have never seen anything like them; he is severe and gloomy, imbued with principles nothing on earth could change; I don't think he is very intelligent; his mind is without refinement; his education is very inadequate; politics and the army—those are the only things that interest him" (quoted in *Horizon History of Russia* 1970: 246).

Queen Victoria may have been a bit unfair to Nicholas: He enjoyed drawing, playing the flute, and attending opera, ballet, and the theater. Furthermore, their conversations, however boring to the young British queen, undoubtedly took place in English, which Nicholas spoke well, as he did French and German. But on the whole her assessment of him is not terribly off the mark as far as most historians are concerned. His reign generally is regarded as a dreary failure, any progress taking place in spite of rather than because of what he did. Nicholas was an autocrat to the core. As he put it to a group of top advisers shortly after becoming czar, "I cannot permit that any individual should defy my wishes, once he knows what they are" (quoted in Crankshaw 1976: 46).

Yet the truth is a bit more complex. Nicholas was determined to serve his country's interests as he understood them. Convinced that he ruled "by the grace of God," Nicholas also fervently believed that autocracy was the best possible form of government for Russia. To his credit, he did not feel the same about serfdom. Thus in 1842 he told a small group of high-ranking officials that there was "no doubt that serfdom, in its present form, is a flagrant evil which everyone realizes." The problem, the czar continued, was that "to attempt to remedy it now would be, of course, an evil even more disastrous" (quoted in Florinsky 1953: Vol. 2, 755). And that was the point. Meaningful reform—moving toward a constitutional monarchy, abolishing serfdom, permitting a free exchange of ideas, especially political ideas—was incompatible with the order Nicholas was sworn to defend.

The bitter truth was that the interests of the Russian people—in other words, Russia's real national interests—were increasingly at variance with the interests of its ruling class and the regime that protected it. The tension between the two was growing each year, while economic, social, and political changes virtually next door in Europe were adding to the strain. It was reasonable to assume that any jolt to the fundamental supports of the system could cause it to collapse. That is why Nicholas feared any attempt to modify serfdom would be "even more disastrous" than the "flagrant evil" it undeniably was.

The czar's solution was to try to stop the clock. The effort began in 1826 with the creation of the innocuously named Third Section of His Majesty's Own Chancery. It administered a new political police that included both a uniformed corps of gendarmes and a network of secret informers. The Third Section did not limit itself, as its predecessors had, to seeking out avowed opponents of the regime. It probed the work of journalists, writers, historians, and others for the slightest hint of dissent. It was assigned to investigate not only "all orders and all reports in every case belonging to the higher police" but "reports about all occurrences without exception." To do the job its secret agents included not only men and women from every level of society but also schoolchildren. In short, the Third Section and its gendarmes provided the model for a modern political police that remained a fixture of Russian life until the end of the 20th century.

The Third Section was complemented by a new criminal code issued in 1845, 54 pages of which enumerated political crimes. These crimes included any attempt to limit the authority of the czar or any expression of such an idea. It was also a crime to spread ideas that might raise doubts about the czar's authority or lessen respect for him as Russia's sovereign. The crime of actually attempting to limit the czar's authority carried the death penalty, while raising doubts about the czar's authority or lessening respect for him was punishable by four to 12 years at hard labor as well as corporal punishment and branding. In other words, when Europe was moving toward more open societies, in Russia it became a crime not only to seek political change but even to discuss the subject.

Nicholas imposed several other measures along the same lines. The same year he set up the Third Section, the czar decreed a censorship law; its 230 articles gave the censors almost unlimited powers. The government also made a sustained effort to control education by limiting lower-class children to elementary-level instruction, regulating the content of private education (and even homeschooling), limiting the

EDICT CREATING THE THIRD SECTION

The edict setting up the Third Section (also translated as "Third Department") was issued in July 1826. Nicholas considered the agency to be his most important weapon against the threats raised by the Decembrists:

> *I assign the following field of activity to this Third Department of My Own Chancery:*
>
> 1. *All orders and all reports in every case belonging to the higher police.*
> 2. *Information about the number of various sects and schisms which exist in the state.*
> 3. *Reports about discoveries of false banknotes, coins, stamping, documents, etc., the search for and the further investigation in connection with which remains in the jurisdiction of the ministries of finance and internal affairs.*
> 4. *Information about all persons placed under police supervision as well as all orders in that connection.*
> 5. *Exile and distribution as to place of suspected and noxious individuals.*
> 6. *Superintendence, supervision, and management of the economy of all the places of incarceration where state prisoners are confined.*
> 7. *All regulation and orders concerning foreigners who reside in Russia, enter, or leave the state.*
> 8. *Reports of all occurrences without exception.*
> 9. *Statistical information which has police pertinence. . . .*
>
> *(Riasanovsky 1967: 219–220)*

autonomy of universities, and banning the teaching of certain subjects at the university level. These efforts reflected a doctrine of "Official Nationality," proclaimed in 1833 by the minister of education. Official Nationality affirmed that a "correct fundamental education" should be based on three "truly Russian saving principles" (Seton-Watson 1967: 220): Orthodoxy—the centrality of the Orthodox Church in Russian life; autocracy—the affirmation of the czar's absolute powers; and nationality—the special qualities of the Russian people that made them such strong supporters of the current order.

Of course, time does not stop, not even for a czar. Russia's industrial sector continued to grow, albeit relatively slowly and mainly in the Urals and in the Moscow and St. Petersburg regions. Steamships made their first appearance on the Volga as early as 1820, five years before Nicholas became czar; by 1837 Russia's first railroad was operating between St. Petersburg and a nearby suburb. The first major railroad, between St. Petersburg and Moscow, opened in 1851. Foreign trade also increased, especially the export of grain via Odessa and the Black Sea. The urban population doubled during the first half of the century to slightly less than 8 percent of the national total. The bad news was that even as Russia moved slowly forward in absolute terms, it was moving backward relatively, as the gap in economic modernization between the empire and most of the major powers of Europe continued to grow.

The Opening of the Russian Mind

There are many ironies associated with the reign of Nicholas I. The czar was reactionary in the fullest sense of the word and committed to holding the line against social and political change. At the same time the demands of maintaining a strong empire in 19th-century Europe required that education be expanded and made available to an ever-widening segment of Russian society. Had he been more discerning, Nicholas undoubtedly would have found it bitterly ironic that during his reign, for the first time in Russia's history, the actions of the czar and the powerful people around him mattered less in the long term than the deeds or opinions of various people who had no power.

Pushing the irony further, it was not what these people did to affect change on the ground that mattered—there was nothing they could do—but what they thought, said, and wrote. As Nicholas and his retinue manned the ramparts of repression and censorship and success-fully blocked social and political reform, words and ideas were flowing around and seeping past them, penetrating into various layers of Russian society, and corroding the foundations on which Nicholas, his ramparts of reaction, and the entire czarist social and political order stood.

The most enduring development by far was cultural, especially in the realm of literature and poetry. The second quarter of the 19th century witnessed an explosion of creative energy among the country's small circle of writers and poets that marked the beginning of what is known as the golden age of Russian literature. This remarkable era, which enriched not only Russian but all of Western culture, usually is dated from the publication of Pushkin's first major poem in 1820 to the appearance of Dostoyevsky's last novel in 1880. The reign of Nicholas, so dreary in almost every other way, was lit up by the major works of Pushkin, Mikhail Lermontov, and Nikolai Gogol, and the first writings of Ivan Turgenev, Leo Tolstoy, and Fyodor Dostoyevsky. It says something about the situation of Russia and the time, and about what must have been lost because of repression, that Pushkin might never have written most of his poetry and prose had he not been exiled from St. Petersburg in 1820 and instead become more deeply involved with the Decembrists and that just over two decades later Dostoyevsky was actually sentenced to death before his sentence was commuted to imprisonment while he stood at the execution ground.

The other major development was political, at least to the degree that political expression was permitted in Russia. It involved a new segment of Russian society that was a direct outgrowth of the spread of education and Western ideas known as the intelligentsia. The term today has a broad meaning, encompassing all kinds of people whose interests lie in the realm of ideas and the arts. But in 19th-century Russia the term *intelligentsia* referred to a much narrower group: educated, socially aware individuals whose main priority in life was to promote beneficial changes in Russian society. They were inspired by European ideas, especially those associated with German romanticism and idealism, which had reached Russia by the 1830s.

The intelligentsia at first consisted of noblemen, but as education spread they were joined by people from the lower classes, the so-called *raznochintsy,* which in Russian means "people of various ranks." Unlike their noble elders, many *raznochintsy* had known poverty and hardship. They were far more alienated from conventional Russian values and were correspondingly more radical in their views, a generational split brilliantly chronicled in the early 1860s by Ivan Turgenev in his novel *Fathers and Sons.*

The Russian intelligentsia began its existence with a debate, set off by the publication of a "philosophic letter" by the nobleman and former soldier Peter Chaadayev. Heavily influenced by Catholicism, an admirer of western Europe, and inclined to mysticism, Chaadayev dismissed Russia as a country without a history that had contributed nothing to civilization. Not surprisingly, the government shut down the journal that had published Chaadayev's polemic, exiled its editor for a year, fired the censor who had permitted the letter to appear, and, on the czar's personal order, declared Chaadayev insane and subject to regular inspection by a doctor. Chaadayev later retreated from some of his more incendiary statements in a tract called *Apology of a Madman.*

But a dam had been breached, and soon other nobles were debating some of the issues Chaadayev had raised. Everyone agreed that Russia had serious problems; the question was how to solve them. By the 1840s two opposing groups had emerged, one conservative and the other liberal.

The conservative Slavophiles argued that Russia had to find solutions based on its indigenous traditions. Following the logic of German idealism, they argued that each nationality was unique. Russia's uniqueness, and its strength, came from three institutions: the czarist autocracy, the Russian Orthodox Church, and the so-called peasant commune, an institution under which peasants controlled their farmland as a community rather than individually. Russia's troubles began when it abandoned its spiritual and cooperative traditions and started to copy the sterile rationalism of the West. The Slavophiles opposed serfdom but not the institution of the czar. The great ogre in their version of Russian history was Peter the Great, who allegedly had changed czardom from a benevolent institution into one based on compulsion. The leading Slavophiles, all highly educated nobles, were Aleksei Khomyakov, Konstantin Aksakov, and the brothers Peter and Ivan Kireevsky.

Opposed to the Slavophiles were the Westernizers, whose leading light was Aleksandr Herzen, the illegitimate son of a wealthy Moscow aristocrat whose family lineage went back to the days of Ivan III. As their name indicates, the Westernizers believed that Russia had to adopt European economic and political models to solve its problems. They originally were political liberals who supported the abolition of serfdom, establishment of constitutional government, and development of capitalism.

A key point in the debate between the two camps concerned the peasant commune, which the Slavophiles said was proof of the inherently and uniquely cooperative nature of the Russian people—one of them called it a "moral choir." According to the Slavophiles, that Russian characteristic stood in total contrast to the supposedly inherent competitiveness of Europeans to the west. The Westernizers countered that the notion of inherent Russian cooperativeness somehow expressed through the peasant commune was nonsense. They argued that the commune as it existed in recent times was a state mechanism of social control and taxation connected to the rise of serfdom. The facts were on the side of the Westernizers, especially with regard to the key practice of distributing land equally among commune members, which did not begin until the 16th and 17th centuries and did not become common until the 18th century.

As Nicholas's reign wore on, the Westernizers increasingly became the dominant group among the intelligentsia. But that did not solve their problems, as the case of Herzen makes clear. The West, it turned out, was far from perfect, much better as a source of ideas than of practical economic policies, above all because of capitalism and the harsh conditions it imposed on millions of workers. Herzen's disenchantment with capitalism began early; by the 1830s, influenced by the ideas of Claude-Henri de Saint-Simon, he had become a socialist. The events of the 1840s made things worse. Forced into exile in 1847, Herzen did not like what he saw in western Europe. He was soon further demoralized by the failures of the revolutions that swept much of the continent in 1848. It seemed clear that the West's foreseeable future would lie with exploitative capitalism, not egalitarian socialism. Socialism, if it ever came, was a long way off. This was a fate Herzen did not want Russia to share.

Herzen's response was an intellectual leap across the Westernizer-Slavophile chasm. He revived a key element of the Slavophile analysis that he and his colleagues had once scorned—the peasant commune. The commune would be his magic carpet for transporting Russia over the wasteland of capitalism directly to the promised land of socialism. Russia's economic backwardness, long considered a curse by patriots concerned for their country's great power status, was a blessing in disguise because it had permitted the survival of the *mir* (the Russian word for both "peace" and "world"), as the commune was often called. The *mir,* in which Russia's peasants protected their economic equality, was proof of their instinctive socialist nature. Russia therefore could build a socialist society on the basis of the peasant commune and avoid the capitalist stage of economic development, with all its terrible flaws.

There were two serious problems with Herzen's upbeat scenario. First, his faith in the peasantry's instinctive commitment to socialism was a fantasy that ignored the harsh realities of peasant life. Rather than being ennobled by instinctive cooperation, life on peasant communes, blighted by extreme poverty, was characterized by jealousy, cruelty, mistrust, and superstition. Notwithstanding the imposed partial equality of commune life, most peasants cared first and foremost about themselves.

Second, Herzen did not explain how to remove the czarist regime, the heretofore immovable barrier to change, nor what kind of regime would replace it. Unlike some of his colleagues, Herzen opposed violence to realize political goals. He was horrified by the idea of a great peasant uprising in which the old order would be entirely destroyed, a vision that so fascinated the famed anarchist nobleman Mikhail

Bakunin. Such a "savage and unrestrained explosion will spare nothing," Herzen warned. Rather than creating a better world, the "rampant spirit of extermination will destroy . . . all those landmarks of human progress that men have created since the building of civilization (quoted in Szamuely 1974: 245). Nor did Herzen have any faith in progress imposed from above by a powerful state, as advocated by Vissarion Belinsky, Russia's leading literary critic of the 1840s, whose contributions to the field of literary criticism include the insidious idea that literature and art have value only if they carry a progressive message. Herzen called that idea "Peter the Greatism" and dismissed it as capable of achieving only "prison equality."

As it turned out, these were not fatal shortcomings for many members of the intelligentsia desperate for a way out of the existing morass. Herzen's idea of a unique Russian route to socialism using the special qualities of its peasants and their communes struck a chord. Under the name of populism it quickly became the prevailing political creed among the Russian intelligentsia. In its various forms it dominated dissident Russian political life for the rest of the century, stamping the revolutionary movement that evolved after 1860 with characteristics it never completely lost.

The Gendarme of Europe

Russian foreign policy under Nicholas I was driven by two imperatives: further expansion of the Russian Empire and a commitment to maintain the conservative order that had been restored in Europe after the defeat of Napoléon. The latter, which added a new and potentially dangerous element to Russian foreign policy, was the logical corollary of everything Nicholas was trying to accomplish in Russia.

Opportunity for expansion was limited and came early in Nicholas's reign, at the expense of Persia and Turkey. Between 1826 and 1828, a war with Persia strengthened Russian control over Transcaucasia, the territory between the Black and Caspian seas south of the Caucasus Mountains today occupied by Georgia, Armenia, and Azerbaijan. Yet another war with Turkey yielded the Treaty of Adrianople in 1829, which gave Russia still more Transcaucasian territory. Four year later the complications of European power politics drove Nicholas to make Russia a protector of Turkey in the Treaty of Unkiar Skelessi. He did not want to see further Turkish decline if it would benefit Russia's European rivals without giving St. Petersburg similar or better gains. The treaty's most important provision from the Russian point of view was Turkey's commitment to close the Black Sea straits to all foreign, and hence British and French, warships.

In Europe itself the battle was against change and against the spread of constitutional and democratic ideas. Russia's problems began in 1830 when a revolution overthrew the conservative monarchy in France and a rebellion in Belgium established that country's independence from Holland. In both cases moderate monarchies were installed, but the dual example immediately spread to Poland, in theory an independent country with Russia's czar as its king but in fact a bitterly restive part of the Russian Empire. The Polish rebellion began late in 1830 and was brutally suppressed by the fall of 1831, at which point Poland was officially incorporated into the Russian Empire and subject to systematic repression and a policy of Russification.

Then came the Revolutions of 1848, which began in France and eventually spread across most of the continent west of Russia. Russia's role was to send an army to crush the Hungarian rebellion against Austria, like Russia a conservative monarchy, an act of intervention that earned Russia the epithet "gendarme of Europe" and the hatred of the Hungarians that persists to this day. Although these revolutions failed everywhere, they had a powerful impact on Russia, and Nicholas ramped up his efforts to stifle subversive ideas. The government eliminated what little remained of university autonomy and intensified censorship. Phrases like "forces of nature" were deleted from physics textbooks and "free currents of air" was cut from cookbooks. According to one official engaged in the effort, after 1848 the number of censors was greater than the number of books published each year.

The Debacle of the Crimean War

The causes of the Crimean War (1853–56) were complex, as half a dozen countries were involved. Three key factors were the continued weakening of Turkey, which by 1850 was generally viewed as the "Sick Man of Europe," the continued growth of Russian power, and a general fear among the European powers that Turkey's further decline would lead to Russian domination of the Balkans and control over the straits leading from the Black Sea into the Mediterranean. When tangled diplomacy finally ended in war between Russia and Turkey, Britain, France, and Sardinia joined the war on the Turkish side, with Austria providing strong diplomatic support.

The Crimean War dragged on for three years before ending with Russia's defeat. The result was a serious setback for Russia but not a

In the bloody Battle of Inkerman in November 1854 during the Crimean War, the Russians unsuccessfully attempted to take the strategic high ground outside Sevastopol from British and French forces in an effort to break the siege of the city, which finally fell in September 1855. (Library of Congress)

disaster. It remained a great power, albeit somewhat chastened and diminished.

The real problem was what would happen to the empire in the long term. The Crimean War once again revealed the backwardness of Russian society vis-à-vis the West. Despite heroic efforts by soldiers and officers alike, the Russian army, more than a match for the Turks, could not cope against modern European military power. To be sure, the key port of Sevastopol on the southern tip of the Crimean Peninsula, where the main fighting took place, held out against French and British naval bombardment for 11 months, a terrible battle chronicled brilliantly by a young Russian artillery officer named Leo Tolstoy. But Russia lacked railroads and even decent roads to supply its troops; the Europeans were better able to supply their armies across far longer supply lines stretching all the way across the sea to Britain and France. Russian artillery could not match superior European firepower, nor could outdated Russian muskets fire as far as modern British and French rifles. The Russian navy, while able to route the Turks, was antiquated by European standards. Overall it became painfully clear that the entire Russian military system, based on serf conscripts, was antiquated and corrupt beyond repair.

Nicholas I, personally devastated by the events that saw most of the European great powers turn against his empire, died in March 1855, apparently a broken man. His son and successor, Alexander II, reluctantly accepted a peace treaty in March 1856 in which Russia gave up southern Bessarabia, with its access to the Danube River delta, and lost its right to keep naval forces on the Black Sea. The new czar thereby extricated Russia from a lost war without excessive damage to its standing as a great power. The question was whether he and his advisers were willing to act on the fundamental problems the war had so graphically highlighted about Russian society.

5

REFORM, REACTION, AND REVOLUTION (1855–1917)

Three czars—Russia's last—ruled between 1861, the year the empire's serfs were emancipated, and 1917, the year its monarchy was overthrown: Alexander II (1855–81), Alexander III (1881–94), and Nicholas II (1894–1917). As personalities, the three men were quite different. Alexander II tended to be shy, emotional, and indecisive but still capable of overcoming his deficiencies by relying on his good sense and stubborn determination to set and stick to reform policies, an ability that was vital in the events that finally led to the emancipation of the serfs. His son Alexander III was a tough, vigorous reactionary, able to adhere without wavering to his policies in part because he never questioned any of his basic beliefs. Nicholas II seems to have combined many of the negative qualities of his father and grandfather without sharing any of their virtues. He was indecisive, stubborn, lacking even a shred of common sense, and incapable of questioning or rethinking any of his reactionary views, even as change was engulfing his country from all sides.

Whatever their personality differences, as political leaders the three were cast from the same autocratic mold. All were despots, true believers in autocracy as the only form of government suitable for Russia. This in turn explains an important commonality in their reigns: each was marked by policies of reaction as well as by programs that actually promoted the strong currents of modernization flowing through Russia during this era. It was the timing that varied. Alexander II began his reign with the emancipation of the serfs, which was followed closely by the rest of an extensive program of change known as the Great Reforms, only to retrench later on. Alexander III came to the throne in the wake of his father's assassination and immediately implemented a vigorous program of reaction and repression known as the counter-reforms, but near the end of his reign he instituted a comprehensive program of economic modernization. Nicholas II floundered as he drifted or was pushed back and forth. He continued his father's economic program for nine years, and then fired its chief architect; reluctantly granted a constitution to stop a revolutionary upheaval, but then did all he could to reverse what he had done; and inaugurated visionary reforms—the vision came from the country's prime minister, not its czar—to help the peasantry economically, but then changed his own electoral law to reduce the peasantry's political weight. His one area of consistency was foreign policy—to his and his country's tragic detriment. Nicholas followed an aggressive foreign policy that led Russia into two wars and was an inept leader in both of them. That unfortunate consistency contributed to a final crisis that was fatal to Nicholas himself, the Romanov dynasty, and the Russian monarchy.

It is a mistake to view that final crisis as somehow inevitable, whatever the virtues or defects of the last three czars. The revolution that brought down the Russian monarchy in March 1917 was above all the product of World War I. Between 1861 and 1914, the year World War I began, Russia made fundamental institutional changes and achieved enormous economic and political progress, albeit in fits and starts. The Great Reforms of the 1860s and 1870s eliminated serfdom and significantly improved the country's government. From the early 1890s until the outbreak of the world war Russia's industrial development was extremely impressive. Efforts to raise agricultural production and improve the lives of the peasantry lagged, but after 1906 there were significant gains in those areas. In the wake of the revolutionary upheaval of 1905, which the monarchy barely survived, Russia gained a constitution and a parliament with limited but not inconsequential powers. The country's middle class grew rapidly. Russia's overall situation was definitely improving, but its creaky social order was still vulnerable to powerful shocks, which World War I brought without letup until the breaking point was reached and passed.

Emancipation and the Great Reforms

The Crimean War, the curtain raiser to the era, highlighted Russia's urgent problems, but it left the regime with enough strength to deal with them. Even before the treaty ending the war was signed in 1856, Alexander II made it clear that policies at home were going to change. He lifted restrictions from non-Orthodox religious sects, ended onerous restrictions on foreign travel, and liberalized censorship. The "thaw" intensified after the treaty was signed and Alexander was officially crowned: The czar cancelled millions of rubles of unpaid back taxes, issued an amnesty allowing the Decembrists still in Siberia and other political prisoners to return home, and suspended army recruiting for three years. The czar and his top advisers well understood that this left untouched the institution Aleksandr Radishchev back in 1790 had called the "grim monster, savage, gigantic, hundred mouthed, and bellowing," and what one high-ranking official now called "the question of questions, the evil of evils, the first of all our misfortunes" (quoted in Mosse, 1962: 41). The time had finally come to deal with serfdom.

Serfdom was always a brutal system and had long hindered Russia's development, but by the mid-1850s it was also a badly corroded institution. It was totally unsuited to the capitalist money economy that was spreading in Russia. Illiterate and unskilled serfs were inefficient laborers, both on the small parcels they farmed for themselves and on the large fields of their landlords' estates. Instead of using their serfs as farm laborers, many landlords let them work in factories or in industries such as transportation in return for a cash payment, a practice that yielded a higher income to both parties. By the 1840s and 1850s landlords were increasingly demanding cash payments in place of labor even from the serfs living and working on their estates. In some of the better agricultural regions, such as in the south along the Volga, landlords actually preferred free to serf labor. None of these practices helped nearly enough, and by the late 1850s most landlords were deeply in debt.

Serfdom was in relative and absolute decline. By the end of the 1850s serfs accounted for just under 40 percent of Russia's total population, slightly less than the number of state peasants. The latter, of course, were also bonded to the land on which they lived and thus likewise required a fundamental change in their legal status. Despite the system's growing difficulties, the nobles did not want to give up their serfs, fearing they could not survive without them. Alexander responded cogently and directly that it was better to abolish serfdom "from above than to wait until the serfs begin to liberate themselves from below" (quoted in Seton-Watson, 1967: 335). The warning resonated strongly against the background of increasing peasant disturbances during the first six decades of the 19th century. The next noble line of defense was to accept emancipation but without granting the peasants land, a proposition the czar also categorically rejected. Slowly he pushed the bureaucratic wheels forward until on March 3, 1861, six years to the day after he ascended the throne, Alexander II, henceforth the "Tsar-Liberator," at last issued his Emancipation Edict granting the serfs their freedom.

The Emancipation Edict did a great deal but left at least as much undone. It freed more than 20 million peasants from the authority of their landlords—about five times the number of slaves liberated after the American Civil War. And unlike the former slaves in the United States, the Russian serfs were liberated with land. The problem was how much land, at what price, and under what circumstances.

Although conditions varied from place to place, the peasants generally received about one-third of the land; the landlords retained the best land, including most of the woodlands and pasture. In a major

THE EMANCIPATION EDICT OF MARCH 3, 1861

The law that emancipated the serfs was more than 400 pages long. Alexander's edict, issued on March 3, 1861, summarized that lengthy legal document for the general population.

Tensions were running high. The government feared that the peasants would react angrily to an emancipation that forced them to pay for the land they believed was theirs as recompense for hundreds of years of unpaid labor, an article of deep faith summed up by a saying the serfs used to describe their relationship to their masters: "We are yours, but the land is ours." Another potential complaint concerned limits on personal freedom. Peasants were free of their landlords but still subject to the authority of their communes. They could not leave their localities unless the commune granted them a passport, a disability that set them apart from the rest of Russia's population.

The government's fears were generally exaggerated. Still, while there was no violent reaction remotely comparable to the great upheavals of the past, official records list more than 1,100 disturbances during 1861 and about 400 annually during the following two years. Stories spread that the nobles and corrupt officials had repressed the true, more generous edict. The Emancipation Edict preceded by just over a month the firing of guns at South Carolina's Fort Sumter, by just under two years Abraham Lincoln's Emancipation Proclamation, and by almost exactly four years the end of the horrific American Civil War, which finally brought freedom to 4 million African-American slaves in the United States.

The following is a small selection of the Emancipation Edict, which was read in churches and publicized in other ways to what was an often uncomprehending peasant audience:

disappointment the serfs had to pay their former landlords for the land, at a price, set by the government, generally higher than what the land was worth. Since peasants were in no position to pay for what they in effect were forced to buy, the government provided them with loans to be repaid over 49 years in installments called redemption payments.

Finally, in most parts of the empire title did not go to individual peasant households but to their communes, which the Emancipation Edict retained. As they did before the emancipation, the communes divided the land up among its member households. The whole system

By the Grace of God, We, Alexander II, Emperor and Autocrat of all the Russias, Tsar of Poland, Grand Duke of Finland . . .

Declare to all Our loyal subjects. . . .

Having called upon God for help, We decided to put this into effect.

By virtue of the aforesaid new regulations the serfs will in due time receive the full rights of free rural inhabitants.

The landowners, preserving the right to ownership of all land belonging to them, allot to the peasants in perpetuity, in return for fixed obligations, the homesteads on which they are settled and, in addition, for the security of their daily lives and the fulfillment of their obligations to the Government, a definite amount of field and other lands, as defined in "Regulations." In return for the use of the land allotments, the peasants, on their part, are duty bound to discharge for the benefit of the landowners the obligations defined in the "Regulations.". . .

In addition, they are given the right to redeem the homesteads on which they are settled, and by agreement with the landowners they can acquire ownership of the field and other lands allotted to them in perpetuity. By acquiring ownership of a definite amount of land, the peasants will be freed from obligations to the landowners on the land they have purchased and will acquire the definitive status of free peasant proprietors. . . .

And now we hopefully anticipate that the serfs for whom a new future has been opened up will comprehend and accept with gratitude the important sacrifice made by the nobility for the improvement of their daily lives. . . .

And now, make the sign of the cross, O Orthodox people, and call upon God to bless your free labor, which is the guarantee of your domestic well-being and common good. . . . (Spector and Spector, eds., 1965: 171–176)

was disastrously inefficient because of two policies, both designed to insure equality. First, the allotments were periodically redistributed, thereby killing any incentive to improve one's land. Second, instead of a unified plot of land, each household was given a series of strips of varying widths (from barely six to over 20 feet wide), scattered across the countryside. The obsession with equality, carried over from pre-emancipation days, was driven by a logical imperative: The commune was collectively responsible for monetary obligations, including taxes; it was crucial that each family be able to carry its own weight.

The commune system and its inherently inefficient system of land tenure was retained because it was the state's proven method of controlling and taxing the peasants. That retention came at a high price. In the post-emancipation era, the system stifled most attempts by industrious or innovative peasants to increase their productivity and improve their lot. Having paid too much for their land to begin with, the peasants were unable to keep up with their redemption payments or with the high taxes the government continued to impose on them, and as a result they fell deep into debt.

Other factors also undermined the peasants' precarious economic position. After emancipation they no longer had free access to the forests and pastureland of the nobles. The spread of industry wiped out many of their cottage industries, which in the past had provided a slim margin of survival to many families. Finally, rapid population growth put increasing stress on limited resources. Debt mounted and the standard of living in many regions declined. When in 1891 the harvest failed, Russia experienced one of the worst famines in its history. As the century drew to a close, the defects rather than the successes of emancipation dominated the rural landscape.

State peasants were freed under more favorable conditions according to a law issued in 1866. Their initial advantage over their ex-serf countrymen eroded over time under the relentless undertow of hard times. Ultimately Russia found itself with a single, hard-pressed, and often demoralized peasant class.

The Great Reforms

Emancipation of the serfs was only the first of Alexander's Great Reforms. In 1864 another decree totally overhauled rural local government by establishing new elected assemblies called zemstvos. The electorate was divided into three categories—landowners, townspeople, and peasant communes—who chose representatives to district zemstvos by a

Peasants in a field about 1870, less than a decade after the abolition of serfdom (Library of Congress)

system weighted according to the value of their land. This ensured that the landowning nobility controlled the local assemblies. Since the local zemtstvos elected the provincial assemblies, landlords were even more preponderant at the provincial level.

The zemstvos had wide responsibility for local services, from education and health care to road maintenance, but their taxing powers were limited. Despite this and other handicaps zemstovs did a commendable job of improving local government. In 1870 a similar decree established new town governments throughout the empire. The town assemblies, elected by a three-class system weighted according to property value, were called dumas.

Meanwhile, in 1863 an educational reform restored autonomy to Russia's universities and opened secondary schools to all classes, not just nobles. An 1864 law overhauled Russia's judicial system, making the judiciary an independent branch of government for the first time. There were three levels of courts, topped by the Senate in St. Petersburg, which served as the final court of appeal. Trials were public and juries decided criminal cases. The new judicial system had its defects, including a shortage of trained lawyers, and in later years the government removed certain cases from its jurisdiction, but on the whole the reform represented a vast improvement over what it replaced and provided Russia with an up-to-date and respectable system of justice.

In 1874 the last of the Great Reforms reorganized military service. All classes of men, not just peasants, became liable to conscription, although the maximum term of six years (nine in the reserve) applied only to those with no education. The conscription term dropped with each level of education completed, down to only six months for university graduates. The 1874 law also abolished corporal punishment in the army, provided education for draftees, and in general dramatically improved the condition of all soldiers in the ranks.

The Great Reforms were a historically important step forward for Russia. They promoted capitalist economic development and the expansion of the middle classes, provided for better treatment of Russia's lower classes, both in civilian and in military life, and raised the educational level of the country as a whole. At the same time, in key ways they were incomplete and left many problems unsolved. Meanwhile, even as he was carrying out his Great Reforms, Alexander II imposed other measures that undermined them, mainly because he feared dissent and instability. The czar was shaken by the Polish rebellion of 1863, which took more than a year to suppress, and even more by an attempt on his life in 1866 by an unbalanced former university student.

Alexander was also deeply concerned with the proliferation of avowed revolutionary groups. The czar first reacted to this threat in 1866 by appointing a conservative education minister, who immediately began to purge the education system of what he considered subversive subjects. Later attention focused on law enforcement. In 1871 cases involving alleged political crimes were removed from the jurisdiction of the courts and transferred to that of the political police. Beginning in the late 1870s several types of political crimes were tried in military courts. In response to growing revolutionary activity, including the assassination of government officials, several decrees expanded the authority of military courts and increased the power of the police to detain and exile people suspected of subversive activity.

Expansion Abroad

Russia expanded in several directions on two continents during the reign of Alexander II. In the Caucasus Mountains resistance by Muslim tribesmen was finally overcome in the early 1860s, allowing Russia to complete its conquest of that region. To the east by the mid-1870s Russian forces had conquered three khanates in central Asia. Russia also made huge territorial gains in the Far East, from the western reaches of the Amur River to the Pacific coast, at the expense of the weakening Chinese Empire. Vladivostok, Russia's main port on the Pacific, was founded in 1860 on territory taken from China. Beyond the Asian mainland an agreement with Japan in 1875 gave Russia control of Sakhalin Island in return for recognition of Japan's control of the Kurile Islands. Russia's only territorial contraction under Alexander occurred even farther east in North America with the sale of Alaska to the United States in 1867.

Things were more complicated and objectives more difficult to realize closer to home. The main focus of attention was the Balkan Peninsula, where rebellions against Turkish rule broke out in 1875 and 1876. The Muslim Turks responded with savage repression and large-scale atrocities against the region's Orthodox Christian population, at which point diminutive Serbia, which itself had endured centuries of Turkish rule before reestablishing its independence earlier in the century and wanted to liberate countrymen living in regions still under Turkish rule, joined the battle in support of the rebels.

Serbia's defeat brought Russia into the war in April 1877, both to further its national interests in the region and to protect the Orthodox Christians suffering under Turkish rule. At great cost in casualties and treasure, the Russians decisively defeated the Turks. In the Treaty of San Stefano (1878), Russia regained southern Bessarabia and greatly strengthened its influence in the Balkans, so much so that both Austria-Hungary and Britain became worried and immediately acted to reduce those gains. The hastily convened Congress of Berlin did exactly that, as the major European powers lined up against Russia. Russia retained southern Bessarabia, but the congress voided the other favorable arrangements under San Stefano involving Serbia, Romania, and Bulgaria. The Congress of Berlin gave Russia a small piece of territory but, more important, dealt it a large diplomatic defeat.

Populism and Revolution, 1861–1881

Whatever Alexander's vexations with Europe's great powers, the greatest hostility his regime and its policies faced was at home. The Great Reforms did not satisfy many of the czar's subjects. The dissatisfied existed in every class of the population, but one small group in particular stands out—the radical fringe of the intelligentsia. They held a variety of beliefs but all agreed that reform was not enough; if Russia was going to solve its problems and become a just and equitable society, revolution was needed, not reform. As Russia was going through its

Great Reforms, its intelligentsia, increasingly dominated by the *razno-chintsy,* was giving birth to the Russian revolutionary movement.

The revolutionaries of the 1850s and 1860s were a new, more militant generation of populists who favored socialist revolution. Their most urgent unresolved issue was how to overthrow Russia's current regime. Some members of the new generation turned to nihilism, a grim, pitiless doctrine that allowed them to overcome Herzen's moral scruples against violence through a rejection of conventional morality. According to nihilism, the current reality was so irretrievably bad that any methods used to destroy it were justified. In effect, destruction for its own sake was transformed into a creative act.

The thinker who incorporated nihilist elements most successfully into his revolutionary scheme was Nikolai Chernyshevsky, a priest's son who began his education in a seminary and eventually graduated from St. Petersburg University. Chernyshevsky's seminal contribution to the revolutionary movement was to use nihilist values to portray an ideal professional revolutionary and thereby provide a model for younger, would-be revolutionaries to emulate. He rendered this service in an artless, dreary, and tendentious novel *What Is to Be Done?*

According to Chernyshevsky, revolutionaries must be full-time activists who do nothing but train and prepare to carry out the great social upheaval that will change the world. Given their noble task of serving humanity, these revolutionaries were not bound by conventional moral codes. Any method that served the revolution was moral. As he put it, "Perhaps the means required by the cause are evil—but if one regards them as evil one should never take up the cause itself" (quoted in Szamuely 1974: 166). Equally important, this moral license covered not only acts against the ruling classes the revolution was to destroy but also acts that might harm the masses of oppressed people the revolution was supposed to benefit.

Here arose a crucial paradox rooted in the long-standing chasm between Russia's educated elite and its peasant masses. Chernyshevsky supposedly was working on behalf of the masses. Yet by virtue of his background and education, he had nothing in common with them, nor any feeling, empathy, or respect for them, notwithstanding the populist axiom about the Russian peasant "instinct" for socialism. In his personal isolation from Russia's masses, Chernyshevsky was no different from any aloof nobleman, bureaucrat, or, for that matter, czar. Russia's peasant masses, Chernyshevsky argued, could only be followers, nothing more; all decisions would have to be made by the revolutionary elite. While revolutionaries were "superior beings, unapproachable by the likes of you and me," the peasant masses were hopelessly inert, concerned only with their immediate needs, "simply the raw material for diplomatic and political experiments" (quoted in Szamuely 1974: 216, 219).

Chernyshevsky himself never engaged in actual revolutionary activities. Still, his published articles made him an influential figure in radical circles and therefore a target of czarist authorities. He was arrested in 1862 (and wrote *What Is to Be Done?* in prison) and later spent 20 years in Siberian exile. Chernyshevsky's fate, if anything, made him more influential than ever. His ideas resonated not only with the next generation of populists but also with a nonpopulist Marxist revolutionary named Vladimir Ilyich Lenin, who so admired Chernyshevsky that 40 years later he borrowed the title *What Is to Be Done?* for his first major revolutionary tract.

Perhaps the most important populist thinker in the generation after Chernyshevsky was Peter Tkachev, who shared Chernyshevsky's view of what a professional revolutionary should be as well as his lack of faith in the peasantry. Tkachev's contribution was to outline in great detail how Russia's professional revolutionaries should organize themselves into a secret, highly disciplined underground political party to overthrow czarism. He further argued that once the revolution was made the elite would have to remain in charge and overhaul society by means of a revolutionary dictatorship. Ordinary people, Tkachev insisted, "are incapable of building, upon the ruins of the old, a new world that would be able to move and develop towards the communist ideal." That task therefore "belongs solely to the revolutionary minority" (quoted in Szamuely 1974: 305). Like Chernyshevsky, Tkachev had no success himself as a revolutionary, but, again like Chernyshevsky, he did influence other populists and made a deep impression on Lenin.

Not all populists agreed with Chernyshevsky and Tkachev—in fact, the conspiratorial outlook was always a minority tendency within populism as a whole—especially after several attempts to organize secret parties to overthrow the regime failed miserably. Peter Lavrov, whose views were close to Herzen's, argued that the only way to make a socialist revolution in Russia that would not turn into another dictatorship as oppressive as that of the czar was to "go to the people" and convince them they had to act on their own behalf. During the summers of 1874 and 1875, about 2,000 of Lavrov's followers, mainly university students, tried to heed his advice. These youthful urban apostles of peasant revolution, about 15 percent of them women, were in for a rude awakening. Their would-be audience in the countryside either did not understand them or would not listen to their message; some fearful peasants even turned the young agitators over to the police. Almost 250 of the naive revolutionaries were put on trial during 1877 and 1878, and although many were acquitted, others received prison sentences of up to 10 years at hard labor or, even after being acquitted, were sent into Siberian exile by the police. The "going to the people" episode dealt a severe blow to the idea that the peasantry had socialist instincts and was ready to make a revolution, a blow from which that article of faith never fully recovered.

This failure reinvigorated the idea of conspiracy but with a nasty twist. The new idea, born of desperation, was that along with conspiracy a "spark" was needed to start a peasant revolution. That spark supposedly could be created by what the revolutionaries themselves called "terror." It is important to keep in mind that to Russia's 19th-century populist revolutionaries, however contemptuous of traditional morality they claimed to be, "terror" did not mean the wholesale slaughter of civilians wherever and whenever possible, as it does to contemporary Islamic terrorist groups. Rather, it meant the assassination of government officials, a tactic that presumably would "disorganize" the government and provide the spark that, finally, would ignite Russia's great peasant revolution.

Terror eventually became the main tactic of a new party called Land and Freedom, organized in 1876. The party soon split, in a significant way. One faction came to reject both terror and the entire concept that Russia's peasantry was the key to a socialist revolution; within a few years it evolved into Russia's first Marxist party. The other faction militantly reaffirmed the strategy of terror and organized a tiny but single-minded party called the People's Will. Since assassinations of government officials had not yet produced the desired results, the People's Will decided to go for broke and assassinate the czar. After several abortive attempts, and with most of its leadership already in jail, on March 13, 1881, the remnants of the group succeeded in their goal. During the czar's regular Sunday-morning visit to a military horsemanship exhibition, one of the members threw a primitive homemade bomb that landed close enough to Alexander II to wound him mortally.

Two eras now came to a close. The first was Alexander II's era of reform. The czar had been planning new political reforms at the time he was assassinated. They were dropped by his son and successor, Alexander III, who launched a period of repression and reaction that lasted his entire reign. The second was the era of populism's monopoly of the revolutionary scene.

It did not take the government long to round up the members of the People's Will who had assassinated Alexander II and hang them. During the 1880s government repression kept the revolutionaries from doing little more than whispering to each other in small groups, some of which chose to gather in foreign exile. But that whispering included the discussion of new ideas, and when revolutionary activity resumed in the 1890s the idea of a peasant revolution had to share the stage with a rival theory called Marxism, a doctrine that designated the factory working class as the agent of the coming socialist revolution. Marxism's origins lay in Germany; however, its influence in Europe was destined to be the most profound in Russia, albeit after first being reshaped into a local variation as much at odds with the original version as it was from populism.

Alexander III and the Counter-Reforms

Alexander III became czar well prepared to carry out a program of reaction and repression. Steadfast and resolute, he had never approved of his father's reforms. His staunchly conservative views had been honed to a sharp edge by his closest adviser and former tutor, the prominent jurist and chief procurator of the Holy Synod Konstantin Pobedonostsev. Pobedonostsev used his formidable rhetorical and debating skills to denounce institutions such as parliamentary democracy ("the great falsehood of our time"), a free press ("one of the falsest institutions of our time"), and public education for the masses (a "vulgar conception of education"). His advice to the czar included the idea that a bloody revolution was preferable to a constitution. Alexander III himself was conscientious and hardworking, willing to take the time to see that his backward-looking policies were fully implemented.

Alexander III's policy of reaction began in 1881 with a supposedly temporary law to strengthen police powers that in fact remained in force until the monarchy fell in 1917. The law subjected a large part of the country to the equivalent of martial law. It allowed the authorities to arrest, imprison, and exile citizens without trial or any other legal proceedings. The next year the police received even more power; they could now bar people who had been placed under "open surveillance" from certain jobs and deny them the right to move from place to place. Meanwhile the political police was reorganized; under the name Okhrana it became notorious for violations of political rights that most other European governments were bound by law to respect.

These measures were followed by laws that together constituted the counter-reforms. During the 1880s a series of decrees tightened press censorship, virtually abolished the autonomy of universities, and weakened the independence of the judiciary. In 1889 the government created land captains, officials with extensive powers to supervise and control the peasantry. The next year a new law increased noble predominance in the *zemstvos* while strengthening the Ministry of Interior's control over those bodies. A law in 1892 had a similar impact on town government: by raising the property qualifications for voting, the law cut the electorate in both Moscow and St. Petersburg by about two-thirds.

Alexander III also intensified the government's Russification efforts directed at non-Russian minorities. While these policies affected nearly all non-Russian groups, they were directed most vigorously against Poles and Ukrainians. The most severe discrimination, however, was directed against the country's Jews, who were treated as aliens unworthy of a place in Russian society. This policy reflected both widely held anti-Semitic beliefs and the particular anti-Semitic attitudes of both Alexander and Pobedonostsev. In 1881 the government played a major role in permitting or, in the case of some officials, even instigating a dreadful wave of pogroms. This outburst of often murderous anti-Jewish mob actions took place in more than 100 southwestern towns and villages. The pogroms were followed by a series of decrees that limited Jewish access to secondary and higher education, barred them from government service, denied them the right to vote in *zemstvo* or city duma elections, and discriminated against them in a wide variety of other ways. Tightened restrictions on where they were allowed to live forced thousands of Jews from their homes.

The reign of Alexander III did see a few positive developments. Russia stayed out of war and in 1894 concluded an agreement with France designed to protect both parties against an attack by Germany, whose growing power was a concern in both Paris and St. Petersburg. To help the peasantry, in 1881 the government reduced redemption payments and two years later established a special bank to provide peasants with credit. Most important, in 1892, in an effort to deal with Russia's chronic inability to balance its budget, the czar appointed Sergei Witte as minister of finance.

Competent and strategically minded, Witte viewed Russia's budgetary problems as symptomatic of a broader and more dangerous problem: its economic backwardness relative to Europe's other great powers. Like Peter the Great before him, Witte believed that Russia's economic backwardness was a threat to its national survival. Having won the czar's confidence, Witte began a comprehensive effort to promote modernization, economic growth, and industrial development. Its centerpiece and foundation was a massive program of railroad construction (including the Trans-Siberian Railroad, still the world's longest) that would both tie the vast empire together and encourage the growth of heavy industries such as iron and machine building, which in turn would stimulate other industries.

To further promote local industrial development, Witte relied on a protective tariff, government subsidies and credits, and a variety of other sophisticated policies. His program yielded impressive results. During the next decade Russia's industrial production doubled, entire new industries developed, and railroad mileage jumped by almost three quarters. Witte neglected the peasantry, however, and his policies helped to expand another dissatisfied lower class, the industrial proletariat, whose discontent became a major new destabilizing factor during the reign of the next, and last, czar, Nicholas II.

Russia Confronts the 20th Century

Nicholas II became czar under inauspicious circumstances. He inherited the throne in 1894 after his father's unexpected death at the age of 48 from a kidney infection and was not prepared to rule. As the new 26-year-old czar himself put it, "I know absolutely nothing about matters of state." This did not bode well for a country only two years removed from the terrible famine of 1891–92 and the epidemic of cholera that followed it. Nicholas then made a bad situation worse. In reaction to increasing talk about possible political reforms to make Russia a constitutional monarchy, in early 1895 he publicly dismissed such ideas as "senseless dreams," a statement that discredited him in the eyes of many moderates and liberals whose support he would some day need.

The czar's foolish statement was followed by bad luck. Nicholas's coronation in 1896 was transformed into a tragedy when a huge Moscow crowd celebrating the grand event stampeded after hearing rumors that the free beer and mugs they had been promised were running out. More than a thousand people died, mainly from trampling or because they suffocated when they fell and were smothered by those who fell on top of them. Meanwhile, the underground revolutionary movement, quiescent for most of the previous decade, was beginning to revive.

The reign of Nicholas II was distinguished by three things. First, compared to previous reigns, major events were driven less by what the czar and his advisers did and more by what the regime's various opponents did, and indeed by what the country's masses did. Second, over time the czar and his officials increasingly found themselves overmatched by

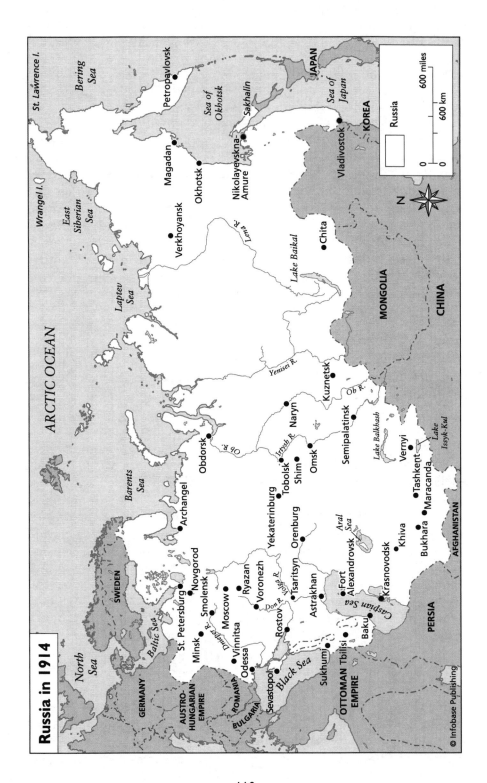

Russia in 1914

ARCTIC OCEAN

St. Lawrence I.

Bering Sea

Petropavlovsk

Sea of Okhotsk

Sakhalin

JAPAN

Sea of Japan

KOREA

Vladivostok

Magadan

Okhotsk

Nikolayevskna-Amure

Wrangel I.

East Siberian Sea

Verkhoyansk

Chita

Lena R.

Lake Baikal

MONGOLIA

CHINA

N

Laptev Sea

Yeniset R.

Kuznetsk

Ob R.

Naryn

Semipalatinsk

Lake Balkhash

Vernyi

Lake Issyk-Kul

Barents Sea

Tobolsk

Shim

Omsk

Obdorsk

Ob R.

Irtysh R.

Tashkent

Maracanda

AFGHANISTAN

Archangel

Yekaterinburg

Orenburg

Aral Sea

Khiva

Bukhara

SWEDEN

Novgorod

Ryazan

Voronezh

Volga R.

Tsaritsyn

Fort Alexandrovsk

Krasnovodsk

North Sea

St. Petersburg

Smolensk

Dnieper R.

Moscow

Don R.

Rostov

Astrakhan

Caspian Sea

Baku

PERSIA

Baltic Sea

Minsk

Vinnitsa

Odessa

Black Sea

Sukhumi

Tbilisi

OTTOMAN EMPIRE

GERMANY

AUSTRO-HUNGARIAN EMPIRE

ROMANIA

BULGARIA

Sevastopol

600 miles

600 km

Russia

© Infobase Publishing

the problems they faced. Finally, Russia suffered disastrous defeats in two wars: the Russo-Japanese war, which shook but did not topple the regime, and World War I, which overwhelmed the czar, the monarchy, and Russia itself and ultimately led to not one but two revolutions in a single year.

The Revolutionary Movement Revives

During the 1890s, stimulated by the widespread anger over the famine of 1891–92, the revolutionary movement revived along two lines. One was essentially an updated version of populism that in 1901 took the form of a new political party, the Socialist Revolutionaries (SRs). The SRs clung to the old vision of a peasant revolution and also resorted to political assassination through their fearless "combat section."

The second tendency was Marxism. Marxism itself grew out of the thinking of the German philosopher and revolutionary socialist Karl Marx, whose ideas were based on his study of the evolution of capitalism in western Europe. According to Marx all societies pass through certain historical stages based on the technology they use to produce what they need to live. In other words, the basis of any society is its economic system. Marx then traced western Europe's evolution from ancient slavery through medieval feudalism and finally to modern industrial capitalism. He argued that at each phase of development the fundamental struggle was between the minority that controlled society's wealth and the great majority that lived in poverty, a conflict Marx called "class struggle." As technology advanced and the economy of a given social order evolved, the class struggle in that social order intensified, eventually leading to its destruction as society passed from one historical stage of development to a higher one. That process had brought western Europe to modern industrial capitalism. Soon, Marx argued, evolving capitalist technology and the class struggle between the capitalists who owned all the wealth and the exploited working class (the proletariat) would lead to a revolution that would destroy capitalism and replace it with socialism.

While Marx believed that socialism was inevitable, he stressed that each historical stage was unavoidable. This meant that any given society had to pass through the capitalist stage before it could achieve socialism. Modern industrial capitalism did two things that made socialism possible. It created vast wealth that, when fairly distributed, allowed everyone to live well, and it created the industrial proletariat, the social class that would carry out a socialist revolution. Once the capitalists had been overthrown, there would be a short, vaguely defined stage Marx called the "dictatorship of the proletariat" during which society would be reorganized on a cooperative socialist basis. Once socialism was established, it would evolve into what Marx called "communism," a perfect society in which each citizen worked "according to his ability" and received goods and services "according to his need."

Marx's most controversial points as far as Russian revolutionaries were concerned were his axioms that each society had to pass through capitalism to reach socialism and that the industrial proletariat was the class that would make the socialist revolution. A crucial corollary of those axioms was that the peasantry was a backward feudal class with no role to play in the coming socialist revolution. The SRs, who desperately wanted Russia to avoid capitalism and continued to accept as a fundamental article of faith that the peasantry was capable of making a socialist revolution, rejected all of this. For Russian Marxists, however, Marx's analysis explained why the populists had failed. The latter had tried to avoid a crucial stage of historical development and had placed their revolutionary bet on the wrong class, the backward peasantry. What was bad news and indeed heresy to the SRs was good news and scientific truth to the Marxists and precisely what drew them to the new doctrine.

Russia's Marxists began organizing in exile in the 1880s under the leadership of a nobleman named Georgy Plekhanov. Like their colleagues in Europe they eventually adopted the name Social Democrats (SDs). In 1898 a group of Marxists based in Russia tried to set up a national organization but were thwarted when the police arrested the delegates attending the founding meeting. A more astute group succeeded in 1903, having wisely chosen to meet abroad, initially in Brussels and then in London, beyond the range of the czar's secret police.

Two Kinds of Marxists

The SDs called their 1903 Brussels/London meeting their "second" congress in deference to the failed "first" congress of 1898. The Second Congress is notable both for the successful founding of the Russian Social Democratic Party and the party's immediate split into two rival factions, Mensheviks and Bolsheviks. The split never healed, as it reflected fundamentally different interpretations of Marxism. In 1912 the two factions formally became separate parties.

The Mensheviks accepted Marx's historical model in its entirety; Russia would have to fully experience its capitalist phase, a historical era that clearly was just beginning. It could not carry out a socialist revolution for a long time, and certainly not before any of the more advanced European capitalist countries such as Britain and Germany. The immediate goal in Russia, therefore, was to overthrow the czar so that a democratic capitalist regime could take power. The turn of the Social Democrats would come later, once capitalism had developed further and the proletariat, currently a small minority of the population, had grown and become the majority. The Mensheviks also wanted to organize the Social Democratic Party along democratic principles, like the Social Democratic parties in Germany and other western European countries.

The Bolsheviks were very different, mainly thanks to their leader, a superb organizer and ruthless infighter named Vladimir Ilyich Lenin, who one year before the Second Congress had published his prescription for revolution, *What Is to Be Done?* Lenin was a Marxist, to be sure, as far as rejecting the populist/SR view that Russia could follow its own road to socialism via a peasant revolution. But as to the structure and functioning of a Marxist political party in Russia, a country where political activity in effect was illegal, Lenin incorporated some key populist ideas into his thinking. In particular he agreed with Chernyshevsky that only full-time professional revolutionaries could ever overthrow the czarist regime. He also endorsed Peter Tkachev's proposals regarding how to organize those professional revolutionaries in a secret conspiratorial party. It therefore is fair to say that although Lenin never admitted it, he modified Marxism by combining it with important elements from Russia's native revolutionary tradition.

Lenin differed from the Mensheviks in yet another crucial way. Even as he rejected the populist/SR idea of skipping capitalism altogether, he could not accept the Menshevik thesis, drawn directly from Marx, of how the capitalist phase in Russia would look. He rejected the Menshevik view that when the czar was overthrown, backward Russia would continue to develop as a capitalist society with the capitalists, or bourgeoisie, as the ruling class and that the socialists could not take power until the proletariat became the majority of the population. To accept this analysis meant that Russia's socialist revolution lay so far in the future that nobody alive in 1900 was likely to see it.

While he considered himself a Marxist, Lenin was above all a revolutionary, driven by an overpowering will to seize power and build socialism. If Marxist theory got in the way of doing that, he was prepared to modify the theory to provide Russia with an immediate route to socialism. He did this basically by arguing that Russia's capitalist phase could

V. I. LENIN AND
WHAT IS TO BE DONE?

Born in 1870, Vladimir Ilyich Ulyanov (he took the name Lenin after he began his revolutionary work) grew up in a comfortable and cultured upper-middle-class home in the Volga town of Simbirsk. The good life was disrupted by the early death of his father and, when Lenin was 17, by his older brother's execution for complicity in a plot to assassinate Alexander III. Despite these misfortunes, Lenin managed to obtain a university degree and become a lawyer.

As a university student Lenin gravitated toward revolutionary circles. Though he eventually turned to Marxism, along the way he absorbed key tenets of Russia's revolutionary populist tradition, in particular Chernyshevsky's concept of the professional revolutionary and Tkachev's blueprint for a revolutionary party. Lenin also accepted Chernyshevsky's and Tkachev's premise that anything revolutionaries did to achieve their goal was morally justified. He demonstrated that in practice by associating with criminals and having his lieutenants engage in activities such as extortion and bank robberies to fill the Bolshevik coffers. Also like Chernyshevsky and Tkachev, Lenin believed the masses could not act on their own, although in his case that contempt was directed at the proletariat, the class Marxists considered the bearer of the coming revolution.

When it came to the revolutionary elite that, Lenin argued, had to control the revolution and the masses, he narrowed things even further. Lenin was absolutely convinced that only under his leadership

be shortened. The problem was that other leading Marxists saw Lenin's modifications as violations of basic Marxist principles. Lenin's response was to deny he was changing anything important and to denounce all critics, even his closest colleagues, in the harshest and most vicious terms.

It was Lenin's inability to compromise that split the party in two in 1903, then made it impossible to heal the rift. At the time the split hardly seemed to matter, as neither the Mensheviks nor the Bolsheviks were able to put even a dent in czarism. But other agents and forces were at work, and soon the czarist regime began to crack on its own, opening up opportunities for frustrated revolutionaries who had done very little to create them.

could Russia's Marxists ever come to power. Many Russian Marxists, mainly but not exclusively Mensheviks, were appalled at Lenin's intolerant beliefs and amoral behavior, and they consistently accused him of operating like a dictator. Yet even they could not have predicted that Lenin would become as dictatorial and ruthless as he turned out to be once the Bolsheviks came to power and he had the means to suppress all those who disagreed with them—to the point of ordering mass murder. In the following selection from *What Is to Be Done?* Lenin responds to the charge that his proposals for organizing the revolutionary party were undemocratic:

> *It is further argued against us that the views on organization here expounded contradict the "principles of democracy.". . . What is the use of advancing "broad principles of democracy" when the fundamental condition of this principle cannot be fulfilled be a secret organization. . . . It is a useless toy, because as a matter of fact, no revolutionary organization has ever practiced broad democracy, nor could it, however much it desired to do so. . . . The only serious organisational principle the active workers of our movement can accept is: Strict secrecy, strict selection of members, and the training of professional revolutionaries. If we possessed these strict qualities, "democracy" and something even more would be guaranteed to us, namely: Complete, comradely, mutual confidence among revolutionists. And this something is absolutely essential for us because, in Russia, it is useless to think that democratic control can serve as a substitute for it. . . . We do not have time to think about the toy forms of democracy. . . . (Lenin 1943: 128–131)*

War and Revolution, 1904–1906

The first five years of Nicholas II's reign went well enough, if the measure is avoiding a major crisis. Russia enjoyed dramatic industrial growth under Witte's management, and there was no serious challenge to the new czar's generally reactionary but, by Russian standards, rather routine political policies.

Economic development accelerated the growth of a middle class of businesspeople and professionals that had been developing since mid-century. Its members, educated and informed about life in Europe, generally supported moderate political reform in the direction of a constitutional monarchy, an idea that also found support among a small group of progressive-minded landlords. The growth of the middle class

Nevsky Prospect, St. Petersburg's main avenue, about 1901 (Library of Congress)

provided a social base for liberal political ideas as an alternative to the reactionary thinking of the supporters of autocracy and the revolutionary thinking of the Marxists, SRs, and other socialists. However, this was still a small social base, and liberals and moderates had little impact on Russian political life during the 1890s.

Trouble started at the end of the decade. Strikes by factory workers laboring under atrocious conditions began to mount in an environment of another famine and a general economic slowdown. The new century brought more unrest in the form of large peasant disturbances in the Ukraine in 1902 and a huge wave of industrial strikes across southern Russia in 1903. These difficulties helped to undermine Witte, whose policies had always been resented by reactionary nobles and bureaucrats who happened to be close to the czar. In August 1903 Nicholas II dismissed his only genuinely competent minister.

One of Witte's major concerns had been to keep Russia out of war, which he feared would disrupt economic development and expose the country's fragile social structure to the strain of modern war against its technologically more advanced rivals. With Witte's cautionary voice gone, the czar's policies in the Far East became increasingly assertive, especially with regard to extending Russian influence into Manchuria and Korea. In both places Russia faced the rising power of the Japanese Empire, whose economic and military strength was widely underestimated.

Despite the looming threat of war Nicholas chose to listen to the likes of his interior minister, V. K. von Plehve. A narrow-minded bigot, in 1903 Plehve had instigated pogroms against Jews to distract ordinary Russians from their grievances against the government and thus serve as a "anti-revolutionary counteraction." In 1904, as tension with Japan mounted, von Plehve opined that a "small victorious war" with Japan was just what Russia needed to quiet popular discontent and to unite the country. One problem with this analysis is that Russia was not prepared for war, while Japan was. In February 1904, without a formal declaration of war, Japanese warships attacked the Russian naval base in the Manchurian city of Port Arthur.

The resulting Russo-Japanese war was a disaster for Russia. Japan was fighting in its backyard, while Russian forces in the Far East were at the end of a tenuous supply line thousands of miles long. Still, the Russians at Port Arthur beat back three Japanese assaults and held out for 11 months before finally surrendering in January 1905. Several weeks later Japanese forces in Manchuria defeated the Russians in the largest land battle of the war, a bitter 12-day struggle that cost Russia 60,000 dead and wounded, 8,000 missing, and 21,000 prisoners. The victorious Japanese were also badly bloodied, suffering an estimated 50,000 casualties. Finally, in May 1905 in the Tsushima Strait between Korea and Japan, the technologically advanced Japanese navy destroyed an outclassed Russian fleet, which had sailed from its base in the Baltic Sea to meet its terrible fate in foreign waters half a world away. Virtually the entire fleet was destroyed or captured in one of the worst naval debacles in history.

Defeat at the front combined with hardship at home to bring matters to the boiling point. For moderates and liberals—including many professionals, a large part of the business community, and even members of the nobility—the government's wartime failures underscored the need for meaningful political change. For them that meant an end to autocratic rule in favor of a constitutional monarchy, to include a national legislative assembly with real powers. About a year before the war began prominent liberals, meeting in the safety of Switzerland, had organized what they called the Union of Liberation to lead the fight for constitutional government. In 1904, as the war dragged on from defeat to defeat, liberals and moderates grew ever more assertive. In defiance of government prohibitions, they organized a series of public meetings to demand change. Organizations of doctors, lawyers, and other professionals added their voices to the chorus, as did a congress of *zemstvo* representatives in November.

An explosion finally occurred in January 1905, triggered by a rather depressing, tragic, but slightly farcical event that could have happened only in czarist Russia. Beginning in 1901, the Russian secret police had been organizing workers into unions that it secretly controlled, in order to divert them from political activity that might threaten the regime. The project was junked in 1903 after several of these supposedly controlled unions joined in the wave of strikes that swept the southern part of the country. It was revived for another run in St. Petersburg in 1904, however, at the behest of the charismatic but megalomaniacal Orthodox priest, Father Georgy Gapon. On Sunday January 22 Gapon led an enormous crowd of workers and their families on a march to the Winter Palace to present a petition to the czar begging him to enact measures to improve their lives. The throng, numbering about 200,000, was armed with banners, pictures of Nicholas, and religious icons. Gapon himself carried the petition on behalf of his flock that he expected to hand directly to the czar. But the czar was not in the palace; instead, the crowd was met by armed troops who opened fire, killing hundreds of men, women, and children and turning that date into "Bloody Sunday."

Bloody Sunday let loose a torrent of strikes, protests, riots, and other forms of defiance and rebellion that are collectively known as the Revolution of 1905. It seemed unstoppable, even after Sergei Witte, urgently brought back into the czar's service, brilliantly negotiated a treaty in September that extracted Russia from the war with Japan while minimizing its losses. On October 26, on the crest of a series of strikes that had ballooned into a general strike in St. Petersburg, the city's workers organized what they called the St. Petersburg Soviet (the Russian word for "council") of Workers' Deputies. Led mainly by Mensheviks, the Soviet included worker representatives from all over the city; it also provided what in effect was a national stage for members of the radical intelligentsia to make their mark, the most notable being the young Social Democratic firebrand Leon Trotsky.

The storm nearly toppled the monarchy and forced Nicholas II, under persistent urging by Witte, to make what the czar called his "terrible decision" to grant Russia a parliament with genuine powers. The promise was embodied in the October Manifesto, drafted by Witte and issued on October 30, 1905, which also promised the people of the empire basic civil rights.

The October Manifesto helped save the monarchy. The revolutionaries in the Soviet ignored it, but moderate and liberal members of the middle and upper classes were largely appeased. They did not want to see a mass revolution from below that would sweep them away along with the czar. The more liberal among them, now organized into the Constitutional Democratic Party (Cadets), pressed for more concessions, but many nervous moderates, whose numbers included leading industrialists and progressive landlords, accepted the October Manifesto and organized their own "Octobrist" Party to translate their attitude into practical support.

By December, as reliable troops returned home from the Far East, the government was strong enough to arrest the members of the St. Petersburg Soviet and crush a Bolshevik-led uprising in Moscow. Those two successes put out the main flames of the 1905 Revolution. Smaller fires continued to burn elsewhere in the empire, but they were ruthlessly stamped out at a considerable cost in lives during 1906. In addition to the army and police, the government enlisted the services of reactionary gangs called Black Hundreds. Apart from their attacks

A crowd in Moscow celebrating the issuing of the October Manifesto by the czar in 1905
(Library of Congress)

and terror tactics against opponents of the regime, the Black Hundreds launched pogroms against Jewish communities in more than 100 cities and towns. The 1905 Revolution was over.

The Duma and the Wager on the Strong

In early May 1906 as he jettisoned Witte for the second and last time, Nicholas II provided his interpretation of the October Manifesto by issuing a new version of Russia's Fundamental Laws. The document was a tremendous disappointment to most liberals and even to many moderates. The czar, while giving significant ground where he had no choice, dug in his heels wherever he could. He made his attitude unmistakably clear by retaining the old formula, "To the Emperor of All the Russias belongs supreme autocratic power." Only the words "and unlimited" had been cut from the old wording, a minor change that provided little comfort to those who hoped Russia would become a genuine constitutional monarchy.

The czar in fact retained the great majority of his traditional powers: He still appointed all ministers, kept complete control over foreign policy and the military part of the budget, and could veto any legislation. He would appoint half the members of the upper house of parliament. The lower house, the Duma, would be elected under a weighted system that favored the propertied and conservative classes. The czar could also dismiss the Duma and call for new elections at any time and, under article 87, could issue emergency laws while the Duma was not in session, although those laws required the Duma's approval to remain in force.

Still, Russia had made progress. The Duma did have real legislative powers, which it proceeded to use. During its 11-year history—there were four elections during that period—it included representatives from archreactionaries on the right to liberals and moderates in the center to revolutionaries—SRs, Mensheviks, and even Bolsheviks—on the left. Between 1906 and the start of World War I in 1914, the Duma enacted important legislation that, among other things, improved the condition of the peasantry, expanded primary and secondary education, and provided the factory working class with minimal protections. The Duma did not make Russia a constitutional monarchy comparable to Great Britain, but its existence belied the claim in the Fundamental Laws that Nicholas II was still a "supreme autocrat."

Nor was Russia's progress limited to political change. Industrial growth, while less than what was achieved under Witte, continued at

Like other Europeans, educated Russians became interested in aviation soon after the Wright brothers made their first successful flight in 1903. In 1910 Mikhail Effimov, a former locksmith, became the first Russian to give a flight demonstration in his native land. His audience included representatives from the Russian military. (Library of Congress)

an impressive rate, and by the outbreak of World War I Russia ranked as the world's fifth-largest industrial power in terms of overall output. The most dramatic changes were in agriculture, where government policy took a new direction in mid-1906 under Prime Minister Peter Stolypin.

Stolypin called his policy the "wager on the strong," by which he meant those peasants capable of achieving prosperity if given the chance. The "wager" was that if millions of peasants were freed from the restrictions imposed by their communes and other anachronistic limits left over from the emancipation, they would succeed and become property owners with something to lose. They would then turn into conservative supporters of the established order, much like peasants in western Europe tended to be. Freed from the inherent inefficiencies of communal ownership, they would also become far more productive and enrich Russia as they prospered. Stolypin's program released peasants from obligatory membership in their communes, allowed them to claim their communal allotments as private property, and, finally, permitted them to consolidate their scattered strips of land into a single plot.

Russia had a parliament with limited powers from 1906 until the fall of the monarchy in March 1917. This picture shows the Duma meeting during that historic month. (Library of Congress)

When his program began in 1906, Stolypin said Russia needed 20 years of peace to transform the countryside. Indeed, after only 10 years the results were visible and impressive. By 1916, about half of all peasant households had left their communes and owned their land privately, and about 10 percent had consolidated their holdings into a single plot. But by then Stolypin's program and everything else in Russia was under a dark cloud. One problem was that Stolypin, the guiding force behind the "wager on the strong," was dead, the victim in 1911 of a revolutionary assassin's bullet. Even worse, Russia was no longer at peace. Since 1914 the empire had been a belligerent in World War I, and it was beginning to buckle under a strain that even the most advanced European powers were finding hard to bear.

A Decade of Contrasts, and World War I

Russia changed a great deal as a result of the Revolution of 1905. What did not change is that it remained a land of extremes. On the one hand, the arts continued to flourish during what was known as the silver age of Russian culture, which began in the 1890s. On the other, the gap between the educated elite and the illiterate and semiliterate masses remained unbridged.

Russia now had a real parliament, but the country continued to experience revolutionary and counterrevolutionary violence. Between 1906 and 1910 the SRs assassinated more than 4,000 government officials, while the government tried to quell violence by executing more than 1,000 people between August 1906 and April 1907 alone, after what were at best perfunctory trials. Even worse, that figure was only a fraction of the total number of executions carried out between 1905 and 1908.

Based on gross production Russia was a major industrial power, but based on per capita production it was badly outclassed not only by major industrial powers such as Great Britain and Germany but by semi-industrialized countries such as Spain and Italy. Meanwhile, as industrial production grew, so did the number and intensity of strikes by exploited factory workers. The Stolypin reforms produced a class of prosperous peasants, but many less capable or industrious peasants sank deeper into poverty. The Russian Empire controlled 40 percent of Eurasia, but millions of non-Russians dreamed of escaping its clutches.

It was with that heavy baggage that Russia entered World War I. About six months before the war began, Nicholas received a memorandum from Peter Durnovo, a former police official warning him of the risks Russia faced in a general European war, but neither Durnovo's nor any other warning could keep the continent's great powers at peace. The war broke out in August 1914 with Russia, Great Britain, and France (the Triple Entente) opposing Germany and Austria-Hungary (the Central Powers), who after several months were joined by the Ottoman Empire.

Within two months, by the end of September, Russia had suffered two disastrous defeats at German hands, and matters deteriorated further after that. The Russian army scored victories over the Austrians, but it was no match for the modern German war machine. Nor was the semi-industrialized Russian economy equal to the demands of modern war. Russia's generals were inept and its political leadership under Nicholas II incompetent. Things were already falling apart when in 1915 Nicholas, against the advice and even the pleading of his chief advisers, went to the war zone and personally took command of the army. This blunder tied him directly to the army's defeats.

Back in the capital, the unpopular empress Alexandra (like so many czarist wives, she was a German) was officially in charge during her husband's absence. She in turn was heavily influenced by the self-designated holy man Grigory Rasputin, whose bizarre activities and behavior added layers of scandal to the rapidly deteriorating situation. By 1916 Rasputin controlled most government appointments.

Rasputin's assassination in December 1916 eliminated him but did nothing to fill Russia's political vacuum. Nicholas refused to consider

PETER DURNOVO WARNS NICHOLAS II ABOUT THE DANGERS OF WAR WITH GERMANY, 1914

Peter Durnovo (1844–1915) had a distinguished government career, heading the police department for a decade within the Interior Ministry and later serving as minister of the interior. During the last decade of his life he served in the upper house of parliament. Nicholas may not have even bothered to read the memorandum Durnovo sent him early in 1914, but in retrospect it reads as if its author was peering into an eerily accurate crystal ball.

> *But in the event of defeat . . . social revolution in its most extreme form is inevitable. . . . The trouble will start with the blaming of the Government for all disasters. In the legislative institutions, a bitter campaign against the Government will begin, followed by revolutionary agitations throughout the country, with Socialist slogans, capable of arousing and rallying the masses, beginning with the division of land and succeeded by a division of all valuables and property. The defeated army, having lost its most dependable men, and carried away by the primitive peasant desire for land, will find itself too demoralized to serve as a bulwark of law and order. The legislative institutions and the intellectual opposition parties, lacking real authority in the eyes of the people, will be powerless to stem the popular tide, aroused by themselves, and Russia will be flung into hopeless anarchy, the issue of which cannot be foreseen. . . . (Golder 1927: 23)*

the political reforms proposed by leading Duma moderates and liberals, which might have won him some badly needed supporters. Meanwhile, by early 1917 the Russian army had suffered 7 million total losses—dead, wounded, missing, and captured—and was crumbling. Russia's major cities, including Moscow and St. Petersburg, were desperately short of food, and during January and February strikes rocked the capital. In March, while Nicholas did nothing, Russia slid into the abyss that Durnovo had warned him about almost exactly three years earlier.

6

THE GOLDEN AND SILVER AGES: RUSSIAN CULTURAL ACHIEVEMENT FROM PUSHKIN TO WORLD WAR I (1820–1917)

Writing in the mid-20th century, the distinguished historian Bertram D. Wolfe noted that the catastrophic setbacks Russia suffered from the 13th century onward deformed the country politically and caused it to stagnate economically and culturally. Having been denied the salutary influences of both the Renaissance and the Reformation, he wrote, Russia "became a strangely silent land." It "remained silent" while Italy, England, Spain, and France flourished and produced literary giants from the 14th through the 17th centuries. Wolfe added that Russia would not "find its voice" for hundreds of years. However, it was worth the wait, for when Russia, that "mighty land," emerged in the 19th century from its long and painful silence "suddenly full throated, it astonished the world" (Wolfe 1964: 17).

This explosion of literary creativity is known as the golden age of Russian literature. It lasted from about 1820 to 1880, the years, respectively, of the publication of the first major poem of Aleksandr Pushkin and the last major novel of Fyodor Dostoyevsky. After a pause of slightly more than a decade during the 1890s, the golden age was succeeded and supplemented by the kaleidoscopic silver age of Russian culture, another remarkable outburst of creativity that ranged across the full artistic spectrum and lasted until World War I. No short survey can do justice to these two remarkable eras, but no book that purports to give even a "brief" history of Russia can claim to have fulfilled its mission without introducing its readers to a national achievement that has so enriched not only Western civilization but the human experience worldwide.

The Golden Age of Russian Literature: Poetry and Early Prose

The golden age did not burst forth quite as suddenly or full-throated as Wolfe implies. It rested on a foundation built during the 18th century by people like Mikhail Lomonosov, who in addition to his impressive scientific endeavors found time to write poetry. More important, Lomonosov did work in linguistics that helped Russian to develop as a modern literary language. Other important 18th-century contributors to literary Russian were the poet Gavrila Derzhavin (1743–1816), Russia's leading literary figure for three decades, and Nikolai Karamzin (1766–1826), a versatile poet, historian, and essayist whose *Letters of a Russian Traveler* became a primary source of information about western Europe to several generations of his countrymen. These men, and others like them but of lesser stature, were essentially local craftsmen whose efforts were strictly of local Russian interest; today their works are known almost exclusively to specialists. Russia's next literary generation was a different matter altogether.

Pushkin and Lermontov

The golden age of Russian literature began with Aleksandr Pushkin (1799–1837), the "Prince of Poets." He is universally acclaimed as the greatest poet in the history of the Russian language—his country's Shakespeare—and the founder of modern Russian literature. Pushkin was only one of a small crowd of notable writers who contributed to the onset of the golden age—his contemporaries included the dramatist Aleksandr Griboyedov (1795–1829) and poets Vasily Zhukovsky (1783–1852), Konstantin Batyushkov (1787–1855), Yevgeny Baratynsky (1800–1844), and Nikolai Yazykov (1803–46)—but his monumental talent so exceeded theirs that, perhaps unfairly, over time their work has been neglected and has received attention mainly from aficionados and students of Russian culture.

Aleksandr Pushkin was born in 1799, the product of a lineage that was at once distinguished and exotic. His father's side traced its roots to a 13th-century Muscovite noble family. His mother's side originated with an African slave named Abram Hannibal—possibly also the son of an Ethiopian prince, hence Pushkin's moniker "Prince of Poets"—who reached Russia as a young boy when he was presented as a gift to Peter the Great. Hannibal rose from that humble station under Peter's mentorship to become a general and a nobleman. Pushkin, his great-grandson, took as much pride in that ancestry, as witnessed by his unfinished novel *The Negro of Peter the Great,* as he did his venerable Russian noble heritage on his father's side.

Notwithstanding his family's declining financial position by the time of his birth, young Aleksandr was raised in comfortable circumstances, surrounded, as was the custom in Russian aristocratic families of that era, by French tutors and governesses. It was Pushkin's good fortune, and Russia's, that he also was surrounded by local peasants, especially his nursemaid, from whom he heard and learned a colloquial Russian free of foreign influences and a wealth of traditional Russian folklore.

Between the ages of 12 and 18 Pushkin received an excellent education at one of the empire's finest schools, but it is generally agreed that he owes his extraordinary feel for the Russian language to the informal education he received from common people who had never set foot inside a school. It was that immersion in his country's authentic popular traditions that allowed him to free Russian literature from the stilted conventions of Church Slavonic that still encased it in the 18th century and forge an expressive and dynamic literary language that we know as modern Russian.

Pushkin's contributions cover the full spectrum of Russian letters, from poetry, short stories, and novels to drama, essays, and works of history. Recognized for his extraordinary promise while still a student, he became a literary star in 1820 with the publication of the poem *Ruslan and Lyudmila.* A series of masterpieces followed, including the historical play *Boris Godunov,* which eventually became the basis of the opera of the same name by Modest Mussorgsky (1839–81), one of the pioneers of Russian opera. Pushkin demonstrated his mastery of prose in works such as the novel *The Captain's Daughter,* which deals with the Pugachev rebellion, and the short story "The Queen of Spades," a frightening tale of an army officer who murders an old woman in a vain attempt to learn her secret of winning at cards. The latter story, like several other Pushkin works, also became the basis of an opera, in this case by Peter Tchaikovsky, widely regarded as the greatest of all Russian composers. In all, by the early 20th century Russia's major composers had produced more than 20 operas based on Pushkin's works.

Most experts agree that Pushkin's supreme achievements are *Eugene Onegin,* a novel written in verse competed in 1830, and *The Bronze Horseman,* a narrative poem written in 1833 but published after the poet's death in 1837. *Eugene Onegin* describes the emptiness and mindlessness that characterized much of upper-class Russian life, as illustrated by the aimless, dissipated life of its hero, Onegin, a classic Russian "superfluous man." As it tells Onegin's story, the novel provides a panoramic view of Moscow and St. Petersburg, the Russian country-side, and many aspects of Russian life. The meaningless duel in which Onegin kills a 17-year-old poet provides an eerie look into the future at Pushkin's own senseless death.

The Bronze Horseman takes its title from St. Petersburg's famed eques-trian statue of Peter the Great by the French sculptor Falconet. It focuses on the conflict between the demands of the state and the fate of ordi-nary individuals who suffer, often terribly, because of those demands, with the Russian state represented by Peter the Great and ordinary people by a government clerk named Yevgeny. Pushkin admired Peter the Great and what he saw as Peter's contributions to Russia, espe-cially the building of St. Petersburg, but he also recognized the heavy sacrifices the czar had imposed on the Russian people. In *The Bronze Horseman,* it falls to the unfortunate Yevgeny to make this point. Having

Aleksandr Pushkin (1799–1837), Russia's greatest poet, whose career marks the beginning of the golden age of Russian literature (Library of Congress)

lost his reason for living when his fiancée is drowned in one of the many floods that plague Peter's cherished St. Petersburg, Yevgeny loses his mind. Standing at the granite base of the Bronze Horseman he denounces Peter, at which point he imagines the statue springing to life and chas-ing him as he flees desperately through the empty city.

Pushkin lived much of his life on the edge. He was exiled from St. Petersburg in 1820 for poems the authorities deemed subversive, a sentence that probably saved him from getting involved with the Decembrist rebellion and suffer-ing accordingly. He provoked the authorities again in 1824 and was banished to his family estate until 1826. Thereafter he lived under a cloud of suspicion and official harassment that included the personal attention of Nicholas I. Despite earning a considerable income from his literary work, Pushkin lived beyond his means and fell into debt. His marriage to a beautiful but empty-headed society woman proved to be his undoing. It further undermined his finances, and in 1837 Pushkin was killed in a duel with a French nobleman who he believed, probably incorrectly, was having an affair with his flirtatious wife. Pushkin's death at such a young age was a cause of national mourning in educated circles. It is not much of an exaggeration to say that after more than 170 years that mourning has never really ceased.

It is unlikely that any Russian lamented Pushkin's death more than a young nobleman and army officer named Mikhail Lermontov (1814–41). Certainly none of them expressed their grief as dramatically as he did in "Death of a Poet," an outburst in verse that blamed Russian society and its various faults for Pushkin's death. Deemed subversive by the authorities, the poem got its author court-martialed and assigned to a frontline regiment fighting in the Caucasus until he was pardoned a year later.

"Death of a Poet" made Lermontov a celebrity. During the next four years he wrote or completed most of the works that won him the status of Russia's second-greatest poet, surpassed only by Pushkin. They include *Mtsyri* (*The Novice*), the story of a young monk who flees his monastery to enjoy a few days of freedom amid nature before dying of exhaustion, and *The Demon*, a narrative poem that tells of a fallen angel who seduces, and kills with his first kiss, an innocent young woman. The Demon is profoundly alienated from all that surrounds him—he tells the young woman, "I am one by all the living hated / By whom all hope is desolated," a sentiment that is essentially autobiographical (Lermontov 1963: 179).

Lermontov's best-known work is the novel *A Hero of Our Time*, published in 1840. Its hero, or antihero, is the soldier Pechorin, one of Russia's "superfluous men," talented people who have no outlet for their gifts in a stifling and repressive society. Pushkin had developed the theme in *Eugene Onegin* and it would appear again in the works of later outstanding 19th-century Russian writers. As for Lermontov, he outlived the publication of *A Hero of Our Time* by only a year. In 1841, the man who had raged so bitterly at the absurdity of Pushkin's senseless death in a duel was killed in exactly the same manner over a trivial point of honor. Lermontov was only 26 years old, more than a decade younger than Pushkin at the time of his tragically premature death.

Gogol and Literary Realism

With Lermontov's passing what had been in effect a golden age of poetry became a golden age of prose. Its first major figure was Nikolai Gogol (1809–52), a descendant of Cossacks and the son of a small landowner in the Ukraine. His earliest successful works, short stories based on Ukrainian folklore, presented an idealized and romantic portrait of rural life, while his inner torments and self-doubts often drove him to produce works of fantasy, such as the short story "The Nose," a tale of a pompous official's desperate search for his missing nose. That said, Gogol is above all considered the founder of Russia's tradition of literary realism that pervaded the golden age all the way to Dostoyevsky and Tolstoy.

Piercing realism, laced with satire and the surreal, was the basis of a cycle of short stories Gogol wrote over the course of about a decade beginning in the early 1830s. Collectively called the St. Petersburg tales, they deal with the grim realities and corruption of urban life. The St. Petersburg tales include "Nevsky Prospect," whose hero is driven to suicide when he discovers that an extraordinarily beautiful woman he sees on St. Petersburg's main thoroughfare is really a prostitute, and "Diary of a Madman," in which a pathetic copy clerk gradually is driven insane by delusions of grandeur. Perhaps the most widely read, and certainly the most influential, of Gogol's short stories is "The Overcoat," the doleful saga of a petty clerk who scrimps and saves to buy a fine new overcoat, only to have it stolen the first day he wears it as he walks home from a party held to celebrate his precious new acquisition. Dostoyevsky reportedly said that "we have all emerged from 'The Overcoat.'"

Gogol's greatest works, the play *The Inspector General* (1836) and the novel *Dead Souls* (1842), brilliantly satirize the greed, corruption, falsity, and general banality of upper-class Russian provincial life. *The Inspector General,* a comedy set in a provincial town, tells of an unscrupulous and opportunistic traveler from St. Petersburg named Khlestakov who arrives in the town under somewhat mysterious circumstances. Mistaken by the local officials and leading citizens as a government inspector, Khlestakov takes advantage of their corruption and resultant readiness to bribe him by fleecing them of a large sum of money. *Dead Souls* chronicles the activities of a swindler named Chichikov, who travels from town to town buying up dead serfs at discount. He then uses these "souls," whose names will not be removed from the tax rolls until the next census, as collateral to secure a large loan and make a huge profit. Chichikov has no trouble finding greedy and dishonest landowners more than willing to participate in his scheme. *Dead Souls* was envisioned as the opening volume of a three-part work modeled after Dante's *Divine Comedy*. But Gogol's chronic depression and melancholy thwarted that plan.

In 1847 Vissarion Belinsky, the country's leading literary critic, bitterly criticized Gogol for publishing a collection of mystical religious essays that excused the social injustices—including serfdom—he had exposed and satirized in his earlier works. Gogol's literary crime, Belinsky wrote in his vituperative "Letter to Gogol," was that he had ignored the injunction that all art must carry a politically progressive message. This rule was sacred to Belinsky and many of his radical intellectual colleagues, none of whom was capable of producing

Nikolai Gogol (1809–52), golden age novelist, playwright, and short story writer and founder of the realist tradition in Russian literature (Library of Congress)

a poem, short story, play, or novel with even the slightest artistic merit. In a phrase that became a byword for totalitarian regimes in the 20th century, including the one that for seven decades would cause Russian artists and the entire country so much misery, Belinsky told Gogol that while Russian readers were "ready to forgive a writer for an inferior book . . . they will never forgive him for a harmful one" (quoted in Hare 1964: 76).

Belinsky's criticism and that of others was hurtful, but Gogol, increasingly driven by conservative religious fervor, was more distressed because he believed his writing was not fulfilling his self-imposed mission of leading people toward God's truth. He spent the next four years fitfully working on part two of *Dead Souls* but then burned his manuscript, leaving for his readers only fragments he apparently overlooked. Less than two weeks later he was dead.

In the end Gogol's literary audience judged him far more kindly than had Belinsky, or than he judged himself. Thousands of mourners attended his funeral in Moscow in February 1852. When a peasant woman who happened to see the huge crowd expressed surprise that the deceased had so many relatives, she was gently informed that the man being mourned was Gogol, "and all Russians are his relatives" (Slonim, 181).

Realism and Turgenev

Several outstanding realist writers made their first appearance on Russia's literary stage in the decade before Gogol's death. The dramatist Aleksandr Ostrovsky (1823–86) began his career by getting into trouble with official censors, but he ultimately managed to produce nearly 50 plays that brought scenes from the lives of ordinary Russians to a wide theatrical audience. Although his plays did not win wide international recognition, they are credited with a key role in establishing an authentic Russian theater.

Aleksandr Goncharov (1812–91) enjoyed his first success in 1847 with the novel *An Ordinary Story*. But his standing as a major Russian novelist rests on *Oblomov,* a massive and somewhat flawed work published 12 years later that focuses on the hapless inertia and slothfulness

SCIENCE DURING THE GOLDEN AND SILVER AGES

Censorship and limited educational opportunities for most of the population were just two of the factors that slowed the development of science in Russia. That is why Mikhail Lomonosov was such an isolated figure. The next Russian to achieve a prominent place in the history of science was mathematician Nikolai Lobachevsky (1792–1856), the father of non-Euclidian geometry, who developed his talents after attending the newly founded University of Kazan. Although Russian scientists at that time still constituted a small circle, Lobachevsky did not work in a void, as did Lomonosov. Several other important mathematicians were working in Russia during Lobachevsky's lifetime. There also was an emerging tradition of excellence in astronomy. In 1839 German-born Frederick William Jacob Struve founded the Pulkovo Observatory, which for a while had the largest telescope in the world. Struve, a world-class astronomer, was the first of four generations of his family to make significant contributions to that field.

of Russia's provincial nobility, as typified by the title character, in the generation before the emancipation of the serfs. Later notable practitioners of the realist approach were the novelist Nikolai Leskov (1831–95), the poet Nikolai Nekrasov (1821–78), and the satirist Mikhail Saltykov-Shchedrin (1826–89). Although Saltykov-Shchedrin is best known as a journalist, his somber family saga, *The Golovlyovs,* ranks as a major 19th-century novel. Fyodor Tyutchev (1803–73), Russia's most gifted poet of that era, stood apart from the realists and is more properly classified as a romantic.

Ivan Turgenev (1818–83) achieved the international distinction that evaded the writers mentioned above. His humane, balanced, and polished portrayals of fellow Russians, from serfs to noblemen to would-be revolutionaries, won him admiration and influence at home and made him the first Russian novelist to win widespread recognition in Europe. Turgenev first gained fame with *A Sportsman's Sketches* (also translated as *A Hunter's Sketches*), a series of 21 short stories that began appearing in the late 1840s and eventually were published in book form in 1852.

Alexander II's Great Reforms were an important stimulus to Russian science, as universities received more resources and greater autonomy. One field in which Russians excelled was biology. It gave Russia its first Nobel Prize in 1904 when Ivan Pavlov was honored for his work in the physiology of digestion. (Pavlov, of course, is best known for his study of the nervous system.) Another Nobel Prize winner in biology was I. I. Mechnikov (1845–1916), honored in 1908 for his work in immunology.

Russia's most celebrated 19th-century scientist was chemist Dmitry Mendeleyev, developer of the periodic table familiar to every student of chemistry and one of the greatest names in the history of that field. By the end of the century Russia also had a core of prominent physicists who laid the foundation for continued excellence in that field during the century to come. Most important among them was P. N. Lebedev (1886–1912), whose contributions beyond his own important research on light pressure included modernizing the physics facilities at the University of Moscow with an eye to making Russia a world leader in that field. Soviet authorities recognized that work by naming the main physics institute at the Soviet Academy of Sciences after him.

The stories laid down a devastating indictment of serfdom. Turgenev did not attack the institution directly (which would have provoked the censors); he simply described realistically the grim lives of Russia's peasants, portraying his subjects as dignified human beings despite the hardships and injustices they endured. Their personal qualities and desires were no different from those of Turgenev's educated readers. Aside from making their author an immediate literary star both at home and in Europe, *A Sportsman's Sketches* is credited with influencing Alexander II in deciding to abolish serfdom.

Turgenev's signature work, the novel *Fathers and Sons,* appeared in 1862. A chronicle of the eternal clash between generations, *Fathers and Sons* introduced the literary world to the young physician Bazarov, who became the paradigmatic fictional representative of Russia's radical generation of the 1860s. Bazarov represented these young radicals because he contemptuously rejected conventional morality, believing instead that rationality and science would bring about human progress.

Fathers and Sons immediately became the most controversial Russian novel of its time. The issue was not its literary merit; most critics agreed it was an artistic success. The disagreement was about politics. Radicals denounced Turgenev for what they saw as an unflattering portrayal of Bazarov, and by extension of the so-called nihilists of the 1860s, while conservatives bemoaned the author's insufficiently harsh treatment of Bazarov and his dangerous ilk. All this distressed Turgenev, who had written the novel to portray the human condition, as he did in *A Sportsman's Sketches* and his other works. In any event, while his subsequent novels are not nearly in the same class as *Fathers and Sons,* that volume and some of his earlier works assured Turgenev a place in the elite pantheon of his country's greatest prose writers.

Dostoyevsky and Tolstoy: Masters of the Novel

The golden age of Russian literature was crowned with the works of Fyodor Dostoyevsky (1821–81) and Leo Tolstoy (1828–1910), the two towering giants of the Russian novel. Arguably they are the greatest of all the world's novelists—the main and irresolvable point of contention being which of them surpassed the other? Radically different in background, outlook, style, temperament, and how they chose to live their lives, they are alike in the most important thing of all: the immense impact each had on both Russian and world literature.

Amazingly, although their lives overlapped so closely, Dostoyevsky and Tolstoy never met. Yet their creative legacies, however different from each other, swirled and circled around each other until they became entwined as the strands of a literary Gordian knot, forever bound together as one of the supreme achievements in the history of Russian and European culture.

Fyodor Dostoyevsky was the son of a miserly Moscow doctor whose dark moods condemned his wife and eight children to life in a gloomy and authoritarian household. After a short, unrewarding stint as a military officer, the young Dostoyevsky turned to writing as a profession, settling in St. Petersburg. The success of *Poor Folk* (1845), his first novel, established him as a major Russian literary figure, but Dostoyevsky struggled financially, largely due to a gambling addiction that would afflict him for decades.

Soon he was in much greater trouble, the result of a flirtation with radical socialist politics. In 1849 the entire group to which Dostoyevsky belonged was arrested and charged with treason. Most were sentenced to death. On a cold December day they were taken to an execution ground to be shot, only to have their sentences commuted to prison terms at the last moment. The commutation was announced when the first group of three convicts (Dostoyevsky was in the second group) was already lined up before the firing squad, blindfolded and tied to stakes.

Four years of prison and hard labor under terrible conditions in Siberia followed for Dostoyevsky, after which he was required to serve two years as a soldier. By then he had long abandoned his fleeting attachment to Western secularism and socialism in favor of an intense Russian Orthodox mysticism and a highly conservative version of Slavophilism. Dostoyevsky was finally allowed to return to European Russia in 1856, his health impaired but his creative powers nourished by his harrowing experiences. He was primed to produce the works that would make his name synonymous with magnificent novels that unrelentingly and unflinchingly plumbed the psychological depths of conflicted and tormented human souls.

Having settled in St. Petersburg, Dostoyevsky almost immediately reestablished his standing as a major writer with several works, most notably *Notes from the House of the Dead* (1861–62), a novel that chronicles his grim prison experiences. In the wake of a collapsing marriage, a disastrous love affair, and an equally disastrous string of gambling losses at European roulette tables, Dostoyevsky published *Notes from Underground* (1864), a pioneering existential work that explores the dilemma of free will and one's ability to choose to be either good or evil.

Arguing against contemporary radicals and socialists who postulated that man was inherently good, Dostoyevsky maintained not only that man by his nature could choose to be evil but that his ability to select that option was the basis of his freedom. Adding bitter irony to the moral dilemma that choice posed, Dostoyevsky's wretched and miserable "underground man" demonstrates his freedom precisely by acting against his own interests, thereby ending up in a state of total unfreedom.

Between 1866 and 1880 Dostoyevsky published his four signature novels: *Crime and Punishment* (1866), *The Idiot* (1868), *The Possessed* (1871–72), and *The Brothers Karamazov* (1879–80). While each stands alone as a masterpiece, they are related as stages and aspects of a life-long intellectual and spiritual quest: Dostoyevsky's tormented effort to resolve his questions about human nature and the painful complexities of human psychology, free will and man's attraction to evil, sin and redemption, and freedom and tyranny, as well as how these are all connected to Christianity and the belief in God. These themes in turn are linked to Dostoyevsky's conviction that his troubled country had to reject western European culture, in particular its rationalism and materialism, which over the centuries had given birth to evils ranging from a soulless Catholicism to an amoral, tyrannical socialism. Russia's salvation, he insisted, lay in its own authentic heritage, in particular the spirituality of Russian Orthodoxy and the communitarian traditions of the simple but instinctually insightful Russian masses.

In *Crime and Punishment,* the first of Dostoyevsky's seminal quartet, the young student Raskolnikov, relying on reason and the logic of nihilism, attempts to assert his free will and affirm his superiority over what he considers the contemptible masses by murdering an aged pawnbroker. He considers the old woman useless to society, while he can use her money to relieve his financial burdens. Raskolnikov ultimately commits not one but two murders and then finds out he is not the great man he thought he was. He is haunted and defeated by guilt as he desperately seeks atonement and peace through a relationship with a young prostitute, who for her part relies on Christian faith rather than reason to cope with the heavy burdens of her life.

In *The Idiot* Prince Myshkin, a fragile, Christlike figure, is destroyed by the wickedness, materialism, and greed of St. Petersburg society. Having tried to spread Christian values of compassion and love, he ends up going insane after inadvertently helping set the stage for the murder of the woman he loves. *The Possessed* (whose title is more literally translated as *The Devils*) is Dostoyevsky's blunt, frontal assault on the revolutionary movement he had briefly been attracted to in the 1840s but which by the 1860s he passionately hated. It is based on an actual incident in which a small revolutionary group under the spell of a charismatic fanatic named Sergei Nechaev murdered one of its own members it suspected of disloyalty. The novel is populated with a cast of ruthless nihilist revolutionaries who have rejected Christianity and the existence of God. Thus freed of any moral restraints, for them any crime is permissible. Because of their ideology they are capable of nothing but destruction, starting with the utterly diabolical Nikolai Stavrogin, the main character. Equally unsavory is Peter Verkhovensky, the actual organizer of the novel's revolutionary group. Secondary characters include the theorist Shigalev, who demonstrates with "mathematical certainty" that the society of the future will consist of a dictatorship in which one-tenth of the population will rule the remaining nine-tenths, who will live in equality as slaves, and the pathetic Kirillov, who demonstrates his free will and affirms the nonexistence of God by killing himself in the service of his monstrously flawed beliefs.

Dostoyevsky achieved what most critics consider his greatest triumph in *The Brothers Karamazov,* a story of parricide in a family that, like Russia itself, is dysfunctional and deeply divided by disparate beliefs. The family consists of Fyodor, the dissolute patriarch; his three legitimate sons (by two wives, both deceased by the time the novel begins) Dmitry, Ivan, and Alyosha; and a fourth, illegitimate, son, Smerdyakov, who lives as a servant in Fyodor's house and commits the murder around which the novel revolves.

The book's central theme is the conflicting ways the three legitimate Karamazov brothers view the world and live their lives. Dmitry, the eldest, like his father is dissolute, hedonistic, and amoral. Through a series of coincidences he will be tried and unjustly convicted of Fyodor's murder. Ivan is a secular intellectual who has rejected Christian faith and belief in God and therefore denies that the concepts of good and evil have any bearing on how human beings should conduct their lives. Because he has discussed his ideas with Smerdyakov and influenced him, Ivan comes to see himself as morally responsible for what his half-brother has done and is consumed with guilt.

Earlier in the novel, however, Ivan explains his world view to Alyosha in an extraordinary episode called "The Grand Inquisitor." Ivan's story, set in Spain during the Inquisition, is outwardly an attack on Roman Catholicism, but it can equally be taken as a denunciation of atheistic socialism, which in Dostoyevsky's view treats human beings as base material creatures devoid of any spirituality. The Grand Inquisitor, his official position as a churchman notwithstanding, does not believe in God and rejects Christ's teachings; he is convinced that man is inherently evil and therefore unfit to make moral choices and live in freedom. He rules a theocratic, totalitarian state that provides for its subjects' basic needs and soothes them with a false faith while keeping everyone under strict control.

Then Christ reappears. Christ returns to earth to confront the Grand Inquisitor for distorting his teachings, but only by his presence: The Grand Inquisitor does all the talking. The Inquisitor imprisons him before he can spread his subversive ideas, namely, "the freedom you stood up for when you were on this earth." That freedom, which the Grand Inquisitor cannot tolerate, is Christ's insistence that people must accept his message strictly on their own volition. No society can allow that kind of choice, the Grand Inquisitor insists, contemptuously asking his silent prisoner, "Or did you forget that peace of mind and even death are dearer to man than free choice and the cognition of good and evil?" (Dostoyevsky: 288, 293). Alyosha, of course, is not convinced, and it is his faith that eventually provides the halo of optimism with which Dostoyevsky ends the book.

Dostoyevsky was not yet 60 when in 1880 he published *The Brothers Karamazov,* and he immediately began working on a sequel with Alyosha as its hero. By then the acclaimed novelist, who had endured so much personal suffering, had found peace and stability in a successful second marriage (in 1867) to his former stenographer. In June 1880 his speech at the unveiling of the monument to Pushkin in Moscow marked another major success. Dostoyevsky appeared to be at the peak of his powers, but the following winter he became ill, and he died in January 1881. To the 30,000 who braved a raw St. Petersburg winter's day to attend his funeral, it did not matter that Dostoyevsky never wrote the projected sequel to *The Brothers Karamazov,* the book he had once anticipated would be the "main novel." They knew that his place of honor at the pinnacle of Russian, and world, literature was permanent.

Leo Tolstoy was an aristocrat who spent both his childhood and most of the last half-century of his long life on his family estate, Yasnaya Polyana ("Serene Meadow") about 100 miles south of Moscow. For almost 20 years between those two bucolic periods Tolstoy essentially drifted. He attended but did not graduate from the University of Kazan; spent several years living an aimless and dissolute life in Moscow and St. Petersburg, an existence laced with the heavy drinking, gambling, and womanizing typical of many Russian noblemen of that time; served as an officer in the army, first fighting primitive mountain tribesmen in the Caucasus and then, during the Crimean War, facing modern European armies in the unsuccessful defense of the Black Sea port of Sevastopol; and finally traveled in Europe, where he developed an intense dislike for the modern West that he retained for the rest of his life. He was already a well-established literary figure in 1862 when he married a woman 16 years his junior and settled for good on his estate. He had written, among other works, *Childhood* (1852) and two other semibiographical volumes. The three gripping stories in *Tales of Sevastopol* (1855–56), set in the year before the city fell to foreign forces during the Crimean War, gave him a national reputation.

In 1862 Tolstoy published *The Cossacks,* a novel that both glorified and idealized the lives of this warrior people, who in Tolstoy's eyes lived wholesome lives close to nature and uncorrupted by civilization. Tolstoy was a devotee of Rousseau; the virtues of a simple life in harmony with nature, such as that of Russia's peasants, as opposed to the artificiality and corruption of civilized life, became an enduring theme in his subsequent work, beginning with *War and Peace,* generally recognized as Tolstoy's supreme achievement and one of the world's greatest novels.

Tolstoy labored on *War and Peace* for seven years before finally publishing this monumental work in 1869—the original Russian text ran to more than 1,800 pages. The novel is a chronicle of Russia's decadelong conflict with Napoleonic France. Its primary focus is on Napoléon's invasion of Russia in 1812 and the national resistance that ultimately resulted in the French emperor's catastrophic defeat and humiliating retreat back to Europe. The novel is an epic in every sense of the word. There are 559 distinct characters, many of whom, including the central historical figures Napoléon, Czar Alexander I, and the Russian commanding general Mikhail Kutuzov, are examined in copious detail. Sweeping overviews and top-to-bottom descriptions chronicle enormous battles, including the bloody collision between the Russian and French armies at Borodino. Turning to the home front, the book gives multifaceted depictions of Russian life, especially that of the upper classes as represented by three families—the Bezhukovs, the Bolkonskys, and the Rostovs. Through it all Tolstoy intersperses lengthy polemical digressions about the meaning of history.

All of this serves to illustrate Tolstoy's main theme of the superiority of the simple, natural, rural life. What matters is not what self-anointed heroes like Napoléon do but the activities of ordinary people, such as the Russian peasants and soldiers who in 1812 dedicated themselves to the common and just cause of expelling the mighty European invaders from their country. Napoléon is portrayed as a pompous, conceited fool, and his efforts to determine the course of history are derided as futile and destructive delusions. Real wisdom resides with Russian peasant soldiers like Platon Kantarev. The pivotal moral character

Leo Tolstoy (1828–1910), one of the two towering novelists of the golden age (Library of Congress)

of *War and Peace,* Kantarev tells a story to Pierre Bezhukov, one of the novel's central characters, in which he reveals to the heretofore uncomprehending nobleman the importance of living by one's own labor, in accordance with God's will and in brotherhood with other men. Despite all that Russia suffers, this insight provides an optimistic ending to the novel.

Anna Karenina, Tolstoy's other great novel, was five years in the writing and went through 17 drafts before its publication in 1877. The novel's main plot involves its title character, a wealthy and beautiful St. Petersburg society woman who abandons her husband and young son for a passionate love affair with the dashing Count Vronsky.

A parallel plot involves a wealthy landowner Levin, a stand-in for Tolstoy. Having come to St. Petersburg only to be rejected by the aristocratic Kitty Shcherbatsky—like Anna, Kitty is infatuated with Vronsky—Levin finds meaning in life by returning to his country estate and immersing himself in farming and an agrarian lifestyle. Levin's productive life on the land turns into genuine happiness when Kitty realizes her error and marries him, a sequence of events that, along with what he has learned from peasants on his estate, helps him to believe in God.

Anna, totally self-absorbed and uninterested in anything beyond her passions and personal desires, suffers a tragic fate. She is rejected by society, driven to despair, and finally commits suicide by throwing herself under a train. The villain in *Anna Karenina* is not any one character but civilized society itself, in particular the world of the urban upper classes, which is filled with people who behave far worse than Anna but know how to cover their transgressions as she did not and whose hypocrisy destroys anyone unable to play by their amoral rules.

The moral judgment that hangs over the conclusion to *Anna Karenina,* like so much in Tolstoy's novels, came from his own life. By the late 1870s he had rejected any secular or scientific rationales that might help him find meaning in life. That led to a religious conversion, not to Russian Orthodoxy or any other established church but to a personal version of Christianity whose message was as critical of established churches as it was of secular life. Tolstoy's eclectic Christianity denied the divinity of Christ; it combined elements of pacifism, anarchistic communism, and a puritanical view of women and sexuality with the idea of returning to nature. It left Tolstoy bitterly critical of almost all existing institutions, including the Russian government and the Orthodox Church, criticism that in 1901 led to his excommunication.

Tolstoy also concluded that art, including his own, had no meaning. He eventually renounced all ties with society and his family, including sexual relations with his wife. Yet even as he worked the land dressed in peasant garb and cobbled his own boots, he continued to write. Aside from *My Confession* (1879), which expressed his new outlook, Tolstoy's notable post-conversion works include the haunting and unnerving short story "The Death of Ivan Ilyich" (1884), the short novel *The*

Kreutzer Sonata (1889), the novel *Resurrection* (1899), and the novella *Hadji Murat* (1904).

In November 1910, after years of domestic tension, having signed away his property to his wife and renounced his copyrights, Tolstoy fled his home, accompanied by his youngest daughter and carrying only a few belongings, seeking refuge from circumstances that he believed

MUSIC DURING THE GOLDEN AGE

Russian music before the 1880s did not approach the heights attained by the country's literature. Nevertheless, Russian composers, beginning with Pushkin's friend Mikhail Glinka (1804–57), began to develop a national style of classical music of considerable quality. Glinka drew much of his inspiration from Russian folk music and Pushkin's poems. His first opera, *A Life for a Tsar,* is a patriotic tale of the exploits of the peasant Ivan Susanin during Russia's Time of Troubles. *Ruslan and Lyudmilla,* an opera based on Pushkin's poem of that name, is considered his finest work.

The brilliant pianist and composer Anton Rubinstein (1829–94), founder of the St. Petersburg and Moscow Conservatories, deserves credit for raising Russian music to a genuinely professional level. He was the first Russian composer to win recognition in Europe. More important, the first graduate of the St. Petersburg Conservatory— one of more than half a dozen Rubinstein founded with his younger brother Nikolai—was Peter Tchaikovsky.

Meanwhile, Glinka's effort to build a distinctly Russian musical tradition by drawing from folk traditions was continued by a group of five amateur—none had professional musical training—but talented composers collectively known as "The Mighty Handful": Mily Balakirev (1837–1910), César Cui (1835–1918), Aleksandr Borodin (1834–87), Modest Mussorgsky (1839–81), and Nikolai Rimsky-Korsakov (1844–1908). The latter three produced the most lasting music, in particular Borodin's opera *Prince Igor* (finished after his death by Rimsky-Korsakov and A. K. Glazunov), Mussorgsky's opera *Boris Godunov* and piano suite *Pictures at an Exhibition,* and Rimsky-Korsakov's orchestral suite *Scheherazade,* which in 1910, more than two decades after it was completed, provided the music for a renowned ballet choreographed by Mikhail (Michel) Fokine.

were hindering his spiritual development. Within days he caught a chill that turned into pneumonia and died at an isolated provincial railway station. Tolstoy's funeral at Yasnaya Polyana took place under very different conditions. Attended by thousands despite government efforts to limit the crowd, covered by most of the world's major newspapers, and filmed by a camera crew using one of the world's most advanced motion picture cameras, it was at once an international media event and a solemn demonstration of respect for a man admired well beyond Russia's expansive borders as a great writer and moral teacher. Given Tolstoy's mission to improve the world and his rejection of modern civilization, it was simultaneously a fitting and an ironic farewell.

The Silver Age of Russian Culture

The end of the golden age of Russian literature did not mean the end of Russia's 19th-century cultural flowering. Although during the 1880s and early 1890s poets and prose writers, even Tolstoy, could not match what had been produced between 1820 and 1880, some of Tolstoy's later works and the early short stories of Anton Chekhov (1860–1904) made those years anything but a literary dark era. However, the brightest cultural torches were in the hands of Russia's composers and painters. Among the former, Peter Tchaikovsky (1841–93), still regarded as his country's greatest composer, holds primacy of place. His major works during this period include two of his most popular ballets, *The Sleeping Beauty* (1889) and *The Nutcracker* (1892), his Sixth Symphony (1893), which many critics consider his masterpiece, and several major operas. Ilya Repin (1844–1930), the most prominent of Russia's 19th-century realist painters, produced several of his most famous works during this period, including *Tsar Ivan and the Body of His Son* (1885), as did Isaac Levitan (1860–1900), whose beautiful landscapes, influenced by both Russian realism and French impressionism, have rarely been equaled.

There is no conventional starting date for the silver age of Russian culture. While some critics date it from the 1898 appearance of the remarkable journal *The World of Art*, the early 1890s would be a less precise but more logical starting point. By then Chekhov had established himself as a master of the short story; within a few years he would be established as a playwright of even greater stature.

Chekhov and Gorky

Chekhov, the grandson of a serf who bought his freedom, was born in Taganrog, a port city on the Sea of Azov. In the wake of his father's bankruptcy and relocation to Moscow, Chekhov began writing humorous short stories under several pen names for a variety of publications to help support the family and put himself through medical school at the University of Moscow. He graduated in 1884, the same year he published his first collection of short stories. Chekhov's success as a writer allowed him to change careers. He abandoned medicine for writing, although he provided free medical care for peasants living on the estate he bought in 1892 and joined in efforts to combat the severe cholera epidemic of 1892–93.

While Chekhov's early comedic works brought him recognition and financial security by the end of the 1880s, his reputation as an outstanding literary figure rests on the serious short stories and plays he wrote after 1890. Many of his best stories, such as "The Duel" (1891) and "Ward No. 6" (1892), depict the frustrations and emptiness he saw in the lives of the provincial upper and middle classes. Chekhov was equally adept at showing how Russians at the bottom of the social ladder lived.

The Island of Sakhalin (1893–94), a series of articles eventually published in book form, is a gripping journalistic account of the conditions convicts and exiles endured on that island off Russia's Pacific coast, thousands of miles from where most of Chekhov's readers lived. "Peasants" (1896) is a brilliantly executed narrative about grinding poverty and hopelessness. Chekhov displays profound sympathy for his subjects, even as he shows peasants treating each other with brutality, deceitfulness, and narrow-mindedness, all unavoidable by-products of desperate lives.

Chekhov reached the peak of his creative powers in four plays: *The Seagull* (1896), *Uncle Vanya* (1897), *Three Sisters* (1900), and *The Cherry Orchard* (1903). All deal with the decline of Russia's provincial gentry. Their status as theater classics lies in how the emotion, hope, and despair expressed by Chekhov's late 19th-century Russian characters have been appreciated by audiences in so many different venues far removed from his original settings in time and place.

The Seagull, the first of these plays, was a failure when it was first staged in 1896. It was rescued a few years later by the newly founded Moscow Art Theater, a central fixture of the silver age, and its avant-garde director Konstantin Stanislavsky, the source of many radical theatrical innovations and the father of method acting. The play was the Moscow Art Theater's first success, and a seagull became its symbol, emblazoned on its stage curtain. The theater had a wide repertory that ranged from ancient Greek dramas and Shakespeare to the works of avant-garde European playwrights like Henrik Ibsen and politically radical Russians like Maksim Gorky. It also staged all of Chekhov's subsequent plays including *The Cherry Orchard,* generally considered his masterpiece. In 1901 Chekhov married Olga Knipper, one of the theater's best actresses, who played one of *The Three Sisters* in its initial production. The marriage, however, was tragically short. By the time Chekhov completed *The Cherry Orchard* in 1903, he was severely ill with tuberculosis. He died in 1904, only six months after the play's successful debut at the Moscow Art Theater.

In 1902 Chekhov resigned from the Russian Academy of Sciences in protest when the writer Maksim Gorky (1868–1936) was denied honorary membership because of his radical political beliefs. Gorky, which means "bitter" in Russian, was the pen name of Aleksei Peshkov, a novelist, short story writer, and playwright from the city of Nizhni Novgorod on the Volga. Born into grinding poverty and orphaned at the age of seven, Gorky had less than a year of formal schooling. He educated himself as he worked his way up from *The Lower Depths,* as the title of his most famous play puts it.

The play, staged with considerable success by the Moscow Art Theater in 1902, presents characters from Russia's urban netherworld as dignified human beings, notwithstanding their flaws, which Gorky did not try to hide; they have been ruined by the injustices of Russian society. Gorky's other works, including the novels *Mother* (1907) and *Childhood* (1913), varied in literary quality and were successful in part because his realistic and moving portrayals of people at the bottom of Russian society were difficult to ignore.

Gorky's radical beliefs led him to his own version of Marxism and an association with the Bolshevik Party; he and Lenin were personal friends. Still, after 1917 Gorky found himself at odds with the Bolshevik regime—he deserves credit for intervening to save many intellectuals during the turbulent era from late 1917 to 1921—and in 1921 he chose to go abroad into his second exile (he had lived in Italy from 1906 to 1913). He finally returned to the Soviet Union in 1928, four years after Lenin's death and—to his great shame—allowed himself to be exploited as a propagandist for Stalin's brutal policies, including the regime's notorious use of forced labor.

Gorky died under unexplained circumstances, possibly as one of the millions murdered by the Stalin regime in whose service he had placed his personal reputation and prestige. That regime considered Gorky the father of socialist realism, the doctrine that art has no intrinsic value and must promote the building of socialism. It paid its respects to the deceased writer by changing the name of his native city to Gorky. Today is it once more known as Nizhni Novgorod.

The Symbolists

Chekhov and Gorky, who were friends, each had one foot outside the silver age, both by virtue of their age (they reached adulthood in the 1880s) and their approach to writing. Younger writers who came of age in the mid-1890s or later had radically different views about art in general and about their own work. Eager to reject convention and experiment with the new, many of them drew on the ideas of the mystical philosopher Vladimir Solovyov (1853–1900), who argued that symbols were not illusions created by individuals but reality itself, as well as the theories of the French antirationalist literary movement known as symbolism. Then, as historian Steven G. Marks has noted, they pushed these ideas "to utopian extremes," rejecting the depiction of the real world in the pursuit of an "ideal higher reality" (Marks 2003, 177–178). At the same time a sense of doom pervaded much of their outlook and work, especially after the Revolution of 1905.

Russia's symbolists were primarily though not exclusively poets. The two outstanding practitioners were Andrei Bely (1880–1934) and Aleksandr Blok (1880–1921). Bely (born Boris Bugaev), who came from an academic family, was a poet, novelist, and literary theorist. Convinced that music held the key to understanding God, he constructed most of his poems as musical compositions, often calling his collections "symphonies"; in his imaginative use of language he is sometimes compared to James Joyce. Bely is best remembered today for his mystical and apocalyptic novel *Petersburg* (1911–13), which pictured Russia as a collapsing world torn by the conflict between East and West.

Aleksandr Blok, like Bely the son of an academic, was Bely's friend and rival; he is considered the genius of the symbolist movement. His first collection of poems in 1904 made him an instant literary icon, but he is best known for two magnificent and chilling poems written after the Bolshevik Revolution in 1918: *The Scythians* and *The Twelve*. *The Scythians,* focusing on the theme of the conflict between East and West, is a warning to Europe to accept Russia as it is. *The Twelve* tells of a murderous, plundering group of 12 Bolshevik soldiers on patrol during a blizzard. When Christ appears as their leader at the end of the poem, unrecognized by the 12 because of the strengthening blizzard, they are revealed as the 12 apostles, and the poem itself as Blok's endorsement of the Bolshevik Revolution, notwithstanding its violence and terror. Blok's effort to, as he put it, "hearken to the music of the Revolution" soon failed in the face of Bolshevik repression of artistic expression, and he died a broken man in 1921 (Slonim 1962: 196). Bely was consumed by the revolution in another way: He survived until 1934, having endorsed it, but as a barely tolerated and largely scorned "relic of the past."

Acmeists and Others

The symbolists were not the only avant-garde innovators of the silver age. Their mysticism did not appeal to poets calling themselves acmeists, a term derived from the Greek word meaning "point of highest achievement." In direct opposition to the dreamy symbolists, the acmeists believed in clarity and precision; they also unambiguously admired the West. Acmeism's founder was Nikolai Gumilyov (1886–1921), whom the Bolsheviks executed for alleged counterrevolutionary activity in 1921, but its most accomplished devotees were Anna Akhmatova (1888–1966) and Osip Mandelstam (1891–1938).

Akhmatova, the pen name of Anna Gorenko, was married to Gumilyov for eight years, an arrangement that did not stop either of them from outside liaisons (Akhmatova's most notable lover being a young Jewish-Italian painter named Amadeo Modigliani). While she established her reputation before World War I writing poems about love and passion, Akhmatova has no greater achievement than *Requiem*, a cycle of poems she wrote secretly during the height of Stalin's tyranny when she was almost completely silenced. In *Requiem*, written in the 1930s in the wake of the arrest of her son, Akhmatova conveys as well as anyone can a sense of the indescribable suffering the Soviet people endured during that dreadful time. Akhmatova's standing as Russia's finest female poet is challenged only by Marina Tsvetaeva (1892–1941), another silver age luminary whose life was thrown into chaos after the Bolsheviks came to power.

Mandelstam, whom many consider Russia's greatest 20th-century poet, was Akhmatova's lifelong friend from the time they met in 1909. He was arrested during Stalin's great purge of the 1930s and died in prison, like so many other creative people in all fields. One silver age poet who did not die in jail but still met a tragic fate at the hand of the Bolshevik Revolution was Vladimir Mayakovsky (1893–1930), a militant apostle of a doctrine called futurism. Mayakovsky's media ranged from poetry to graphic art. He admired Lenin, joined the Bolshevik Party as a teenager well before the revolution, and fervently supported the Soviet regime. However, by the late 1920s Mayakovsky found himself out of favor as Stalin consolidated his hold on power. In despair, he committed suicide in 1930.

The silver age produced a host of other poets and prose writers, some of whom do not fit easily into any literary category, including Ivan Bunin (1870–1953) and Yevgeny Zamyatin (1884–1937). A distinguished poet as well as a superb writer of prose, Bunin is best known for his short story "The Gentleman from San Francisco" and was the first Russian writer to win the Nobel Prize (1933); he became an émigré in 1920. Zamyatin wrote the pioneering and prophetic dystopian novel *We*; completed in 1920, it was first published abroad, in English, in 1924. Miraculously, Zamyantin was allowed to emigrate from the Soviet Union in 1931.

The silver age also included an astonishing creative outpouring in painting, music, and dance. Talented avant-garde painters coalesced into a variety of rival schools. Mikhail Vrubel (1856–1910) and Vasily Kandinsky (1866–1944) were symbolists. Natalya Goncharova (1881–1962) and Mikhail Larionov (1881–1964), who also happened to be husband and wife, were drawn to the simple style and bright colors of peasant art and called themselves primitivists; later they moved on to a new style they called rayonism. Kazimir Malevich (1878–1935), Vladimir Tatlin, and Mayakovsky, pioneers in abstract art, were cubo-futurists. Following the outbreak of World War I Malevich moved on to a new form of abstract painting he called suprematism, determined to use his art to launch "the beginning of a new culture."

The silver age also saw a host of outstanding Russian painters who stand outside these categories. They include Valentin Serov (1865–1911), the greatest Russian portraitist of his time, and the young Marc Chagall (1887–1985), who was just beginning his career as Serov's was coming to an end.

No single silver age composer equaled Tchaikovsky, but several did achieve enormous and lasting international stature. Aleksandr Scriabin, a symbolist mystic with revolutionary and grandiose ideas about music, believed the arts could be used to achieve universal brotherhood and an end to human suffering. Notwithstanding his delusions, Scriabin was an extremely gifted composer and pianist who anticipated the future by accompanying some of his performances with multimedia presentations.

The composer, conductor, and pianist Igor Stravinsky (1882–1971) wrote the music for three of the most celebrated ballets of all time: *The Firebird* (1910), *Petrushka* (1911), and *The Rite of Spring* (1913). American audiences since 1940 know his work from Walt Disney's classic animated

Vaslav Nijinsky (1889–1950), the greatest male ballet dancer of the silver age of Russian culture (Library of Congress)

film *Fantasia*. Sergei Rachmaninoff (1873–1943), more traditional than either Scriabin or Stravinsky—he once said that he had no use for composers who abandoned melody and harmony—wrote superb, enduring, and difficult piano concertos along with magnificent symphonic pieces. Another great Russian musician was the legendary opera basso Fyodor Chaliapin (1873–1938), whose triumphant performances took him from Russia to Europe's great opera houses and across the Atlantic to the United States.

Russian ballet meanwhile set the standard for the world. During the first decade of the 20th century the Imperial Maryinsky Ballet was graced by three legendary ballerinas: Matilda Kschessinskaya (1872–1971), Anna Pavlova (1881–1931), and Tamara Karsavina (1885–1978). While all were magnificent, Enrico Cecchetti, the renowned Italian coach who taught each of them and many other outstanding dancers as well once commented, "Pavlova has that which can only be taught by God" (Lincoln 1998: 258). Male dancers of the era included Mikhail (Michel) Fokine, also a gifted choreographer who created the *Dying Swan,* Pavlova's signature performance, and the incomparable Vaslav Nijinsky (1889–1950), whose soaring leaps, during which he seemed to be suspended aloft, awed and amazed audiences wherever he performed.

Sergei Diaghilev and the Ballets Russes

The silver age of Russian culture, the final artistic flourishing of the old regime before its catastrophic collapse, is by its very nature and place in history a phenomenon filled with contradictions. Some of the most interesting involve the person and career of Sergei Diaghilev (1872–1929). The man who pulled many of that era's most creative strands together by founding a performing company that drew on the talents of Russia's best composers, dancers, opera singers, and painters, was not an artist himself—he once said, "I think I have no real gifts"—but an aristocratic former law student turned bourgeois impresario. The company he formed, the Ballets Russes, mesmerized audiences in Europe, the United States, and even Latin America but never performed in Russia. And while the Ballets Russes would enrich cultural life at many levels in the West before and after World War I—there is a direct link, for example, from the choreography of the Ballets Russes to the postwar musicals of Broadway and Hollywood—the advent of Communist totalitarianism in Russia cut off the company and its priceless artistic legacy from the land of its original inspiration.

The genesis of the Ballets Russes was an extraordinary journal called *The World of Art,* which Diaghilev founded in 1898 with the artists Lev Bakst (1866–1924) and Aleksandr Benois (1870–1960). The journal drew together avant-garde artists from every medium and with many points of view to celebrate how art can uplift the human soul and to explore how artists, with their unique abilities to transcend the mundane and grasp what Diaghilev called the "mysteries of . . . divine nature," could literally transform the world (Marks 2003: 178). *The World of Art* lasted for six years, after which Diaghilev started another journal, *The Golden Fleece.* Then, after presenting several productions of works by Russian composers in Paris, he established the Ballets Russes.

Beginning in 1909 (the company was officially founded in 1911), Diaghilev brought Pavlova, Karsavina, Nijinsky, Fokine, and other great Russian ballet dancers to Paris. Chaliapin was there too, and during the Ballets Russes' first historic season in Paris, Diaghilev alternated ballet with opera on succeeding nights. The dancers performed to music by Stravinsky (who was unknown when Diaghilev commissioned him to compose the score for *The Firebird,* which made its debut in 1910), Rimsky-Korsakov, Borodin, and other Russian and European composers. They danced in stunning costumes and on lavish sets designed by distinguished painters such as Konstantin Korovin, Nikolai Rerikh, Benois, and especially Bakst, which by themselves were works of art. The scenery and costumes of the Ballets Russes were so innovative and spectacular that Bakst, who produced them for 12 ballets between 1909 and 1914, was justly considered one of the company's stars.

The Ballets Russes created something entirely new, using ballet "to blend kaleidoscopic combinations of sight, sound, and motion into intense musical pictures that left the stunned audiences of Paris breathless" (Lincoln 1998: 293). At the end of the 1909 season, Benois accurately summed up what had taken place: "Not Borodin, not Rimsky-Korsakov, not Chaliapin nor Golovin or Diaghilev triumphed in Paris, but all of Russian culture" (Suzanne Massie 1980: 435). Looking at it from another perspective, art historian Suzanne Massie has written that Russian art at the dawn of the 20th century "was a wonder of the world" (Suzanne Massie 1980: 434). At a minimum the performances of the Ballets Russes between 1909 and 1914 constituted the sterling quintessence of Russia's silver age.

Russia had many serious problems as the 20th century began, but it undeniably had come a long way since the days, not that far in the past, when it had been a "strangely silent land." Who could have imagined the totalitarian silence that would soon cover that land?

7

SOVIET RUSSIA: UTOPIAN DREAMS AND DYSTOPIAN REALITIES (1917-1953)

During 1917 Russia underwent two revolutionary shifts in power, one entirely negating the other. The first, in March,[*] brought Russia to the threshold of a genuine parliamentary regime; the second, in November, pushed the country into the clutches of a one-party dictatorship, the chaos of civil war, and, ultimately, into the black hole of Communist totalitarianism.

In early March a spontaneous upheaval broke out that almost immediately attracted millions of Russians into its ranks and within a week brought down the autocracy. Power fell to the leading elements of the country's moderate and progressive-minded elite—liberal nobles, civic-minded businessmen, and prominent members of the professions. These groups, who for decades had been at the forefront of creating civil society in Russia, quickly organized what they called the Provisional Government.

Russia's new leaders were tied together by an important common thread: They were people of property from Russia's middle and upper classes, and they all therefore had something to lose, quite possibly everything, if events careened entirely out of control. All hoped their country would continue in the capitalist-parliamentary path of the West that it seemed to have been following since the Great Reforms. They considered the overthrow of the czar the end of the revolution, the place where it had to stop. Indeed, however much they despised

---

[*] *Russia in 1917 was still using the flawed Julian calendar adopted by Peter the Great; by the 20th century it trailed the modern Gregorian calendar by 13 days. All Soviet historians, most Russians, and some Western historians refer to the "February" and "October" revolutions, respectively. This volume follows the Gregorian calendar, and thus refers to the "March" and "November" revolutions.*

Nicholas personally, many of them had not wanted to abolish the monarchy but favored a genuine constitutional monarchy on the British model.

While they understood the need for more reforms and were prepared to offer some response to the needs and demands of the lower classes, the people in charge after the events of March 1917 were against further drastic change; additional reforms would be enacted gradually and only after order and discipline had been restored. Over a period of several months they were joined in the Provisional Government by socialists of various stripes—SRs, Mensheviks, and others with varying degrees of commitment to political pluralism, democracy, and socialism. But not even these socialists, whatever their ultimate goals, were ready for radical change beyond what had been accomplished in March and the succeeding few months.

In November, after continual disorder, power was seized in a military coup by a small militant group committed to the premise that the process of change had merely just begun. Its members rejected both capitalism and parliamentary democracy, the latter seen as nothing but the tool of the class they most hated, the middle class, or bourgeoisie. They wanted to remake society entirely. As Marxists they looked to the establishment of a new society based on the abolition of private property in favor of public ownership of the country's productive wealth and on cooperation instead of competition. In these goals this group was not fundamentally different from some of the other socialists who after March joined Russia's new government and cooperated with liberals and moderates. The key difference is that this group was not willing to wait to achieve its goals. To that end it was determined to set up a dictatorship and rule alone. This group was the Bolshevik Party, and its indispensable leader was Vladimir Lenin. Its success in seizing and holding power set the course for the next seven decades of Russian history.

The Provisional Government, Petrograd Soviet, and Dual Power

Beginning March 8, 1917, a week of riots, mutinies, and demonstrations brought down the Romanov dynasty, which had ruled Russia since 1613, and with it the Russian monarchy, whose roots stretched back to the grand princes of Muscovite Russia. By the time Nicholas II formally abdicated late on March 15, Russia had a Provisional Government in place. It was led officially by Prince Georgy Lvov, a *zemstvo* notable, but its most important members were foreign minister Pavel Milyukov, the leader of the Constitutional Democrats and a distinguished historian, and justice minister Aleksandr Kerensky, the most left-wing member of the new government, with views ranging from liberal to mildly socialist.

Kerensky was pivotal; he was the only member of the Provisional Government who belonged to another key body that had formed at the same time as the Provisional Government—the Petrograd* Soviet of Workers' and Soldiers' Deputies. This lineal descendant of the 1905 St. Petersburg Soviet had no clearly defined or stated purpose other than to defend the revolution in general and the interests of Russia's working classes and rank-and-file soldiers in particular. In its composition and actions it combined the trappings of a government, a political convention, and a mob. Above all, by its very presence the Soviet undermined the authority of the Provisional Government, something the latter, given its many weaknesses, could not afford.

The relative strength of the two bodies was convincingly demonstrated on March 15 when the Soviet issued what it called its "Order Number 1," which instructed enlisted military personnel serving in units stationed in and around Petrograd to choose representatives to the Soviet and proclaimed that the Soviet would now be their ultimate authority. It was an order the Provisional Government did not dare challenge.

The Provisional Government was in a precarious situation. Whatever its pretensions, in reality it represented the interests of a tiny upper crust of Russian society, and only the more forward-looking part at that. Most ordinary Russian workers, peasants, and soldiers were not particularly interested in Western-style parliaments, the rule of law, or the other legal issues so important to the moderate and liberal educated elite. Nor did the masses care about Russia's war aims, another issue of major importance to the leaders of the Provisional Government. Thus the Provisional Government had virtually no influence with peasants, who made up the vast bulk of the country's population, or with workers in the cities, who numbered only 3 million but were concentrated in key cities like Petrograd and Moscow and therefore were a threat to any government they opposed.

Making matters worse, the czarist police had been dissolved at the time the Provisional Government took charge, leaving the new regime without a civilian force to control Russia's masses. As Order Number 1 showed, it could not count on the military either. Army and navy units

---

* When World War I began, the name of Russia's capital city was changed from the Germanic "St. Petersburg" to the Russian "Petrograd" ("grad" is derived from the Russian word for "city," "gorod").

might or might not listen to its orders. As its first minister of war grimly put it, "The Provisional Government has no real power of any kind and its orders are carried out only to the extent that this is permitted by the Soviet of Workers' and Soldiers' Deputies. . . . One can assert bluntly that the Provisional Government exists only as long as it is permitted to do so by the Soviet of Workers' and Soldiers' Deputies" (Quoted in Pipes 1990: 306). The imbalance became more pronounced as soviets were established in other cities across Russia, including Moscow. Such was the state of affairs Russians called "dual power."

Other factors added to the Provisional Government's burdens. Since that government was self-appointed rather than elected, its members did not believe they could undertake major social reforms. Only a nationally elected Constituent Assembly could establish a fundamental body of law, and only the new parliamentary order that body of law created could legislate social change. Because of the complex logistics of arranging such an unprecedented national election in an enormous empire engaged in a world war, the balloting for the Constituent Assembly could not be scheduled until November.

The delay left Russia with a government that even its own members believed lacked the authority to tackle urgent problems. That agenda included peasants' demand for land reform to transfer noble-owned properties into their hands as well as the demand by the non-Russian national minorities, almost half the country's population, for some form of local autonomy. The Provisional Government did issue several major human rights decrees that guaranteed a wide range of civil and political liberties and put an end to all religious, national, and class discrimination. It also abolished the czarist secret police. But these measures carried little weight with the land-hungry peasantry or the poor urban population suffering from wartime shortages and other hardships.

The one decisive action the Provisional Government did take, to remain in the war on the Allied side and mount a major new military offensive, made its problems much worse. The offensive, which began in late June, ended in total defeat by the Germans. The Russian army then collapsed. Hundreds of thousands of demoralized and angry soldiers, unable to take any more, deserted and headed home. As that was happening, the Provisional Government faced a mutiny of soldiers in the capital who feared they would be transferred to the front. Once the mutiny began, it was encouraged and eventually led by the Bolsheviks, who turned it into an uprising known as the July Days.

Revelations that Lenin and the Bolsheviks had accepted German money to fund their activities helped the government rally enough soldiers to its side to put down the uprising. Lenin, a warrant out for his arrest, fled the capital and went into hiding. Still, the government's narrow escape in fact left it weaker and looking more vulnerable than ever. Meanwhile, neither several reshufflings between May and September that brought moderate socialists into the cabinet nor the appointment of Kerensky as prime minister did anything to stabilize the situation.

Lenin, the Bolsheviks, and the November Revolution

Against this chaotic background Lenin, who made it back to Russia from exile in Switzerland in April, plotted and schemed. Lenin's goal from the beginning was to overthrow the Provisional Government and establish a one-party Bolshevik dictatorship. As the only major political party of the center or left that refused to support the Provisional Government, the Bolsheviks were able to exploit the deteriorating conditions in the spring and fall to gain support among the disaffected workers and soldiers in and around Petrograd. They also gained several prominent new recruits from among the radical intelligentsia, most notably the Social Democratic firebrand Leon Trotsky, a dynamic speaker and brilliant organizer who before 1917 had stood aloof from both Bolsheviks and Mensheviks and, indeed, often clashed with Lenin. When Trotsky joined the Bolshevik Party in 1917, Lenin found a right-hand man whose skills both complemented and enormously enhanced his own. Together the two men formed a powerful historic partnership.

Vladimir Lenin (1870–1924), founder of the Bolshevik Party and leader of the Soviet government from 1917 to 1924 (Library of Congress)

The Bolshevik eclipse caused by the July Days came to an end when the Provisional Government faced another coup in early September, this time by conservative forces led by the general Lavr Kornilov. To help with its defense, the government released Bolshevik leaders from prison and even supplied arms to the party's militia, the Red Guards. During the days that followed the failed Kornilov coup, Bolshevik strength among the Petrograd workers and soldiers grew so that by mid-September the party held a majority in the Petrograd Soviet. Shortly thereafter it won a majority in the Moscow Soviet.

Lenin now decided the time had come to overthrow the government. At first only Trotsky among the party's Central Committee members supported him. For all their bluster and years of pining about revolution, when the moment of truth arrived the other members, to put it bluntly, lost their nerve. It took Lenin a month, until the end of October, to convince his timid colleagues to make a grab for power. The coup itself, organized mainly by Trotsky (Lenin was still in hiding), began during the late night and predawn hours of November 6–7 when armed Bolshevik detachments seized key points throughout the city. It was successfully concluded late in the evening of November 7,[*] the official date of the Bolshevik Revolution, when the party's militia occupied the Provisional Government's headquarters at the Winter Palace and arrested most of its ministers (Kerensky fled the city). Russia's eight-month experiment with democracy was over. The Soviet era in Russian history had begun.

Securing Bolshevik Power

The Bolsheviks moved quickly and ruthlessly to secure power. On November 8 they issued two decrees that millions of Russians had been waiting to hear. The Decree on Peace called for immediate negotiations to end the war and announced that the Bolsheviks were prepared to sign a separate peace with Germany if the Western Allies chose to continue fighting. When the Allies did not follow suit, the Bolsheviks signed their separate peace with Germany, the Treaty of Brest-Litovsk, in March 1918.

The Decree on Land abolished all private property ownership of land and called for all farmland to be transferred to the peasantry. Essentially, it legalized the seizures of land by the peasantry that had been taking place, often violently, in many rural areas for several months. Far more problematic for many Russians, the Bolsheviks also announced their new government, the Council of People's Commissars, or *Sovnarkom*, which included only Bolsheviks. This immediately aroused a storm;

---

[*] *October 25 according to the Julian calendar; hence the Soviet Union's "Great October Revolution."*

most Russians active in political life assumed that any new government would include several parties and be subject to the will of the people through elections. They correctly saw the new regime as laying the foundations for a one-party dictatorship, something virtually everyone opposed. Most Russians, whatever their political views, did not want to exchange the czarist autocracy for another form of dictatorship.

The months of November and December made it clear that this was precisely what the Bolsheviks intended. Within a day of announcing their new government, they banned the nonsocialist press. In the following weeks they won control of Russia's major cities, although in Moscow it took 10 days of hard fighting. In December they set up "revolutionary tribunals" to suppress opponents of the regime and outlawed the Cadet (Constitutional Democrat) Party, labeling its leaders "enemies of the people." This mark of Cain would come back to haunt and destroy many of those same Bolsheviks after Lenin's death when Joseph Stalin led the party. On December 20 the Bolsheviks raised the Russian secret police from its grave under the name of the Cheka, the "Extraordinary Commission for Combating Counterrevolution and Sabotage."

The new regime did not dare stop the elections for the Constituent Assembly, which stood as the fulfillment of a generations-old dream. The elections, reasonably free despite Bolshevik efforts at intimidation, were held in late November, with the Bolsheviks finishing a poor second to the SRs, who won a solid plurality (41 percent to the Bolshevik total of 24 percent). Lenin had no intention of listening to the will of the people as expressed in the first national election in Russia's history. The Bolsheviks allowed the Constituent Assembly to meet for exactly one day, January 18, 1918, before closing it down by force, one measure in an expanding policy of repression. In April the Cheka arrested hundreds of anarchists. In June 1918 the Bolsheviks expelled the Mensheviks and the SRs from the country's soviets. The stage was now fully set for civil war.

Russia's Civil War

The basic cause of the civil war was established the day the Bolsheviks set up their one-party regime. It did not matter that in December a splinter group from the SRs briefly joined the government; these Left SRs had no real power, and in any case they left the government in protest against the Treaty of Brest-Litovsk. Even before the end of 1917 some conservative generals and politicians began organizing to oppose the regime, and the first armed clashes began as early as February 1918. That opposition grew after the Treaty of Brest-Litovsk was signed in March. The treaty was unpopular in many circles across the political spectrum, as it cost Russia about a million square miles of the western part of the czar's former empire (including all of the Ukraine) and approximately 60 million people (mainly non-Russians).

There is no specific date or single event that officially marks the beginning of the civil war, no clear opening salvo as occurred when Confederate guns fired the first shot of the American Civil War at Fort Sumter at 4:30 A.M. on April 12, 1865. Instead, over several months skirmishes turned into battles that turned into full-scale, fratricidal war. By June many Mensheviks, SRs, Left SRs, Cadets, and others with varying beliefs had decided that only armed resistance could dislodge the Bolsheviks from power. The Bolshevik government announced the war to the country on June 29 when it proclaimed that "the socialist fatherland is in danger." That turned out to be the death knell for Nicholas II, who had ended up in Bolshevik hands after the November revolution. The former czar and his family—Alexandra, four daughters, and one son, the former heir to the throne—were being held prisoner in the Urals region. To keep the royal family from falling into the hands of advancing anti-Bolshevik forces and becoming a symbol around which their opponents could rally, local Bolsheviks acting on Lenin's orders executed them and burned their bodies.

Those fighting the Bolsheviks (the Reds) were known collectively as the "Whites." Although at first glance the Whites appeared to have the advantage of broader public support than the increasingly dictatorial regime, they suffered from serious disadvantages. The Whites were not a single movement but an assortment of groups divided by divergent political beliefs, ranging from socialist to arch-conservative and monarchist. These groups often failed to cooperate with each other; at one point they were split into 18 governments and factions. When the fighting began, the Bolsheviks controlled the center of the country, including the main cities and industrial centers, while the Whites had to operate from the periphery, their armies separated by huge distances and unable to coordinate their campaigns.

Real power on the White side lay with former czarist military officers, who made no effort to appeal to the country's masses, especially the peasantry. In fact the White generals (and the one admiral among their top leaders) alienated the peasants by refusing to confirm that they could keep the land they had seized. The Whites received some help from the Allies, who in 1918 intervened with supplies and troops in the hope the Bolsheviks could be overthrown and Russia brought back into the war against Germany and the other Central Powers. That intervention continued after Germany's defeat in November 1918, but its scope was always very limited and not nearly on a scale sufficient to overcome the Whites' deficiencies.

The Bolsheviks had plenty of their own troubles. It seems fair to say that in the turmoil of 1918, just as in 1917, the odds were stacked against *any* group, Bolsheviks included, remaining in power for long. That they did so is explained by more than the ineptitude or misfortune of their opponents. Between 1918 and 1921, when the civil war ended, the Bolsheviks demonstrated organizational skill, unity, unbreakable will, and utter ruthlessness, all of which they needed to defeat their opponents. The key to their success was Lenin, who during the civil war reached the summit of his political career as his party's unquestioned leader and the embodiment of the qualities that enabled it to prevail.

Lenin, of course, had plenty of help from colleagues like Leon Trotsky, a man without military experience who organized the Red Army that bested the White generals on the battlefield; Joseph Stalin, an efficient troubleshooter prepared to use any means necessary to achieve his ends; Mikhail Tukhachevsky, a former czarist army second lieutenant who by virtue of his capabilities, which would not have counted for much in the class-bound old regime, rose to command the Red Army; and Feliks Dzerzhinsky, a Pole of noble blood who turned the Cheka into a massive instrument of political terror in the service of the Bolshevik regime. There were many others as well, from unheralded but skilled propagandists to merciless Cheka agents, but Lenin and the unchallenged leadership he provided still was the rock upon which the Bolsheviks built their victory.

One of the many ways in which the Cheka served the regime between 1918 and 1921 was in the mobilization of resources for the war effort. The Red Army needed weapons, ammunition, fortifications, uniforms, means of transport, and much more. Nothing was more vital than food, and the Bolsheviks stopped at nothing to get what they needed. One tactic was to form "Committees of the Poor" whose job was to wage class war in the villages and seize food from prosperous peasants (called *kulaks*, the Russian word for "fists"). These groups were soon joined by "Food Requisition Detachments" armed with machine guns and ordered to take whatever the regime wanted from the peasantry—food, tools, farm animals, or anything else deemed necessary to the war effort.

Deprived of these basic necessities, many peasants, most of whom were not kulaks, struggled to survive. Conditions were no better in the

LENIN, THE CHEKA, AND THE USE OF TERROR

During the civil war the Bolsheviks consciously carried out a policy of political terror they frankly called the Red Terror. A key tool of that policy was mass execution, which the Cheka carried out on many occasions. The worst example of this, which arguably constituted genocide, took place between 1919 and 1920, when the regime killed or deported an estimated 300,000 to 500,000 Cossacks in the southern part of the country between the Don and Kuban rivers. Lenin militantly supported these acts. For him mass executions and the terror they caused were justified because they served the revolution. He gave graphic instructions on how to terrorize the population in a telegram he sent in August 1918 to Bolshevik officials facing a peasant uprising in the region around the town of Penza, about 400 miles southeast of Moscow.

> *Comrades! The kulak uprising in your five districts must be crushed without pity. The interests of the whole revolution demand such action. . . . You must make an example of these people. (1) Hang (I mean hang publicly, so that the people see it) at least 100 kulaks, rich bastards, and known bloodsuckers. (2) Publish their names. (3) Seize all their grain. (4) Single out the hostages per my instructions. . . . Do all this so that for miles around people see it all, understand it all, tremble and tell themselves that we are killing kulaks and will continue to do it. (Werth 1999: 72)*

It is worth noting that the "kulaks" Lenin contemptuously referred to as "rich bastards" were nothing more than peasants who through hard work and efficiency had managed to attain a decent standard of living somewhat better than their neighbors. Kulaks were not "rich"; at most they enjoyed a small measure of prosperity by the very modest standards of that time and place. Anticipating that his order might cause some problems, Lenin added that in that case Penza party leaders should "find tougher people."

The Cheka found many such people. About a year after Lenin's telegram, a Cheka newspaper in Kiev, *The Red Sword,* published the following justification for its activities. In doing so it expressed as well the view of the party leadership:

> *We reject the old systems of morality and "humanity" invented by the bourgeoisie to oppress and exploit the "lower classes." Our morality has no precedent, our humanity is absolute because it rests on a new ideal. Our aim is to destroy all forms of oppression and violence. To us, everything is permitted, for we are the first to raise the sword not to oppress races and reduce them to slavery, but to liberate humanity. . . . Blood? Let blood flow like water! . . . For only through the death of the old world can we liberate ourselves forever . . . (Werth 1999: 102)*

cities, where desperate people increasingly turned against one another in the struggle to survive. As historian William Henry Chamberlin reported:

> The law of survival of the fittest found its cruelest, most naked application in the continued struggle for food. The weaker failed to get on the trains to the country districts, or fell off the roofs, or were pushed off the platform, or caught typhus and died, or had the precious gifts of the foraging taken by the ... hated guards who had boarded the trains as they approached the cities and confiscated surplus food from the passengers. (Chamberlin 1965: 345)

The Bolsheviks seized control, or "nationalized," all industry in Russia. This allowed the regime to direct all production to the war effort. Private trade was forbidden. Lenin's government also made use of forced labor, often with the help of the Cheka, for construction projects, transport, and other difficult tasks. These policies were eventually given the name War Communism, which reflected both the military struggle that provided its context and the fact that some of the policies—such as nationalizing industry, suppressing private trade, and abolishing money—clearly matched Marxist concepts of a socialist society. Most of the policies associated with War Communism were emergency measures designed to win the civil war, but Lenin and other Bolshevik leaders, as well as the party's rank and file, strongly approved of them from an ideological perspective because they looked like the first steps toward the socialist society they were determined to construct.

The New Economic Policy and the Ban on "Factions"

The last major battles of the civil war were fought in 1920. By the end of the year the last significant White force, with French help, was evacuated from the country via the Black Sea. The Bolsheviks then tried to export their revolution to Europe by sending the Red Army into Poland, the intent being first to ignite a socialist revolution there and then spread the revolution to Germany. But the Poles had other ideas. They rallied against the invaders from the east and drove the Red Army out of their country.

The end of the civil war thus left the Bolsheviks with half a cup. They had triumphed in Russia. Some non-Russian western parts of the old czarist empire had broken away and established their independence—Poland, Finland, and the Baltic states of Lithuania, Latvia, and Estonia—but most of the former czarist patrimony was in Bolshevik hands. At the same time the country they ruled was in ruins. Industrial production had plummeted and, worse, so had food production, which by 1921 was less than half of what it had been in 1913, the last full year before World War I. In some areas farmers planted 70 percent less than before the fighting began.

When food did not reach the cities, desperate urbanites scattered to the countryside to find sustenance. Moscow lost half its population, Petrograd more than two-thirds. Wherever they were, people struggled desperately to survive. Far too often their efforts were in vain: between early 1918 and the beginning of 1921, an estimated 5 million people in Russia died from hunger and disease. Nor did the end of the fighting restore food production quickly enough; as a result during 1921 and 1922 Russia suffered one of the worst famines in its history, with another 5 million people starving to death. Only a massive international relief effort led by the American Relief Administration directed by future president Herbert Hoover prevented the death toll from going even higher.

It was against this background of victory combined with hardship and distress that in March 1921 the party (officially called the Communist Party since 1918) gathered to decide policy at its 10th Party Congress. As the meeting was about to begin, it was interrupted by news of a rebellion against Bolshevik rule by sailors at the Kronstadt naval base, on an island not far from Petrograd in the Gulf of Finland. It was one of numerous uprisings, mostly by peasants, that the Bolsheviks faced after defeating the Whites. What made the revolt so disturbing was that the Kronstadt sailors had a long history as militant revolutionaries. Many had previously been strong supporters of the Bolsheviks; now they accused the party of setting up a dictatorship and betraying its socialist ideals. The Bolsheviks put the rebellion down after a fierce, bloody 10-day battle, but even in victory many of them were deeply shaken. After all, if the Kronstadt sailors had turned against them, what did that say about their policies? As Lenin himself put it, despite their victory over the Whites, the Bolsheviks had "failed to convince the broad masses."

The shock of Kronstadt and the wider crisis it represented led to a dramatic change in policy. Despite great reluctance on the part of many party members who enthusiastically supported War Communism as a major step toward socialism, Lenin concluded it had to go. Demonstrating a flexibility many of his colleagues lacked, he argued that for the Bolsheviks to remain in power the country had to recover economically, and economic recovery could not be accomplished at the point of a gun. In its place Lenin proposed what he called the

New Economic Policy (NEP), a program he admitted was a "strategic retreat."

The NEP consisted of several components. First, food seizures from the peasantry were ended and replaced by a progressive tax. This meant that for the first time since 1918 peasants had an incentive to produce as much food as possible since they could sell and profit from any food they did not consume themselves. The NEP also undid much of the nationalization of industry. Russia's major industries and businesses—the largest factories (which employed 80 percent of the country's factory workers), railroads, and banks—remained in government hands. The Bolsheviks called these enterprises "the commanding heights" of the economy and considered them crucial to building a socialist economy in the near future. The remaining thousands of small factories and workshops, retail outlets, and other businesses were returned to their former owners, if they were still alive, or leased to other entrepreneurs, and new businesses were permitted as well. Private trade was legalized as the only way to move agricultural products and other goods and services from private producers to consumers. The result was what is known as a mixed economy, one that combined elements of socialist state control and private enterprise.

Lenin was ever the flexible politician, with his eyes firmly fixed on maintaining the Bolshevik dictatorship. Therefore, while loosening the economic reins, he tightened the political ones. In 1921, with all opposition *outside* the party destroyed, this meant tightening control *inside* the party, a policy implemented at the pivotal 10th Party Congress. Lenin faced disagreement from some leaders about restrictions on party members during the civil war—it is worth noting that they had no problem with repressive measures against *non*-Bolsheviks—and the increased concentration of power in the hands of Lenin and his closest associates.

By 1921 these dissenters were openly expressing their views. Lenin feared that expressions of dissent, even within the party, could get out of hand, cause a party split, and threaten the exclusive Bolshevik grip on power. He therefore urged that any organized "factions" within the party be banned. In effect, having banned all political discussion outside the party's confines, Lenin now found it necessary to ban it inside the party as well. The resolution banning factions caused considerable debate at the congress before finally being adopted. In the future those guilty of violating "party unity," a concept whose definition obviously lay with the top Bolshevik leaders, could be expelled. There was considerable unease, even among party leaders, with the resolution. One leader, in supporting it, did so despite his concern that some day it might "well be turned against us." He was right. Lenin would not live to see that day, but many of his colleagues did, to their great sorrow.

Old and New Problems, 1922–1924

The work of building and perfecting the one-party dictatorship continued during and after 1921. Shortly after the end of the 10th Party Congress about a third of all members were expelled from the party, a measure that rid it of many dissenters. In 1922 the Cheka, officially a temporary body, was abolished, only to reemerge instantly with even more powers as a permanent body, the State Political Administration, or GPU (after 1923 the Unified State Political Administration, or OGPU). One of those new powers was the right to arrest party members.

Another crucial development in 1922 was Joseph Stalin's appointment to the newly created party post of general secretary. Lenin selected Stalin for this position because he wanted someone who could effectively control the annoying dissenters who continued to make their voices heard at major party meetings. Stalin immediately began using this post, which gave him the power to place party members in important jobs, to build a network of supporters in key positions. Lenin meanwhile dealt with defeated non-Bolsheviks whose very presence he considered a threat. Following his call for "model" trials to intimidate any potential political opponents, several SR leaders were tried and convicted on the trumped-up charge of "counterrevolution," and some were executed. Stalin would use Lenin's model far more extensively and with much deadlier effect in the 1930s.

As the Bolshevik leadership tightened the political screws, the NEP did its work on the economic front. For the Bolsheviks that was both good and bad news. The good news was the recovery itself. By 1923, as peasants planted their crops and sold their surpluses to private traders, the country had enough food. Industrial recovery, while slower, also continued at a respectable rate. The bad news was that wherever the economy was making large strides it was on the basis of capitalism, not socialism. This applied not only to the peasants and the growing class of prosperous kulaks, but also to private traders and businesspeople the Bolsheviks bitterly called "Nepmen."

In contrast, the socialist "commanding heights" lagged behind. They lacked modern technology, funds for investment, and skilled managers; the party bureaucrats who ran many enterprises had few business skills. In short, as the Bolsheviks saw it, recovery under the NEP was exacting too high a price: the revival of capitalism in Russia, with the kulaks and Nepmen playing the role of the new bourgeoisie. This was not the Russia they had risked and sacrificed so much to build. The writing of a new constitution for the "Union of Soviet Socialist Republics (USSR)," the official name of the former Russian Empire until 1991, did not change the unpleasant fact that by 1923, in an economic sense, Russia was moving further away from socialism with each passing day.

Lenin's Last Struggle

The issue of the NEP and where it was taking Soviet Russia did not emerge in time to become a major concern for Lenin. Rather, his concerns were personal and political, and they were interrelated. In mid-1922 Lenin suffered the first of three strokes that in fewer than two years would kill him. The first one disabled him for five months, and during his forced inactivity Lenin began to take a critical look at his revolution. He did not like what he saw. The regime was becoming increasingly corrupt. Officials were using their positions for personal gain, treating ordinary citizens with contempt, and in general behaving much like officials had behaved under the hated czars.

Why Lenin suddenly noticed this is uncertain, but it should not have surprised him. Like czarist officials in Imperial Russia, Bolshevik officials in Soviet Russia were part of a dictatorship. They were not restrained by any independent outside force, such as a free press or rival political parties that could unseat them legally and peacefully. Lenin's problem was that he did not understand that a socialist dictatorship, like any other kind of dictatorship, governs dictatorially. Its officials inevitably are imperious and very likely to be corrupt. Unwilling to consider any modification in the Bolshevik dictatorship—his lifelong goal—Lenin had no solution to the problems he saw, which he considered inconsistent with socialism.

The best Lenin could do was to focus on one official who seemed to be most closely identified with these undesirable developments, which Lenin called "bureaucratism." That man was the recently appointed general secretary Joseph Stalin, a Bolshevik since the party's earliest days and for many years one of Lenin's most trusted aides and associates. Lenin seems to have feared Stalin's motives and decided that his power had to be strictly limited.

After his second stroke in December 1922, when he knew he would never return to active political life, Lenin composed what is most commonly known as his political "Testament," in which he evaluated each of his top lieutenants and possible successors. He found all wanting in one way or another, although it was clear that he considered Leon Trotsky the outstanding member of the group. Lenin strongly implied in the "Testament" that no one person should succeed him but that authority should lie with a collective leadership. In an explosive "Postscript" to the "Testament," written in January 1923, Lenin urged that Stalin be removed from his position as general secretary, which Lenin understood was the key source of Stalin's growing power. Both documents were kept secret from most party leaders until after Lenin's death. Despite his weakness Lenin continued to try to undermine Stalin. In early March he urged Trotsky to take the offensive against Stalin at the upcoming 12th Party Congress that he himself was too ill to attend. For reasons that still remain a mystery, Trotsky declined to follow Lenin's entreaties.

Lenin's third stroke in March 1923 left him an invalid. He lingered, unable to influence events while his closest comrades-in-arms, among them Stalin, began to maneuver and position themselves for the expected power struggle. Vladimir Lenin died on January 21, 1924, leaving to those comrades the issues of who would succeed him and how the effort to build socialism in Soviet Russia would be continued.

From Lenin to Stalin

Russia during its troubled history has endured two especially painful periods. The first was the Mongol conquest and its aftermath, which subjected the country to destruction on a staggering scale and left it with a suffocating legacy of economic backwardness and autocratic rule. The second was the Stalin era. Between 1929, the year Stalin consolidated his power, until his death in 1953, the Soviet government was directly responsible for the deaths of between 10 and 20 million of its citizens. Millions more who survived had their lives destroyed by the same policies, including forced labor under unbearable conditions, that killed so many of their countrymen.

The Stalin regime silenced and murdered artists, persecuted, imprisoned, and sometimes killed scientists; and terrorized and impoverished tens of millions of ordinary citizens. In addition, because it failed to prepare the Soviet Union for an invasion by Nazi Germany that clearly was coming, it bears indirect responsibility for the deaths of many of the 27 million Soviet citizens who perished during World War II in the Nazi-Soviet theater, when two totalitarian regimes, each in its own way representing the worst of humanity, locked horns in a merciless fight to the death. Indeed, the Stalin regime was directly responsible for a significant number of those wartime deaths because of its inexcusable blunders prior to and immediately after the German invasion, wasteful tactics on the battlefield, and brutal policies on the home front. The Stalin era in short was a national catastrophe—imposed on tens of millions of Ukrainians, Belarusians, and all the other national minorities of the Soviet Union no less than on its Russian citizens. It concentrated the misery caused by more than two centuries of Mongol tyranny into a quarter of a century. That the killing was done and the suffering imposed in the name of building a perfect egalitarian socialist society adds an element of bitter irony to one of the most egregious examples of a government's oppression of its own people in all of history.

The road from Lenin to Stalin was bumpy and pitted but also short and straight. A number of different factors were in play. On the one hand, Stalin's triumph was a straightforward example of the ruthless and skillful pursuit of political power. On the other hand, the policies he introduced after consolidating power, in particular rapid industrialization and the collectivization of agriculture, while very much part of his personal agenda, had origins that transcended both the leader and his agenda. Their economic and social roots lay in fundamental Bolshevik principles and in the concerns that emerged among many party leaders and rank-and-file members in the 1920s about how the country was developing under the NEP.

The succession struggle began with maneuvering in 1923 when Lenin lay dying, and went through several rounds between 1923 and 1929. In 1923 Trotsky seemed to be Lenin's logical successor. His brilliant leadership during the November coup and the civil war gave him a revolutionary pedigree second only to Lenin's. But notwithstanding his many talents as a revolutionary and his ability to deal with crises that overwhelmed most of his colleagues, Trotsky was an inept politician once things settled down. He paid no attention to the nuts and bolts of placing supporters in key positions within the party bureaucracy, which is where power lay once Bolshevik rule was consolidated during the civil war.

This is precisely where Stalin excelled. By 1923 he was one of the six members of the Politburo, the party's top policy-making body. His power was reinforced and augmented by his position as general secretary, and he held several other major posts as well. He also had an excellent sense of timing, knowing when to take a firm position on an issue and when to make and break political alliances. Stalin had another major advantage: His main rivals tended to underestimate him, in part because unlike them he was not an intellectual with a flair for public speaking or writing. In 1923 none of his colleagues realized how much power Stalin had accumulated by virtue of his control of the Communist Party political machinery.

Other major players in the ring included the partnership of Grigory Zinoviev (1883–1936) and Lev Kamenev (1883–1936), both of whom detested Trotsky and, like Trotsky, did not appreciate Stalin's political skills or understand the power he had quietly accumulated. Compared to Trotsky and Stalin, both men were mediocrities. Also important, mainly as an ally rather than as a contender for power, was Nikolai Bukharin (1888–1938), the party leader with the strongest credentials as an economist and, by the mid-1920s, the leading defender of the NEP.

During the first round in the struggle for power every major leader united against Trotsky. For reasons that remain unexplained, Trotsky did almost nothing to defend his position. Most notably, after Lenin's "Testament" was read to the party's Central Committee in early 1924, Trotsky did not force the issue of removing Stalin as general secretary. After that single reading, he allowed the document to be suppressed, and with that Stalin to survive. By 1925, although he still sat on the Politburo, Trotsky had given up his last bastion of power, his position as commissar of war, which had given him control of the Red Army. Although Trotsky still had significant influence, he stayed on the side-lines in 1925 while Stalin crushed Zinoviev and Kamenev in a fierce but short struggle. With that victory, Stalin was able to place two of his loyal allies, Vyacheslav Molotov and Klement Voroshilov, on the Politburo in place of his demoted opponents.

Trotsky entered the political ring again in 1927 as an ally of Zinoviev and Kamenev, only to be defeated again by Stalin's political machine and expelled from the party he had done so much to bring to power exactly a decade earlier. In 1929 Stalin ordered Trotsky deported from the Soviet Union. That same year Stalin also turned on Bukharin and his associates, and by year's end he had consigned all of his rivals to political oblivion. Stalin was securely in place as Lenin's successor.

This struggle for power at the top took place against the background of disagreements within the party over the NEP and the direction in which it was taking Soviet Russia. By the mid-1920s the NEP had accomplished its assigned task and brought about the country's economic recovery. For many Bolsheviks, however, the NEP as an economic tonic was as bad as the disease it had cured. While it had enabled Russian peasant agriculture to feed the country and gradually restored most industries to a semblance of health, the NEP had not produced the economic surpluses needed to build a modern industrial infrastructure, the basis of any socialist society. Furthermore, the NEP was promoting the growth and prosperity of social classes—kulaks and Nepmen—who favored capitalism, not socialism. The kulaks were especially dangerous because they were tightening their grip on the rural economy and becoming increasingly influential in local rural politics as well.

These problems and others led the party into what is known as the "Industrialization Debate," a wide-ranging discussion between 1924 and 1928 about economic development, the building of modern industry, the nature of socialism, and the future of the NEP. One of the issues raised was how to extract more resources from the peasantry to finance industrialization. Critics of the NEP, led by Trotsky, argued that this had to be done and suggested raising taxes on the peasantry and increasing the prices of the goods they used while paying them less for the grain and other agricultural products they sold. The problem was how the peasants would react to such policies, for they certainly would oppose them as vigorously as they could. Trotsky was the leading critic of the NEP and Bukharin its leading defender, while Stalin avoided taking a firm position on this or any other issue; instead, he used the Industrialization Debates of the mid-1920s to maneuver and build his political strength.

Meanwhile, by the mid-1920s the Bolsheviks were not popular with any major social group. The peasants showed no interest in joining Bolshevik-run collective farms. They wanted to farm their land as individual families and run their own village affairs in the 350,000 communes that dated from before emancipation of the serfs. Women, who supposedly were to be liberated from capitalist oppression by socialism, were more interested, if they lived in urban areas, in Western fashions than sexual equality, and, if they were peasants, supported their men in preferring traditional ways of doing things to Bolshevik ideas. Most artists, writers, and other intellectuals who had at first rejected the revolution continued to do so, and some who initially had supported it became disillusioned. Workers in state-run factories were dissatisfied with poor working conditions and low wages. The young, supposedly the country's future, also snubbed the party. This was true even of candidates for Communist Party membership, who, according to one official report, "were not interested in political education, but preferred organizing dance parties instead" (Brovkin 1998: 114).

In short, notwithstanding its unquestioned control of the government, by 1929 the Communist Party, rather than moving closer to the reality of socialism, was watching its vision drift further beyond the horizon. For some, including Bukharin and his associates, the NEP was not to blame. For others, including Stalin when he finally took a firm stand on the matter after disposing of Trotsky, the NEP was indeed the problem. That became clear at the end of 1929, when Stalin and his supporters finished consolidating their power and turned to building socialism as they saw fit.

The Second Bolshevik Revolution: The First Five-Year Plan

The events of the 1930s, during which Soviet society underwent fundamental and wrenching changes imposed by the regime, is often called the "second" Bolshevik Revolution. With equal logic it is also called Stalin's "revolution from above." Stalin's program for building socialism, the core of this traumatic event, drew on ideas first raised during the 1920s, all of which his regime took to extremes previously not considered possible. The overall concept was to industrialize as rapidly as possible according to a plan.

In 1929 this strategy gave birth to the First Five-Year Plan, a 1,000-page document developed by many of the Soviet Union's leading economists. Its targets for industrial growth were extremely ambitious, especially given the country's limited resources. To put it simply, for the targets to be reached everything had to go right. Stalin immediately raised those targets and then declared the plan operational, before it was officially adopted or even fully drafted.

The plan depended on getting more resources from the peasantry. To that end peasants were to be gradually moved from their small, supposedly inefficient individual farms to collective farms: large units in which many families, 100 or more, worked together supervised by Communist Party officials. The party's central planners would determine how much the peasants would be paid for their crops. The original plan called for collectivizing 20 percent of the peasantry in five years and doing it voluntarily. How that would be accomplished with peasants who had shown absolutely no interest in giving up their property and way of life and adopting a communist lifestyle was not addressed.

By 1929, however, Stalin and his leading colleagues had decided that collectivization would proceed much faster than the planners had called for and that the peasants would be moved whether they liked it or not. The new schedule called for placing most peasants on collective farms within three years; in certain areas, including the key grain-producing regions, the process was to be completed in a matter of months.

Collectivization and Dekulakization

To their great sorrow the peasants soon found out just how determined the Stalin regime was. Full-scale collectivization began in December 1929. Although the government preferred voluntary compliance, individuals or villages that resisted faced overwhelming force. Stalin called on heavily armed units of the secret police and the army and on thousands of specially selected party cadres to crush resistance and get the job done. By March 1930 more than half of the Soviet Union's peasants had been placed on what supposedly were collective farms. In reality, however, almost nothing had been prepared. Party workers, fearing they would be punished if they did not show sufficient enthusiasm, strove to exceed the targets they had been given.

The resulting chaos and disorganization was compounded by the destruction of farm machinery and tools and the death of millions of farm animals. Sometimes this was done deliberately by the peasants

PEASANT RESISTANCE TO COLLECTIVIZATION

The peasants resisted collectivization in various ways, especially during the first dreadful months of the campaign in early 1930, when more than 1,600 cases of armed resistance were reported. Most resistance was passive, as many peasants destroyed their property or killed and ate their farm animals rather than give them up to the collectives. Others fought back with whatever weapons they had. Most resistance consisted of killing party officials or secret police agents directly in charge of what was taking place in individual villages. Larger and more organized revolts were less common but still took place in many places, especially in non-Russian areas such as the Ukraine, parts of the north Caucasus region, and Kazakhstan. When this happened, the government reacted with destructive fury, as the following eyewitness account of events in the Ukraine along the Dnieper River reveals:

> In 1930, in the Dniepropetrovsk region, thousands of peasants armed with hunting rifles, axes, and pitchforks, revolted against the regime. . . . NKVD units and militia were sent. For three days . . . a bloody battle was waged between the revolting people and the authorities. . . . The revolt was cruelly punished. Thousands of peasants, workers, soldiers, and officers paid for the attempt

themselves; sometimes the cause was neglect or incompetence. In any event the chaos was so widespread that the government retreated and allowed about half the peasants to leave the collectives. However, that was only a temporary step back on a relentless forced march; within two years more than two-thirds of the country's peasants were on collective farms. By 1936 about 90 percent were collectivized.

Some peasants escaped collectivization by being consigned to a worse fate. They were the kulaks, the country's best and most successful farmers. To Stalin and other party leaders they were by definition "counterrevolutionaries," dangerous enemies of socialism, who had to be "liquidated as a class." A few, deemed less dangerous than the others, were allowed to remain in their home districts as pariahs, stripped of all their possessions, to survive as best they could. Many others were arrested and sent to the Soviet Union's growing network of labor camps. Most kulaks, numbering in the millions, were deported to remote parts

During the 1930s peasants from villages around Moscow view a poster depicting prosperous peasants, or kulaks, as pigs. (Associated Press)

with their lives, while the survivors were deported to concentration camps. In the villages of Ternovka and Boganovka . . . mass executions were carried out near the balkis [ravines]. The soil of this region was soaked in blood. After these executions, the villages were set on fire. (Kravchenko 1950: 99–100) of the country. The journeys alone, with peasants packed into long trains of boxcars without sufficient food, medical care, or protection from the elements, killed people by the thousands.

Those deportees who made it to their destinations in the far north, central Asia, or Siberia were placed in "special settlements," which often consisted of nothing but bare ground in a region of desert, barren steppe, or marshy forest. If local authorities supplied any food or help in building shelter, it was meager at best and did not come until many people had already died. The death toll quickly mounted into the hundreds of thousands. Children suffered the most: A report that reached the Politburo in early 1932 revealed that in many areas the death rate for them was 10 percent per month.

Yet even that does not cover the full measure of the suffering collectivization caused. Although the program was supposed to increase food production significantly, the chaos of the process and bad weather caused poor harvests in both 1931 and 1932. This did not stop the government from taking the grain and other crops it needed to feed the cities and meet export targets. That left peasants in certain areas, especially the grain-producing regions of the Ukraine and north Caucasus, without food. When peasants began to starve en masse, the government responded by doing everything it could to make sure they did not steal any of the food they had grown.

The result was catastrophic famine. During 1932 and 1933 5 million people died in the Ukraine alone. This did not bother Stalin; the crisis helped break the back of any remaining resistance to collectivization. Decades later a survivor referred to the famine that Stalin's policies had caused as "execution by hunger." The toll for the Soviet Union as a whole, including the north Caucasus where about a million died, reached 7 million.

Collectivization gave the Stalin regime control of the country's agricultural production and was thus considered a success. And in fact the system that emerged from the maelstrom of the early 1930s lasted until the end of the Soviet Union nearly 60 years later. The problem is that it never worked. Whether they labored on collective farms, where their pay was based on how much the farm produced, or on larger state farms, where they were paid a straight wage, Soviet peasants made indifferent workers.* There simply were no rewards for working hard

---

* Henceforth, references to the collective farm system will encompass all types of farms.

in collective farm fields. Instead peasants focused their attention on the small private plots where they could grow vegetables and fruit and sell their surplus, and on the few livestock they were permitted to keep for their own use.

The peasants could not have survived without those private plots. Nor could the Soviet Union as a whole have managed, as those plots, 3 to 4 percent of the country's farmland, produced a third of the country's fruit, vegetables, meat, milk, and eggs. When Stalin died in 1953, grain production was below the level of 1913. In the long run, after Stalin died and the Soviet leadership had to provide its people with a better standard of living, the collective farm system's lack of productivity turned a country that under the czars had been a major grain exporter into the world's largest grain importer.

Industrialization

Collectivization of agriculture was not an end in itself. It was a means to the end of rapid industrialization. The goal was to build a modern industrial base within a decade that would enable the Soviet Union to become a modern military power. Stalin dictated what in fact was an impossible rate of growth because his egomania demanded such an accomplishment. According to him the Bolsheviks were "bound by no laws" and could achieve anything if they had the will. Stalin also demanded that most investment go to heavy industry—such as iron, steel, coal, machine tools, and electric power—rather than industries producing consumer goods because only heavy industry could provide the basis for long-term economic growth. A choice had to be made between investment and consumption, and that meant the Soviet people would have to reduce their consumption.

While Stalin carried this policy to an extreme, his basic assumptions reflected traditional Bolshevik thinking. The same applies to Stalin's emphasis on building a powerful military establishment. He starved the civilian economy to feed the military, but the idea that war would decide the struggle between socialism and capitalism dated back to Lenin, and was accepted by the party leadership as a whole, including the men Stalin bested in the struggle for power.

The emphasis on breakneck speed caused enormous problems and wasted vast amounts of scarce resources. Materials arrived at construction sites before they could be used, or they did not arrive on time and caused delays. Untrained workers ruined complicated machin-

A combine factory in the city of Rostov-on-Don during the 1930s industrialization drive (Library of Congress)

ery. Accidents were common as underfed, overtired workers raced to complete dangerous jobs without proper safety precautions. Many of the goods produced on excessively stringent timetables were useless, even as they were counted toward the fulfillment of the plan's quotas.

176

Invaluable resources went to dubious and expensive projects Stalin decided were vital, including a canal to link the Baltic and White Seas that proved to be useless. The canal was too shallow and narrow for the large boats and barges used to transport military supplies, exactly the purpose for which it had been built.

That said, and although very few major targets actually were met, a great deal was built during the First Five-Year Plan, and also during the Second Five-Year Plan, when many of the projects initiated under the first plan were completed. Between 1929 and 1937 steel production in the Soviet Union rose from 4 to 17 million tons. Oil production went from under 12 to more than 28 million tons, coal from 35 to 128 million tons, and electricity generation from 5 billion kwh to 36 billion kwh. Entire new industries were built, such as the automobile, tractor, and aviation industries, as well as entirely new industrial complexes, above all the Magnitogorsk iron and steel complex near the Ural Mountains, and the Kuznetsk coal-mining and metallurgy complex in central Siberia.

By the end of the 1930s about 80 percent of all industrial production came from new or modernized factories. The first two five-year plans also dramatically increased the country's military production capability; it could now produce everything from rifles and ammunition to tanks and aircraft, although there was a great deal of waste in this sector too. For example, during the early 1930s the Soviets rushed new tanks and airplanes into production so rapidly that technological advances made them obsolete within a few years. But the industrial capacity and technical skills necessary to build these modern weapons had been developed, as had the ability to mobilize resources for war. By 1941 the Soviet Union was producing some of the most effective tanks, artillery, and rifles deployed by any country during World War II.

At a terrible price the Soviet Union had become the world's second leading industrial power, trailing only the United States, a status it held until surpassed by Japan during the 1980s. Nevertheless, because of the inefficiencies of centralized planning in managing advanced and complex industries, a grossly oversized military sector that drained resources and talent from the rest of the economy, the absence of market mechanisms to spur innovation, and a system of collectivized agriculture that could not feed the country at a level comparable to capitalist systems, the Soviet planned economy that emerged in the 1930s was plagued by inherent faults that eventually would cause it to crumble beyond repair.

Women were employed in factories in large numbers during the industrialization drive of the 1930s. These women, shown about 1940, are lathe operators. (Library of Congress)

The Gulag

In 1934 the Soviet regime established a new agency it called the Gulag, an acronym for Chief Administration for Camps. The Gulag camps were places of forced (or slave) labor. Like so much else from the Stalin era these camps dated from the time Lenin was in charge. The key difference was size and function.

Under Lenin the camps remained relatively small and were used mainly for projects related to the war effort against the Whites. Not until the mid-1920s, when Stalin was consolidating his position as Lenin's successor, did the issue arise of using forced labor in a systematic way as part of the effort to build a new socialist society. The decision to use forced labor to build socialism was taken in 1929, the same year the First Five-Year Plan began. Over the next few years collectivization and dekulakization led to an enormous growth in the number of inmates and a corresponding expansion of the camp network. Both the size of the camps and the expanded role their inmates played in the economy led to the formal establishment of the Gulag.

As it developed the Gulag consisted of labor camps run from Moscow, a huge network of "colonies" managed by local authorities, and special settlements populated by exiles rather than prisoners. There are no accurate figures for how many people passed through the Gulag. One reasonable guess is that between 1929 and Stalin's death in 1953, 18 million Soviet citizens were held at one time or another in the camps and colonies, while another 6 million may have passed through the special settlements. Many of them died in these hellish places.

Gulag camps were located everywhere in the Soviet Union, from remote Siberia to the centers of the country's main cities. Slave laborers worked on many of the most important projects of the First and Second Five-Year plans, especially in construction and mining. During the 1930s, among many other tasks, Gulag laborers built the Baltic–White Sea Canal, worked on railroad construction in Siberia, mined gold in the Kolyma region of eastern Siberia (increasing production from 511 kilograms in 1932 to 33,360 kilograms in 1936), and harvested lumber from northern forests. During World War II they also produced weapons, built factories, and constructed airfields. After the war, in addition to working in construction, mining, and a host of other areas, Gulag laborers played a central role in the crash Soviet project to build an atom bomb, doing everything from mining uranium under absolutely appalling conditions to building the structure that housed the country's first atomic reactor.

A special unit of the Gulag, organized in 1938 by Lavrenty Beria, one of Stalin's closest henchmen and the newly appointed head of the secret

Gulag labor camps were set up all over the Soviet Union during the 1930s. This labor camp was located in eastern Siberia. The fence on the right hides a work gang. The corner hut is for guards armed with machine guns. This picture was taken in 1954, the year after Stalin died. (Associated Press)

police, held scientist and engineer prisoners to work on high-tech projects. The services of these so-called special design bureaus included developing weapons that played an important role in World War II.

Living and working conditions in the Gulag ranged from barely survivable to lethal. Inmates were often literally worked to death. Millions died, although just how many is not known. During the war years, annual mortality rates of 10 to 20 percent were common in the camps, and during 1942–43 they reached 25 percent for the Gulag as a whole. By war's end more than 2 million people had died in the Gulag's camps and colonies, a figure that does not include deaths in special settlements. Only the special design bureaus, whose inmates were highly valued because of their vital skills, were exempt from the terrible conditions.

There was a bitter irony to the Gulag system. Because its labor seemed to be so cheap, it was used in a colossally wasteful way on projects of little or no economic utility, such as the White Sea Canal or

CONDITIONS IN THE GULAG

Working conditions in the Gulag were inhumanly harsh. The following is an account by a prisoner who had the good fortune to be released during World War II. Conditions in the lumber camps where this man worked were among the worst in the Gulag. Making matters even worse, workers doing heavy labor such as construction or felling trees received a food ration of about 1,400 calories per day, barely enough to sustain a person confined to a prison cell and doing no physical labor.

> . . . The working conditions were almost always deadly for us. We were forced to work in temperatures of -40° [F]. Only when the cold was even more intense than this were the men sent to their barracks. Rain and snow storms were disregarded. We had to cut trees in the forests even when the snow was waist deep. Falling trees would hit the workers, who were unable to escape in the deep snow. In the summer, while mowing in this marshland, the men had to stand knee deep in water or mud for 10 or 11 hours. The same thing happened in the turf pits. . . . Influenza, bronchitis, pneumonia, tuberculosis . . . malaria, and other diseases decimated our ranks . . . The men were compelled to work by force . . . [C]amp authorities would force prisoners to work by beating, kicking, dragging them by their feet through the mud and snow, setting dogs on them, hitting them with rifle butts, and by threatening them with revolvers and bayonets. (Cited in Dallin and Nicolaevsky 1947: 37–38)

railroads in remote regions that led nowhere and ended up never being used. Beyond that, Gulag labor required prison camps, guards, and a huge bureaucracy. It also was far less efficient than free labor. In short, it was much more expensive than it appeared at first glance. As a result the Gulag as a whole actually retarded Soviet economic development rather than promoting it. It thus not only was a massive moral crime but a major economic failure as well.

The Great Terror

Beginning in 1933 the frantic pace set during the First Five-Year Plan mercifully began to moderate, albeit only slightly. The Second Five-Year Plan, which covered the years 1933 to 1937, while mandating ambitious growth targets, also called for consolidation, in particular completing projects dating from the previous plan and focusing more on quality. The worst of collectivization was over, and the return of order along with concessions to the peasantry regarding private plots and livestock helped agriculture recover from the poor harvests of 1931 and 1932. At the 17th Party Congress, which met in January 1934 and officially adopted the Second Five-Year Plan, an attitude of relative moderation seemed to prevail.

Significantly, Stalin was not the only star of the Congress. The delegates enthusiastically applauded the speeches of Sergei Kirov, the powerful head of the party organization in Leningrad, as Petrograd was renamed in 1924. Kirov was a staunch supporter of Stalin, but he also had a reputation of being a moderating force on party policy. Kirov's popularity was such that some delegates secretly suggested he replace Stalin as general secretary, a suggestion Kirov rejected out of hand. After the congress Kirov spoke publicly about improving conditions for both workers and peasants, welcome news in a country where during the First Five-Year Plan the standard of living had plunged.

It all turned out to be the calm before the storm, a tempest so furious and powerful that it shook the entire Soviet system. In December 1934 Kirov was murdered by an unbalanced former party member, an act most likely arranged by Stalin. A huge wave of arrests and deportations to the Gulag followed, 40,000 in Leningrad alone, as Stalin's propaganda machine trumped up warnings about foreign spies, disloyal party members, insidious followers of the exiled Trotsky, and other alleged enemies of the Soviet state infiltrating the country. The great purge, or Great Terror (the terms are used here interchangeably), entered a dormant phase for a while before flaring up into a colossal fireball in 1936 and burning its way through Soviet society until 1938.

It is difficult to understand why Stalin would launch such a destructive purge, but most historians agree that the fundamental cause was his intense paranoia and determination to wield absolute power beyond any possible challenge. Stalin certainly wielded dictatorial power in 1934, but it was not absolute. Other Communist Party leaders like Kirov had their own bases of power, as did army generals. This made all of them Stalin's targets. Beyond that there were people around who still remembered Lenin and whose memory of past events challenged Stalin's version of history, especially his spurious claim that he had been Lenin's number-one disciple and virtual coequal in the history of Bolshevism, the November Revolution, and the establishment of the

Soviet state. Such old-timers, including several of his former rivals, were also targets of Stalin's purge.

The Great Terror shifted into high gear in August 1936 with the first of three public show trials, the other two following, respectively, in 1937 and 1938. The overall purge campaign from 1936 on was managed by the fanatical Stalin loyalist Nikolai Yezhov, head of the People's Commissariat of Internal Affairs (NKVD), the agency that controlled the secret police. The prosecutor at the show trials was Andrei Vyshinsky, a one-time Menshevik turned militant Stalinist. In those trials almost every surviving Bolshevik leader from the Lenin era was accused and convicted of plotting crimes against Lenin and Stalin, offenses that were absurd on their face and could not possibly have occurred.

In every case these former tough revolutionaries and party stalwarts confessed in open court, broken by NKVD physical torture and excruciating psychological pressure. For example, the court heard from Zinoviev how "[m]y defective Bolshevism became transformed into anti-Bolshevism and through Trotskyism I arrived at fascism." The arch villain in the prosecutor's account was Trotsky, whom Stalin could not put on trial as he had been deported and now lived in exile in Mexico. Virtually every defendant was executed; those who were not disappeared forever into prison camps. The 1936 trial claimed Zinoviev and Kamenev; the 1937 trial disposed of 17 former Trotsky supporters who had long since repented and transferred their support to Stalin; and the 1938 trial convicted Bukharin and several other former members of Lenin's Politburo. Meanwhile, because Stalin feared the military might turn against him, a secret one-day trial in 1937 led to the execution of Mikhail Tukhachevsky, formerly the army's chief of staff and its most influential officer in terms of military doctrine, and seven other senior Red Army commanders.

These trials constituted only the tip of a giant iceberg. Stalin not only slaughtered his former rivals; he decimated his own supporters, the people who had carried out collectivization and industrialization. The victims included 1,108 of the 1,966 delegates at the 17th Party Congress and 70 percent of the Central Committee members they elected. The purge also decapitated the military, wiping out the majority of the top-ranking military officer corps down to the level of divisional commanders. Half of all military officers—35,000 men—were imprisoned or shot. Even the NKVD, the organization that carried out the terror, was purged.

Accomplished artists, writers, and scientists disappeared into prisons and labor camps, never to emerge. So did millions of ordinary people. Available official records are incomplete (or destroyed) and thus understate the total number of victims. Yet even according to them, during the peak of the purge, between August 1937 and November 1938, the NKVD arrested at least 1.6 million people and shot 700,000. The latter figure means that during a period of 16 months the NKVD shot 1,500 people *per day*. One widely cited estimate maintains that during the Great Terror 900,000 people were shot and 3,000,000 sent to labor camps, where they died in droves

THE GREAT PURGE AND TERROR

The terms "great purge" and "great terror" are used interchangeably for good reason. During the Great Terror, arrests often took place for no discernible reason. Total loyalty to the regime and a sincere devotion to Comrade Stalin were no protection against the NKVD. Anyone arrested faced brutal interrogation and either execution or, more often, a long sentence in a labor camp. Rank was no help: No organization in the Soviet Union was more ravaged by the purge than the Communist Party itself. Aleksandr Solzhenitsyn, the Nobel Prize–winning novelist, described how no one ever knew what to expect because arrests of the "most varied kind" could come out of nowhere:

> They take you aside in a factory corridor after you have had your pass checked—and you're arrested. They take you from a military hospital with a temperature of 102 . . . and the doctor will not raise a peep about your arrest—just let him try. They take you right off the operating table . . . and drag you off to a cell. . . . Or . . . you try to get information about your mother's sentence, and they give it to you, but it turns out to be a confrontation—and your own arrest. In the Gastronome—the fancy food store—you are invited to the special order department and arrested there. [Only high-ranking people would be in such a store.] You are arrested by a religious pilgrim you have put up for the night "for the sake of Christ." You are arrested by a meterman who has come to read your electric meter. You are arrested by a bicyclist who has run into you on the street, by a railway conductor, a taxi driver, a savings bank teller, a manager of a movie theater. Any one of them can arrest you, and you notice the concealed maroon-colored identification card only when it is too late. (Solzhenitsyn 1973: 10)

from maltreatment. One thing is clear: During the great purge the Soviet regime killed far more Communists than did the Nazi regime in Germany and more Red Army generals than the Germans managed to kill during all of World War II.

The great purge ended as suddenly as it began. By late 1938 it had badly disrupted many aspects of Soviet society, including the economy. Meanwhile, the Soviet Union, along with the rest of Europe, faced the rising threat of Nazi Germany. In November 1938 Stalin removed Yezhov as head of the NKVD (he was later arrested and shot) and replaced him with Beria. Mass arrests and executions ceased, although steady, controlled repression did not. Stalin's control of the Soviet Union was as absolute as any dictator has ever achieved. Only one job related to the purge was left undone, and that was completed in 1940 when an NKVD agent murdered Leon Trotsky in Mexico.

A Totalitarian Regime

The 20th-century term "totalitarianism" refers to rule by a one-party state exercising complete dictatorial control over a society's political, intellectual, cultural, and economic life. The foundations of Soviet totalitarianism lie with the Bolshevik Revolution itself, whose claims on Russian society were total from the start. But those claims were not realized until Stalin's industrialization drive and the subsequent Great Terror. No regime, even with the most modern technology, can ever exercise absolute control over a society, but the Soviet regime under Stalin came closer than any contemporary competitor, even Nazi Germany. By the end of the 1930s there was no way an ordinary citizen could get around the party-state's multiple levels of control. Any places or practices that afforded Soviet citizens some temporary shelter from the state were nothing more than small cracks and crevices in a huge totalitarian block.

Aside from the NKVD and its network of spies and agents, the state controlled all information outlets and access to all benefits and services from jobs to education to medical care. Under the doctrine of socialist realism, which mandated that artists and writers endorse the Soviet Union's "move to socialism," the regime turned culture into a propaganda vehicle for Stalin's policies. History was rewritten to legitimize those policies.

Even the natural sciences had to conform to Stalinist requirements. For example, Stalin supported crackpot theories suggesting the environment could affect heredity that contradicted basic genetic knowledge. Relying on such theories, he insisted that Soviet agronomists could miraculously raise food production by subjecting seeds to extreme conditions before planting. Geneticists who correctly argued that this was impossible paid for their forthrightness with their jobs and sometimes, as in the case of the world-famous Nikolai Vavilov, with their lives.

Meanwhile, staggering inequalities were covered up. While most ordinary citizens did without, Stalin and the Communist Party leadership lived in luxury, often in the same homes that had belonged to Russia's richest families under the czars. Such was the Soviet system in the late 1930s as the storms Stalin had let loose on his country finally abated. The relative calm that followed was deceptive and short. A new storm, this one unleashed on all of Europe and much of the world by Adolf Hitler, was about to begin.

The Soviet Union and World War II

The road to World War II was paved by appeasement and deceit. The appeasement was by the Western democracies, primarily Great Britain and France, who tried to buy Hitler off by caving in to his territorial demands. That policy reached its disgraceful nadir in September 1938 at a conference in the southern German city of Munich, when Britain and France agreed that Germany could annex strategic territory belonging to Czechoslovakia, the only democratic country in eastern or Central Europe, in return for a promise of peace. This inevitably emboldened rather than satisfied Hitler, and in 1939 he seized the rest of Czechoslovakia and made new territorial demands on Poland.

At this point Soviet deceit entered the picture. Stalin knew Hitler had ambitions of seizing vast areas of Soviet territory. He also knew the Soviet Union was not ready for war, especially in the wake of what his purges had done to the military. Stalin's goal was to turn Hitler westward against France, Britain, and the rest of western Europe and buy as much time as he could. Meanwhile, the Soviet Union would rebuild its strength while the Germans and the democracies fought and exhausted each other.

To get the deal he wanted, Stalin openly negotiated with Britain and France for a common defense against Hitler while secretly negotiating with the Germans as well. The result was the notorious Nazi-Soviet pact of August 1939, in which the two sides promised each other neutrality if the other got into a war and divided Poland and most of eastern Europe between themselves. The pact opened the door for Germany to attack Poland, which it did on September 1, 1939, marking the start of World War II in Europe. Britain and France, which after Munich had realized the futility of appeasement and promised to defend Poland, declared

Joseph Stalin, Soviet dictator from the mid-1920s until 1953, at the World War II Teheran (Tehran) Conference in 1943 (Library of Congress)

war on Germany. The Soviet Union meanwhile seized eastern Poland, as specified in the Nazi-Soviet pact, leaving Hitler free to overrun the rest of Poland and then turn his war machine against the European democracies to the west, without fear of being attacked from the east.

For two years Stalin adhered strictly to the terms of the 1939 pact, which included supplying Nazi Germany with raw materials its army needed for its military campaigns against the Western democracies. Meanwhile, the Soviet Union prepared for war. Much was accomplished, but it proved impossible to repair the damage the purges had done to the officer corps in only two years. Worse still, in May and June 1941, despite highly creditable reports from several sources, Stalin refused to believe that Hitler was about to break his treaty and attack the Soviet Union. As a result Soviet troops were totally unprepared for the massive onslaught that began in the morning hours of June 22, 1941, when the German army smashed into the Soviet Union along a 2,000-mile front. Staggered by the news, Stalin left it to Foreign Minister Molotov to break the news to the Soviet people on the radio and a week into the war suffered what apparently was a short-lived nervous breakdown. A series of catastrophic defeats followed as German armies surged toward Moscow, Leningrad, Kiev, and other key targets. They eventually were halted at the very gates of Moscow and Leningrad by a combination of Hitler's military blunders, bitter early winter weather, the sheer scale of the task they faced, decisive action by newly installed Soviet commanders, and countless battlefield heroics by rank-and-file Soviet soldiers. Soviet forces actually recovered some ground around Moscow, but Leningrad, virtually surrounded, was subjected to a 900-day siege that cost the lives of 1 million Soviet citizens, 600,000 of whom died of starvation.

The year 1942 brought new disasters, especially in the Ukraine. Not until the titanic battle of Stalingrad, a city on the Volga River, a horrific struggle that lasted from the summer of 1942 through February 1943, did the tide finally turn. By then millions of Soviet soldiers and civilians were dead and many cities and towns in ruins. And the Germans still occupied vast parts of the country.

Russians call World War II "the great patriotic war" or the "great fatherland war."[*] The savage crimes that German forces perpetrated against the Soviet Union as a whole were exceeded only by the Holocaust, the Nazi campaign of genocide against Europe's Jews. Of the 6 million Jews murdered in the Holocaust, more than 1 million were Soviet citizens, who in the first stages of the invasion were rounded up and murdered by specially recruited German units. Many Soviet citizens who hated Communist rule, especially in the Ukraine, initially welcomed the Germans as liberators, but the brutal treatment they received soon turned most of them against the invaders.

Once Stalin recovered from the shock of the German invasion, he proved to be an able war leader, and the Soviet government effectively mobilized the country's resources and reorganized its armies to take on the German invaders. In December 1941 the United States became part of what British prime minister Winston Churchill called the "Grand Alliance" of his country, the United States, and the Soviet Union, and by 1942 the Soviet Union was receiving massive crucial shipments of war matériel and other lend-lease supplies from the United States. But in the end it was the heroism and ability to endure of Soviet soldiers and civilians alike that broke the back of the German army at Leningrad,

---

[*] *Non-Russian Soviet citizens, under the influence of government propaganda, also spoke of the war in those terms until the Soviet Union collapsed. Certainly that has changed in most of the 14 non-Russian countries that emerged from the former Soviet Union in 1991, although probably not, at least among the older generations, in Ukraine and Belarus.*

Stalingrad, and in massive confrontations like the Battle of Kursk in 1943, the greatest tank battle in history.

The Soviet people displayed their fortitude countless times, enduring enemy brutality alongside recklessly cruel treatment by their own government. The Gulag continued to take its grim toll throughout the war; in addition, on Stalin's orders the Soviet military executed 150,000 of its own soldiers, fully 15 divisions, most of whom had done nothing more than break through German lines after their units were encircled and link up with other Soviet forces or escape from prisoner of war camps. (By comparison, the United States executed a total of 125 soldiers during the war, almost all for violent crimes against civilians or fellow soldiers.) Units made up of former Gulag prisoners, the so-called penal battalions, were used for near suicidal mass frontal assaults against heavily fortified German positions; penal battalions also cleared minefields—by marching through them. Behind those unfortunate soldiers were NKVD troops with orders to shoot anyone who hesitated to

The World War II memorial in Volgograd, the city formerly known as Stalingrad, that was the site of the decisive Soviet victory over invading German forces between August 1942 and February 1943. The statue of "Mother Russia," standing more than 150 feet tall, is the focal point of a series of monuments that begin at the bottom of the hill called Mamayev Kurgan. More than 34,000 Soviet soldiers, a fraction of the total that fell in the battle, are buried on the east slope of the hill at the foot of the statue. (4780322454, 2007. Used under license from ShutterStock, Inc.)

move forward or tried to retreat. Those NKVD troops were also posted behind regular army troops to prevent "unauthorized retreats." By the time the war ended, an estimated 27 million Soviet citizens were dead. Every segment of the population suffered terribly, apart from the Communist Party leadership, which continued to enjoy its luxurious lifestyle amid all the deprivation. Worst hit was the generation whose men bore the brunt of the fighting. At war's end only 38 percent of that age group still alive were males. The war effort was an act of collective bravery and strength that lent new truth to the saying, "Only the Russians can conquer Russia."

Stalin's Last Years, 1945–1953

The Soviet Union emerged from World War II in a paradoxical situation. It was a devastated land. Aside from its staggering human losses, the country had suffered horrendous physical destruction: 70,000 villages, 40,000 miles of railway, and half of all urban housing lay in complete ruin. Internationally, however, the Soviet Union was a superpower second only to the United States. The Red Army stood astride all the countries of eastern Europe and controlled almost half of prewar Germany, including territory more than 100 miles west of Berlin. Communist parties loyal to Moscow were major political forces in France, Italy, and Greece. Never, even after the Napoleonic Wars, did Moscow hold the fate of so much of Europe in its hands.

The Cold War

The main consequence of the westward expansion of Soviet power in Europe was the Cold War. Soviet policy, as Prime Minister Molotov described it many years later, was to "expand the borders of the Fatherland as much as possible." Molotov added, "it seems that Stalin and I coped with this task quite well" (Kort 1998: 13). By 1948 Poland, Romania, Bulgaria, Hungary, and Czechoslovakia had Communist governments under Soviet control. The next year Moscow set up a puppet Communist state, the German Democratic Republic, in the Soviet-controlled parts of the defunct Third Reich.

As the Soviet Union went about imposing Communist regimes on the countries of eastern Europe and turning them into satellites, however, it provoked a defensive reaction by the United States, Britain, and other democratic countries. All feared the extension of Soviet power farther into Europe, especially in light of the dreadful postwar conditions there. Soviet pressure on Turkey and Iran intensified those

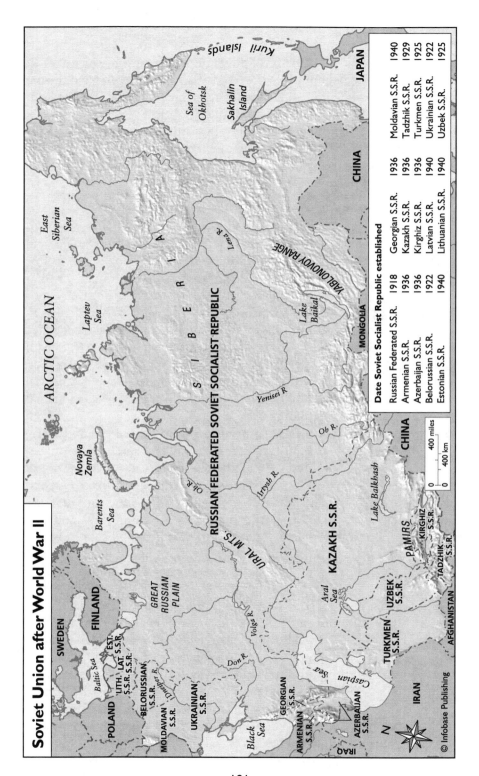

Soviet Union after World War II

ARCTIC OCEAN

Barents Sea

Laptev Sea

East Siberian Sea

Kuril Islands

Sea of Okhotsk

Sakhalin Island

JAPAN

CHINA

Novaya Zemla

S I B E R I A

Lena R.

YABLONOVOY RANGE

Lake Baikal

MONGOLIA

RUSSIAN FEDERATED SOVIET SOCIALIST REPUBLIC

Yenisei R.

Ob R.

Irtysh R.

URAL MTS.

Ob R.

GREAT RUSSIAN PLAIN

KAZAKH S.S.R.

Lake Balkhash

CHINA

SWEDEN

FINLAND

Baltic Sea

EST. S.S.R.

LAT. S.S.R.

LITH. S.S.R.

POLAND

BELORUSSIAN S.S.R.

Dnieper R.

MOLDAVIAN S.S.R.

UKRAINIAN S.S.R.

Don R.

Volga R.

Aral Sea

UZBEK S.S.R.

Black Sea

GEORGIAN S.S.R.

ARMENIAN S.S.R.

AZERBAIJAN S.S.R.

Caspian Sea

TURKMEN S.S.R.

PAMIRS

KIRGHIZ S.S.R.

TADZHIK S.S.R.

AFGHANISTAN

IRAQ

IRAN

N

0   400 miles

0   400 km

© Infobase Publishing

Date Soviet Socialist Republic established			
Russian Federated S.S.R.	1918	Georgian S.S.R.	1936	Moldavian S.S.R.	1940
Armenian S.S.R.	1936	Kazakh S.S.R.	1936	Tadzhik S.S.R.	1929
Azerbaijan S.S.R.	1936	Kirghiz S.S.R.	1936	Turkmen S.S.R.	1925
Belorussian S.S.R.	1922	Latvian S.S.R.	1940	Ukrainian S.S.R.	1922
Estonian S.S.R.	1940	Lithuanian S.S.R.	1940	Uzbek S.S.R.	1925

concerns. The result was the breakdown of the wartime alliance against Germany and the beginning of the Cold War, which intensified during the remainder of Stalin's lifetime and continued for over three-and-a-half decades beyond his death. Moscow would eventually lose that Cold War, and much more in the process, as the stress it placed on the Soviet system contributed to its eventual collapse. Molotov, who lived into his mid-90s, missed that historic event by only five years.

The Lesser Terror: The Last Purges and Plots

During the war the Stalin regime eased certain restraints on the people to win their support and strengthen the war effort. The Russian Orthodox Church was allowed to choose a patriarch for the first time in 30 years. The peasantry was given more freedom to manage their private plots and were paid higher prices for their output. But hopes that these policies would continue after the war were misplaced. Stalin now demanded a rapid economic recovery and set excessive growth targets that once again depressed the standard of living of both industrial workers and peasants. A crash program to develop an atomic bomb, aided by a highly successful espionage effort against the American program during the war, achieved success by 1949. The role of Gulag labor in the economy actually grew, reaching its all-time high in terms of its share of industrial production between 1950 and 1952.

Meanwhile arrests and purges continued, albeit on a much smaller scale than during the 1930s. Immediately after the war hundreds of thousands of people were deported to the Gulag from territories that had been under German control during the war, from the Baltic states in the north to the Ukraine in the south. Hundreds of thousands of returning prisoners of war and people whom the Germans had used as slave laborers met the same fate, all condemned, at a minimum, for being "socially dangerous" because they had been exposed to foreign influences.

Beginning in 1946 the campaign to exorcise foreign influences evolved into a full-fledged purge of intellectuals and an attack on foreign culture—among other things, jazz was banned. This purge was known as the *Zhdanovshchina,* after Andrei Zhdanov, at the time Stalin's favorite and apparently in line to become his successor. Zhdanov's critique of Russian cultural figures included calling the esteemed poet Anna Akhmatova "a whore and a nun." Although Zhdanov died under mysterious circumstances in 1948, and many of his associates were then purged in what is known as the Leningrad Affair, the purge that bore his name continued. The *Zhdanovshchina* included a vicious anti-

Semitic campaign during which many Jewish cultural leaders were murdered and the entire Soviet Jewish community was put at risk. The period 1948 to 1953 is aptly known as the "Black Years of Soviet Jewry."

By 1953 Stalin clearly was planning another purge, this one directed at both the Jewish community and members of his inner circle. The intended victims were spared when he suffered a massive stroke. Stalin died on March 5, 1953. His successors now faced the task of reforming and stabilizing one of the most murderous regimes in human history.

8

SOVIET RUSSIA: REFORM, DECLINE, AND COLLAPSE (1953–1991)

The basic institutions of the Soviet system were conceived and built between the Bolshevik Revolution of November 1917 and Stalin's death in March 1953, a period of slightly more than 35 years. The country's Communist Party leadership then spent another 38 years struggling to reform those institutions to enable the Soviet system to compete with the world's modern capitalist societies. To that end the leaders had to make the economy more efficient and productive, stabilize the Communist political system, and deal with a growing number of serious social problems.

Three leadership teams with three very different approaches tried, and ultimately failed, to cope with these tasks. Between 1953 and 1964, Nikita Khrushchev directed an energetic, albeit often spasmodic and poorly conceived, reform effort. With Khrushchev at the helm the Communist Party leadership ended Stalin's terror while preserving and trying to improve the basic institutions of Soviet life inherited from the Stalin era. From 1964 until 1982, the Communist Party leadership headed by Leonid Brezhnev rejected many of Khrushchev's reforms as potentially destabilizing and relied instead on the status quo, tinkering here and there in the hope that stability was the best solution to the country's problems.

Meanwhile, under both sets of leaders the Soviet Union competed for world influence with the United States and its allies in the Cold War. It was an extremely expensive and burdensome struggle whose inherent dangers were exponentially compounded by the Soviet-American nuclear arms race it produced.

After a short transition period, beginning in 1985 the dynamic new leader Mikhail Gorbachev, having concluded that the Soviet Union's problems were turning into a systemic crisis, returned the party to the path of reform. Gorbachev went far beyond anything Khrushchev had contemplated as he tried to overhaul the Soviet system while preserving its fundamental socialist framework. That radical effort proved to be more than the system could stand, and, rather than fixing what was broken, it unleashed forces that caused the Soviet Union to collapse.

Khrushchev and the Problem of Reform

The issue of reform emerged immediately after Stalin's death, even as the small group who had been the late dictator's top aides and supposedly were going to govern together as a "collective leadership" began their maneuvering in an incipient power struggle. The key players in that struggle were Georgy Malenkov, who seemed to be Stalin's heir apparent and in the days immediately after the dictator's death garnered the key positions of prime minister and senior party secretary; Lavrenty Beria, the secret police chief and therefore the most feared by his colleagues; Vyacheslav Molotov, who had served Stalin for long periods as both foreign minister and prime minister; and Nikita Khrushchev, a tough, efficient party boss who at different points in his career had headed its organizations in the Ukraine and Moscow.

Yet even as they schemed against each other, Stalin's successors understood that they could not rule as Stalin had. During Stalin's continuous waves of terror—greater or lesser—no one in the Soviet Union had been safe, not even members of the Communist Party elite. Even they were at risk of losing everything at a single stroke. Governance by terror therefore had to end. That in turn meant something had to be done to improve the lives of the Soviet people as a whole lest popular discontent lead to instability that could threaten the entire regime.

The early moves in the struggle for power took place within the context of these imperatives and therefore in effect brought about two key reforms in Soviet life. First, the new leadership promised the people an improved standard of living. Within a month, by lowering prices on a variety of foods and consumer goods, it took a small first step to deliver on that promise. Second, the leadership as a body made political changes to prevent any one of them from accumulating absolute power. This in turn assured the Soviet Union's new leader he would not be able to rule by terror, which had left no Soviet citizen safe, not even top party leaders. Thus within days of Stalin's death Malenkov, the prime minister, was forced to give up his position as senior party secretary, a post, soon to be called "first secretary," that went to Khrushchev.

Perhaps more important, in June 1953 Khrushchev organized a coup in which the dreaded and hated Beria was arrested and the secret police purged. In December Beria and several of his top aides were executed. The result was that for the first time since Stalin's rise to power, the secret police, reorganized in 1954 as the KGB (Committee of State Security), was brought under the supervision of the party's Central Committee and thereby under the control of the party leadership as a whole, where it remained for the remainder of the Soviet Union's existence. That crucial change did much to guarantee that the Soviet Union would never again be ruled by an all-powerful dictator. In the future the Soviet leader would be the head of the Communist Party oligarchy, its most powerful member to be sure, but still a politician dependent on the support of his colleagues to remain in power.

With Beria out of the way only two contenders remained for the top spot in the Soviet political hierarchy—Khrushchev and Malenkov. In early 1955 Malenkov resigned as prime minister, and while he remained a member of the Communist Party leadership, Khrushchev clearly now was in charge.

The party leadership meanwhile had continued with reforms and efforts to improve life for ordinary citizens, including paying collective farmers more for their crops and reducing taxes on their private plots. An amnesty announced in March 1953 (before Beria's arrest, and actually his idea) had led to the quick release of about 1.5 million Gulag inmates (out of about 5.5 million), although most of those released were common criminals and only a smattering were political prisoners. By 1955, however, the number of released political prisoners had risen to 90,000. In 1954 Khrushchev launched a massive program to grow grain in the steppe region of central Asia, his so-called virgin lands program, a risky undertaking given the unreliable rainfall in the region but yet another sign of his determination to raise the country's standard of living as quickly as possible. In foreign affairs, during 1953 the new Soviet leadership moved to ease tensions with the West by helping to arrange an armistice that ended the Korean War. Other measures included a summit meeting with American, French, and British leaders in mid-1955 in Geneva, the first such meeting since the end of World War II.

These were all small steps, and not all of them were supported by everyone in the top leadership. In fact the entire issue of reform was controversial. From the start the burning question was how much reform could the system stand? Everyone was glad to see Beria gone, and no one wanted a return to Stalin's terror, but that was as far as the consensus went. The great fear was that the reform process could run out of control and threaten the power of the party leadership, or even the rule of the Communist Party itself. The specter of runaway reform loomed ominously as early as mid-1953 during an anti-Soviet outbreak in East Germany and appeared again during three major uprisings in the Gulag during 1953 and 1954. These events placed additional obstacles in the path of those who believed in further, more substantial reform.

The most vigorous proponent of reform was Khrushchev. Born into a peasant family in 1894, Khrushchev had labored as a mechanic in the coal-mining industry before joining the Communist Party in 1918. Over the next quarter century he worked, and clawed, his way up the party hierarchy. Although hampered by his limited formal education and crude manner, Khrushchev was highly intelligent. His interests ranged well beyond politics, from the techniques of modern farming to the technology of advanced machinery, and as he once told the British ambassador to the USSR, to rereading Tolstoy's *War and Peace* every year.

Like Malenkov, Molotov, and his other colleagues, Khrushchev had served Stalin and carried out many of his most oppressive policies. Unlike them, however, he had not remained isolated from ordinary people, cut off from the realities of daily Soviet life by high Kremlin walls and legions of guards. As boss of the Ukraine and Moscow, Khrushchev continually visited collective farms and factories and knew firsthand how the people lived. During World War II he had served in the army as a political officer (with the rank of general) and had been the horrified witness to the consequences of Stalin's methods when millions of Soviet citizens welcomed the Germans as liberators.

A true and passionate believer in the virtues and superiority of communism and an impatient man determined to see those virtues benefit the Soviet people, Khrushchev was committed to implementing real change. He also understood that the single greatest barrier to reform was Stalin's reputation, which provided legitimacy to those opposed to change. After all, if Stalin was everything a generation of Soviet propaganda claimed he was, surely the institutions and policies he left behind did not require serious modification. His reputation therefore had to be cut down to size. Khrushchev also wanted to consolidate his place at the top of the Soviet hierarchy, which as of 1955 was hardly secure. By early 1956 the confluence of those objectives and the nature of the obstacles he faced led him to a policy known as de-Stalinization.

Khrushchev's Secret Speech and Its Repercussions

Khrushchev launched de-Stalinization in 1956 at the Communist Party's 20th Party Congress, its first since Stalin's death. His vehicle was a dramatic four-and-one-half-hour speech, called the "secret speech" because it was given in a closed session from which outside observers were barred. Of course, its contents soon became widely known, and they were shocking, at least to Khrushchev's audience in Moscow, for whom Stalin had been infallible. Khrushchev accused Stalin of being a mass murderer who had persecuted thousands of loyal Communists. Included in Khrushchev's long list of Stalin's Communist victims were the grim statistics from the 17th Party Congress of 1934, the majority of whose delegates and Central Committee members Stalin eliminated during the great purge. Stalin's blunders during World War II likewise had cost the Soviet Union huge numbers of lives, Khrushchev bitterly noted. Beyond that Stalin had violated party norms by promoting a "personality cult" that glorified him beyond recognition.

The speech, to put it mildly, was an eye-opener for the stunned delegates, but Khrushchev left out as much as he put in. He said nothing about Stalin's *non*-Communist victims, including the millions of peasants victimized by collectivization. In fact nothing Stalin did before 1934, all of which Khrushchev had supported as creating the basis for socialism in the Soviet Union, was subject to criticism. Instead Khrushchev's message was that the Soviet system, while in need of reform, was fundamentally sound, as was the Communist Party Stalin had led for a quarter of a century. Of course, leaders like Malenkov and Molotov, who stood closest to Stalin during the period of the late dictator's most savage crimes and blunders—closer than had Khrushchev—were tarred by the speech, even if only indirectly. And that also served the politician who delivered it.

The problem, as Khrushchev's rivals feared, was that the speech and de-Stalinization itself could lead to trouble when people sought more change than Khrushchev was willing to permit. The most serious difficulties occurred in Eastern Europe, first in Poland and then in Hungary, two countries that had little love for either communism or Russia. In Poland riots and demonstrations between June and October 1956 forced Khrushchev and his Kremlin colleagues to accept a change in the Polish Communist leadership. That and subsequent reforms, including the dismantling of the hated collective farms, brought order to Poland.

In Hungary a new Communist leadership was not enough to pacify the population. As in Poland protests against poor conditions and the local Communist rulers brought a reformist party leadership to

Nikita Khrushchev, Soviet leader from 1953 to 1964, at the UN General Assembly in 1960
(Library of Congress)

power, but that only encouraged the Hungarians who wanted to see their country enjoy genuine freedom. Demands for reform turned into a full-fledged revolt against Communist rule and Soviet control. The fateful step was taken when Imre Nagy, a party official with a reputation as a reformer and the newly installed prime minister, announced that Hungary would no longer be a one-party dictatorship and was leaving the Communist bloc to become a neutral nation, like neighboring Austria. That precipitated massive Soviet military intervention. Thousands of Hungarians were killed in the fighting that followed, while more than 200,000 fled to the West before the revolt was crushed. Nagy and several colleagues, tricked into leaving the Yugoslav embassy where they had taken refuge, were brought to Moscow and eventually executed.

The backlash of the Hungarian revolution nearly toppled Khrushchev. In June 1957 Malenkov, Molotov, fellow Stalin loyalist Lazar Kaganovich, and several other party leaders joined together in a plot to remove Khrushchev from office. The plotters actually had a majority on the Presidium, the party's top decision-making body (the former Politburo). But Khrushchev, insisting on following party rules, brought the issue to the Central Committee, the body to which the Presidium was technically responsible and where his supporters held sway. A tumultuous eight-day meeting followed at which Malenkov, Molotov, and Kaganovich were accused of direct responsibility in the unjust arrests and murder of fellow Communists under Stalin.

As the most recent and comprehensive biographer of Khrushchev has noted, the June 1957 Central Committee meeting went much further than Khrushchev's 1956 secret speech and was "the closest Stalin's henchmen ever came to a day of reckoning" (Taubman 2003: 323). The details were kept secret from the Soviet public, which was informed only that members of what was labeled the "anti-party" group had been dismissed from their posts. That sounded a lot like Stalin's old politics, but Khrushchev's victory included a far more important political reform: This time all the losers in the power struggle survived. It was Stalin's murderous politics that, finally, was dead. While consigned to political oblivion, Malenkov, Molotov, and Kaganovich—the latter tearfully phoned Khrushchev begging for his life—were given minor administrative positions and later allowed to retire on pensions.

In October 1961 public insult would be added to the injury of political defeat when Khrushchev denounced Stalin in open session at the Communist Party's 22nd Congress. He and various other speakers linked Malenkov, Molotov, and Kaganovich to Stalin's crimes. After the congress all were expelled from the Communist Party. Yet the three, who themselves had cut short so many lives, lived to ripe old ages and had the pleasure of seeing their nemesis Khrushchev removed from power seven years later. They all also outlived him, in relatively comfortable retirement, by many years.

Khrushchev at the Helm

Like Stalin's politics and the "anti-party" group, the Gulag met its end during 1956 and 1957, when most of its camps and other facilities were closed down and the great majority of their inmates released.[*] Millions of Stalin's victims finally returned home, reemerging in the words of poet Olga Berggolts as if "from the bottom of the sea" (quoted in Cohen 1982: 91). Along with millions of joyful reunions their unexpected return from the Gulag netherworld also produced uncounted awkward and painful encounters, a situation aptly described by the poet Anna Akhmatova when she wrote, "Two Russias are eyeball to eyeball—those who were imprisoned and those who put them there" (quoted in Cohen 1982: 27).

Meanwhile, Khrushchev, one of those who had "put them there," doggedly pursued his eclectic reform agenda. It was a daunting list that ranged across the spectrum of Soviet life and required far more resources than were available to the Soviet leadership. For example, according to the Sixth Five-Year Plan approved by the 20th Party Congress, the Soviet Union would dramatically raise production in heavy industry and at the same time increase the availability of consumer goods. Khrushchev added to his burden of promises in 1957 by announcing that within four years the Soviet Union would match the United States, the world's best-fed country, in the output of milk, meat, and butter.

Where would the government find the resources to deliver on these promises? One potential source was the country's bloated military establishment. But, even though between 1955 and 1957 the Khrushchev regime had demobilized more than 2 million troops—leaving the Soviet Union with a still formidable military numbering 3.6 million—any savings were eaten up by the soaring costs of developing and deploying technologically advanced weapons such as ballistic missiles and nuclear submarines. In more of a hurry with each passing year and

---

[*] The Gulag's formal dissolution, according to a decree by the Ministry of Internal Affairs, took place in January 1960.

burdened by demands he could not ignore from interests he called the "steel eaters," Khrushchev was driven to resort to questionable methods that often failed and in the process wasted precious resources that should have been put to better use.

Still there were significant successes. There was a slow but steady increase in the earnings of state employees and an increase in the minimum wage. Collective farmers, who technically did not work for the state, also benefited from increased wage rates. There was also a dramatic increase in the size and availability of old-age pensions, enough to improve the lives of millions of elderly people. An effort was made, albeit only partially successful, to extend high-quality education to the children of ordinary workers and peasants, and a crash program to build new housing provided better quarters to more than 100 million Soviet citizens who had lived in cramped, dreary conditions under Stalin.

All of these efforts were flawed—Khrushchev's prefabricated housing often deteriorated very quickly, for example—but they considerably improved the lives of the people. In a country that had claimed to be the world's pioneer in the building of socialism, they helped reduce the extreme inequalities that pervaded Soviet society during the Stalin years.

A model of Sputnik, the world's first artificial satellite, launched in October 1957, which put the Soviet Union ahead of the United States in the space race (Associated Press/Zentralbild Picture Service)

The most spectacular success of the Khrushchev era was in the area of rocketry and space exploration. Khrushchev strongly supported the development of ballistic missiles, which he believed represented both the technological wave of the future and a way to reduce military expenditures, since missiles could replace expensive aircraft and the personnel needed to fly and service them. Of particular interest were intercontinental ballistic missiles (ICBMs), which with a range of more than 5,000 miles could be launched from the Soviet Union and reach the United States with their atomic warheads.

It turned out there was another benefit to ICBMs: Modified versions of those huge rockets could be used for space exploration. Thus on October 4, 1957, the Soviet Union launched *Sputnik,* the world's first artificial satellite. The launching thrilled Khrushchev and his countrymen and shocked the United States. Then a Soviet series of space firsts culminated in April 1961 when Soviet test pilot Yury Gagarin was launched into space and became the first man to orbit the earth. Khrushchev was ecstatic. At a lavish diplomatic reception honoring the event Khrushchev spoke with immense pride—in some ways speaking as much about himself as his country—about how "once illiterate" Russia, dismissed by others as a "barbaric country," had become the world leader in space (quoted in Taubman 2003: 492).

Gagarin's flight, it turned out, was also the pinnacle of Khrushchev's political fortunes, which by 1961 were running afoul of a growing number of problems. One ill-conceived reform was the decentralization of economic decision making and management, introduced in 1957 shortly before the showdown with the anti-party group. Khrushchev abolished more than 140 central government ministries and replaced them with 105 local planning units, a change that did nothing to improve efficiency and led instead to confusion and competition for resources among the various units, each of which cared primarily about itself rather than the Soviet Union as a whole. It did not help when the number of these units was reduced to 47 in 1962.

Nor did efforts succeed to make the collective farms operate more efficiently. Early in his tenure Khrushchev had reduced taxes on the peasantry's private plots, a policy that both improved their meager standard of living and increased the food supply for the population at large. But several years later Khrushchev turned against his own reform, in part because private farming, even on a small scale, violated his Marxist principles. When Khrushchev applied fiscal and other types of pressure to make the peasants pay more attention to their collective farm responsibilities as opposed to their private plots, the main result was reduced production from those plots and less food for the country as a whole.

The virgin lands program had mixed results. Good weather in 1957 and 1958 led to bumper harvests, which strengthened Khrushchev politically. But poor weather in 1959 reduced the grain harvest, both in the virgin lands and in the Soviet Union's traditional agricultural regions. In 1962 food shortages and price increases led to a large protest demonstration in the city of Novocherkassk that turned into a massacre

SERGEI KOROLEV (1907–1966): SOVIET ROCKET GENIUS

Sergei Korolev's life in many ways stands as a symbol for what was wrong with the Soviet Union. Born in the Ukraine, Korolev trained as an aeronautical engineer and quickly established himself as one of his country's leading experts in the development of liquid-fueled rockets. Then, like so many other scientists, he was arrested during the peak purge years of 1937–38, allegedly for selling information to the Germans. He ended up in one of the worst parts of the Gulag, the dreaded Kolyma gold mines in eastern Siberia, the "land of the white death," which became a mass graveyard for countless tens of thousands of prisoners. Korolev was saved from almost certain death by the intervention of Andrei Tupolev, one of the Soviet Union's leading aircraft designers. Tupolev was himself a Gulag prisoner but in one of the Gulag's special design bureaus, where inmates, all highly trained scientists and engineers, lived in tolerable conditions while working on advanced scientific and weapons projects for the Soviet state. Tupolev requested Korolev's transfer to his facility. Korolev was finally released from prison in 1944 to serve as part of a team investigating German rocket technology.

After Stalin's death Korolev focused on the development of Soviet ICBMs, and by August 1957 his design team had built and successfully tested the R-7, the world's first operational ICBM, with a range of more than 4,000 miles. But Korolev's passion was space flight, not weapons of war, and he used his skill at bureaucratic infighting to divert resources to that end, despite opposition from powerful officials whose only concern was the military. It also was his good fortune

when troops fired on demonstrators, who were carrying portraits of Lenin, killing 26 and wounding almost 90.

In 1963 dry weather and strong winds turned the virgin lands region of central Asia into a vast dustbowl, largely because of agricultural methods that did not take proper account of the semi-arid climate. The drought also hit central Russia, the Ukraine, and other traditional grain-producing areas. No longer able to impose Stalin-type hardships on the people, the Soviet leadership was forced to endure the humiliation of buying almost 11 million tons of grain from several capitalist nations, including—adding insult to injury—almost 2 million tons from the United States.

that the mighty R-7 could not only propel nuclear warheads thousands of miles but also had the power to lift satellites into space. On October 4, 1957, an R-7 launched the world's first artificial satellite, *Sputnik* (companion), into space. A series of dramatic firsts followed, all based on the R-7 or modified versions of that rocket, including the first dog in space and the three unmanned Luna missions in 1959 that reached the moon (respectively a flyby, landing, and an orbiting that took the first photographs of the side of the moon that faces away from the earth). In 1961 a modified R-7 with improved upper stages launched the first human into space—Yuri Gagarin, who completed one orbit before returning safely to earth. Despite access to far fewer resources, both material and scientific, than his counterparts in the United States, Korolev put the Soviet Union into the lead in space flight and kept it there into the mid-1960s.

It is unlikely, given America's technological superiority in numerous key areas, that the Soviet Union could have won the race to the moon once President John F. Kennedy committed the United States to achieving that prize. For that Korolev needed a much bigger rocket, a huge vehicle he named the N-1. The N-1 never flew. Whatever chance the Soviets had of winning the race to the moon ended in January 1966 when Korolev died from botched surgery. Ironically, because of his country's obsession with secrecy, the man known in life as the "Chief Designer" received the public recognition he deserved only after his death, beginning with a hero's funeral and burial in the Kremlin Wall.

Korolev's legacy has lived on. As the 21st century began every one of the Soviet and (since 1991) Russian manned space flights had taken place aboard launch vehicles based on his R-7. Direct descendants of the R-7 are still lifting payloads into space and are considered the most reliable space launch vehicles in service.

Khrushchev and Culture

The Stalin era was a dark and destructive age in the history of Russian culture, by far the most repressive since Muscovite times. It is to Khrushchev's credit that under his leadership that terrible era came to an end. To be sure, there was nothing like the cultural freedom enjoyed in the democratic West, nor, for that matter, did Soviet artists, writers, and musicians have the freedom of expression their counterparts enjoyed in Imperial Russia during the 19th and early 20th centuries. The Communist Party of the Soviet Union still determined the limits on artistic expression. But those limits became far less restrictive, and artists who exceeded them did so at the risk of their careers, not, as was the case under Stalin, their freedom or lives. At the same time, it was not always clear what those limits were, as Khrushchev extended or limited them according to the political pressures he was under from conservative forces within Soviet ruling circles or, sometimes, according to his own arbitrary personal agenda or motives.

Soviet cultural life began to revive, albeit haltingly, almost immediately after Stalin's death, a period that received its unofficial title from a novel called *The Thaw* by Ilya Ehrenburg (1891–1967), a talented novelist and journalist who during his long career had shown occasional flashes of independence while serving mainly as an apologist for Stalin. The pace of change quickened in 1956 after the 20th Party Congress, most notably with the publication of Vladimir Dudintsev's *Not by Bread Alone,* an exposé of party corruption. The upheavals in Poland and Hungary in the fall of 1956 led to a crackdown that put Dudintstev under a cloud and culminated in the persecution of Boris Pasternak (1890–1960), one of the many pre-revolutionary poets silenced during the Stalin years.

Pasternak ran afoul of the authorities in 1957 when he allowed his novel *Dr. Zhivago* to be published abroad. The book focused on the individual's fate during times of upheaval and raised serious questions about the Bolshevik Revolution. Making matters worse, *Dr. Zhivago* was both a commercial and a critical success, winning its author the Nobel Prize in literature in 1958. A torrent of official abuse poured down on Pasternak, who, it turned out, had only three more years to live.

But the cultural genie was out of the Stalinist bottle, and Khrushchev—whose fundamental commitment to de-Stalinization did not change—did not want to imprison the genie in that vessel again. By 1959 Dudintsev was restored to good standing.

During the mid-1950s a youthful group of talented poets came of age, among them Yevgeny Yevtushenko, an admirer of Pasternak. In the decades to follow Yevtushenko would use his art and his international celebrity status to extend the limits of reform; he walked a fine line between dissidence, which the authorities would tolerate, and outright dissent, which they would not. In 1961 Yevtushenko published "Babi Yar," a stunning, emotional denunciation of Soviet anti-Semitism. In 1962 came "The Heirs of Stalin," eerie and ominous, which warned that despite the reforms since 1953 Stalin's heirs were still alive and powerful and that a Stalinist reaction was therefore possible. That same year Khrushchev personally intervened to permit the publication of Solzhenitsyn's *A Day in the Life of Ivan Denisovich,* a novella that became a literary bombshell by exposing the horrors of Stalin's labor camps to the general Soviet population as never before.

Khrushchev's tolerance for artistic expression was fickle as well as erratic, and it most definitely did not extend to modern art. In December 1962, while visiting an exhibition of standard socialist realist art in the Manezh Exhibition Hall near the Kremlin, Khrushchev was directed to an exhibition of modern art elsewhere in the building. It was not a serendipitous detour but rather a scheme by conservatives who wanted to enlist the first secretary in their effort to curb unconventional artistic expression. Khrushchev did not disappoint them, at least in terms of his initial reaction. Among his printable remarks, which included threats against the artists, was the observation that a "a donkey could do better with its tail" (Medvedev 1984: 217).

But Khrushchev's response to the exhibit went further, and in doing so showed that times truly had changed. After his initial outburst the Soviet premier demanded to meet the person in charge of the exhibition. That happened to be a tough former paratrooper turned sculptor named Ernst Neizvestny. In spite of what he later called "the fear in the air," Neizvestny did not back down in the face of harsh criticism, a daring act that would have been inconceivable under Stalin, and bluntly told Khrushchev that he knew nothing about art. The two men argued back and forth until Khrushchev ended the conversation with words that showed how far the Soviet Union still had to go, but also with a simple gesture that revealed how far it had come. As Neizvestny later recalled, "My talk with Khrushchev ended like this. He said, 'You're an interesting man—I enjoy people like you—but inside you there are an angel and a devil. If the devil wins, we'll crush you. If the angel wins, we'll do all we can to help you.' And he gave me his hand" (Medvedev 1984: 218).

Foreign Affairs and the Cuban Missile Crisis

Immediately after Stalin's death his successors moved to relax tensions with the West. Over the next three years that approach evolved into what Khrushchev called "peaceful coexistence," a doctrine that repudiated the assumption of the Lenin and Stalin eras that the struggle between capitalism and communism would be settled by war. It was a logical and an essential step in a world of nuclear weapons. But "peaceful coexistence" did *not* mean normal relations, or even coexistence as that term is normally understood. The struggle to spread communism would continue. It would be peaceful insofar as it directly involved the nuclear superpowers. But in the developing world of Asia, Africa, and Latin America, the Soviets would continue to promote what Khrushchev called "wars of national liberation" to help overthrow pro-Western regimes and bring Communists to power.

The continued commitment to expanding Communist power led to periods of tension and several crises during Khrushchev's tenure in power. One source of continual tension was Berlin, the former German capital. Like Germany itself Berlin had been divided into four Allied occupation zones at the end of World War II. By 1949 the United States, Britain, and France had combined their zones into the German Federal Republic (West Germany) while the Soviets set up the Communist German Democratic Republic (East Germany). In 1955 West Germany became a member of the Western military alliance the North Atlantic Treaty Organization (NATO), while East Germany entered the Soviet-dominated Warsaw Pact. Paralleling that arrangement, Berlin, which lay deep inside the Soviet zone and therefore after 1949 inside East Germany, was divided into East Berlin and West Berlin.

The tense and awkward arrangement led to several of the major crises of the Cold War. By 1961 the most urgent Berlin issue facing the Soviets and the East German regime was the huge flow of refugees to West Berlin, especially young people seeking a better life. Berlin was the escape route of choice because, unlike the fortified border between the two Germanys, there was no physical barrier between the two Berlins. By 1961 the exodus had reached thousands of people per week. It was at once a constant humiliation for both East Germany and the Soviet Union and a potentially crippling loss of skilled manpower for the East German regime. With Soviet approval the East Germans responded in August by building a barbed-wire fence through the center of the city that quickly was supplanted by a concrete structure that came to be known as the Berlin Wall. The Wall did its job, stopping the flight of East Germans to freedom. It also became a symbol of both the Cold War and the inability of Soviet-style communism to compete successfully with Western democratic capitalism in providing the things that most people, at least in Europe, seemed to value.

Following the relative success of the Berlin Wall, Khrushchev blundered into the disaster of the Cuban Missile Crisis. By 1962, along with a host of domestic concerns, the Soviet leader had to contend with serious foreign policy problems. Most urgent was the Soviet Union's military inferiority vis-à-vis the United States, especially in the area of ICBMs. The United States had several times more ICBMs than the Soviet Union, the American missiles were technologically more advanced, Washington was deploying new missiles at a faster rate than Moscow, and the newer Soviet missiles were plagued with technical problems. Under sharp criticism from hard-liners within the party leadership for slighting military needs in favor of civilian economic priorities, Khrushchev looked for a way to redress the military imbalance with the United States quickly and cheaply without waiting for a new generation of Soviet missiles to come on line.

At the same time Moscow was concerned about a newfound ally, Fidel Castro, the Communist dictator of Cuba who had come to power in a revolution in 1959. The United States had already mounted an unsuccessful invasion of Cuba in 1961 using Cuban exiles, and both Castro and Khrushchev expected the Americans to make another effort to bring down the Communist regime only 90 miles from Florida.

In the spring of 1962 Khrushchev came up with a plan to solve both foreign policy problems at once. He would secretly place Soviet medium-range (1,200 miles) and intermediate-range (2,500 miles) nuclear missiles in Cuba. With that one stroke Khrushchev believed Moscow could partially redress its nuclear imbalance with Washington and protect Castro and his Communist regime from another U.S. invasion.

The result was the Cuban Missile Crisis of October 1962. In the short run it brought the world to the brink of nuclear war; in the long run it undermined Khrushchev at home and contributed to his fall from power two years later. The Soviet plan was reckless. Ignoring cautionary advice from a few of his more independent-minded advisers, Khrushchev disregarded both the strong possibility the missiles would be discovered before they were deployed—the United States had Cuba under constant surveillance—and the likelihood that President John F. Kennedy would react strongly to stop a deployment that violated Washington's most fundamental security imperatives. The plan also had a curious element of unreality. One proposal for hiding the missiles after they were installed called for them to be covered by palm fronds to make them look like palm trees. However dubious that idea, it rested on the equally unrealistic assumption that well before these weapons reached their launching pads the United States would fail to detect and be alerted by dozens of Soviet ships docking in Cuba laden with huge suspicious cargoes and then not notice 80-foot-long transport vehicles lumbering along narrow rural roads.

The Soviet plan unraveled in mid-October when U.S. intelligence planes discovered construction sites before any missiles could be made operational. President Kennedy then ordered a blockade around Cuba to prevent further Soviet military matériel from reaching the island and demanded that the missiles already there be withdrawn. For almost two weeks the superpowers faced each other at the nuclear brink until, as U.S. secretary of state Dean Rusk put it, the Soviets "blinked." They had little choice in the face of overwhelming American military superiority, both strategically and in the skies above and seas around Cuba. The face-saving formula that resolved the crisis called for all Soviet missiles to be removed in return for a public American promise not to invade Cuba. The United States also secretly promised to remove its intermediate nuclear missiles from Turkey, which Kennedy had planned to do in any case since they were obsolete.

The End of the Khrushchev Era

The resolution of the Cuban Missile Crisis gave Castro the security he needed. In 1963 two important agreements provided both the United States and the Soviet Union with small measures of additional security: a direct "hot line" teletype between the White House and the Kremlin to improve communications during any future crisis, and a partial nuclear test-ban treaty (signed by Great Britain as well) that banned all atmospheric nuclear tests.

But Khrushchev himself was vulnerable. Dissatisfaction with his leadership within top Communist Party circles, already widespread, mounted. A second round of de-Stalinization that had followed the 22nd Party Congress included the wholesale renaming of places and things named after Stalin—most notably, the city of Stalingrad was now to be Volgograd—but little else. Khrushchev's efforts at further reforms, including a program to divide the Communist Party in half—one branch responsible for industry and the other for agriculture—produced nothing but confusion and further eroded his base of support. By the fall of 1964 even some of his closest aides and former protégés were plotting against him. They prepared carefully, both in the Presidium and in the Central Committee, and in October 1964 Khrushchev was removed from power. A terse announcement informed the Soviet people of his "request" to be relieved from his duties because of ill health. He was allowed a comfortable retirement, albeit in obscurity—all public mention of him stopped—and under constant surveillance by his successors.

The Khrushchev era was an amalgam of failure and success. His reforms did not make the centralized Soviet economy an efficient competitor of the economies of the Western democracies. As a staunch Leninist Khrushchev made no effort to modify the one-party dictatorship that ruled over the Soviet Union. Yet he played a pivotal role in removing the most unbearable parts of the Stalinist inheritance. The secret police terror was ended, the Gulag was dissolved, the country's standard of living improved considerably, and the range of permissible cultural expression was broadened significantly. By 1964 life in the Soviet Union was both quantitatively and, more important, qualitatively better than it had been in 1953. Whatever his faults and failures, Nikita Khrushchev had served his country far better than most of Russia's leaders, whatever their titles or claims to fame.

Khrushchev's career probably was best summed up by Neizvestny, who was informed nine years after the famous confrontation at the Manezh art exhibit that Khrushchev's will had designated him to create his tombstone. Neizvestny responded brilliantly with a bronze bust surrounded by two interlocking marble columns, one black and one white, respectively, symbolizing the negative and positive aspects of Khrushchev's career.

This small episode in Soviet history contains another touch of irony. Because he was so disliked by those who deposed and then succeeded him, Khrushchev was denied the honor of internment in the Kremlin wall with other deceased Communist Party dignitaries. The bust over his grave therefore stands several miles distant in the cemetery of the beautiful Novodevichy Monastery, coincidentally the final resting place of many of Russia's greatest writers, musicians, and painters, among them Gogol, Chekhov, Scriabin, and Serov. When one considers each group's respective contributions to Russian life, it seems fair to conclude that Khrushchev, on balance, more appropriately belongs among the artists in the Novodevichy cemetery than with the Communist functionaries whose ashes are stuffed in and alongside the Kremlin Wall.

Brezhnev and the Era of Stability

The leadership team that succeeded Khrushchev was headed by Leonid Brezhnev, a protégé of the deposed first secretary who had turned against his benefactor. Moderate and careful but also a skillful bureaucratic infighter, the bland Brezhnev contrasted well with Khrushchev, at least as far as the Communist Party leadership was concerned. The new team included Alexei Kosygin, an economic specialist as prime minister; Nikolai Podgorny, Brezhnev's main rival for the top spot who soon would be pushed aside; and Mikhail Suslov, the party's chief ideologist and kingmaker.

Two key points defined this team. First, even though Brezhnev emerged as its most powerful member and retained that position for

18 years, the Communist Party leadership operated as an oligarchy. Whoever was at the top was there because he satisfied the interests of the most powerful branches of the party bureaucracy. Not only were Stalin's personal dictatorship and terrorist methods now a part of the past, so were Khrushchev's radical, haphazard attempts at reform that often threatened the positions or comforts of other top leaders or their clients. Second, the main value that governed all policy initiatives was the stability and security of the existing system and those—in particular the top party leadership—who benefited from it.

It was acceptable to tinker with the system, including the economy, to make things work better, but comprehensive reforms that might threaten job security or lead the regime into uncharted waters that might prove unpredictable and therefore destabilizing were out of the question. In foreign policy the same caution dictated a dual approach: a military buildup to match the overall strength of the United States, alongside efforts to improve relations with Washington and its allies. The most important objective with regard to improved relations with the West was a nuclear arms limitation treaty to help prevent nuclear war.

A third element was also crucial to understanding how the Soviet Union evolved during Brezhnev's long tenure, which lasted until his death in 1982. Because the Soviet leadership with its total commitment to stability was unwilling to undertake reforms that might have resolved key economic, political, and social problems, those problems festered and grew worse. Over time stability turned to stagnation, and by the early 1980s stagnation was evolving into a systemic crisis, a chain of events Brezhnev and his colleagues ignored. By then they themselves were in the process of departing from the scene, but their inaction had put their country and society at risk.

The first order of business for the Brezhnev regime was retrenchment—reversing several of Khrushchev's policies it considered ill-conceived or dangerous. Within a month of taking control the new leadership restored the unity of the Communist Party. In the fall of 1965 it abolished Khrushchev's decentralized economic planning units and restored the central ministerial system of managing the economy. An important Khrushchev promise also went by the board. In 1961 he had told the Soviet people that the "foundations of communism" would be laid by 1980. In its place the new leadership assured the people that they were living in the age of "developed" or "mature" socialism, a satisfactory and prosperous state of affairs that was permanent rather than transitory and therefore required no significant changes or improvements.

In cultural policy another area of retrenchment occurred. In 1965 two prominent Soviet writers, Andrei Sinyavsky and Yuli Daniel, were arrested for publishing essays and works of fiction abroad that were critical of the Soviet system. Their writings had been published for almost a decade under the respective pseudonyms of Abram Tertz and Nikolai Arzhak. These arrests were disturbing to the Soviet literary and intellectual community because the "crime" involved was nothing more than writing, not any overt act of defiance. At their trials Sinyavsky and Daniel courageously refused to admit any guilt; they were nonetheless convicted and sentenced, respectively, to seven and five years at hard labor.

A revealing sign of the times was the end of Khrushchev's de-Stalinization campaign. In 1965 Stalin's wartime leadership, which Khrushchev had criticized so severely, was praised by a number of generals in their memoirs. Some party leaders, concerned that de-Stalinization had undermined the party's authority, wanted a more extensive rehabilitation of the late dictator at the 23rd Party Congress in 1966. That did not occur, largely because memories of Stalin's terror were still vivid and an extensive rehabilitation therefore remained controversial among

Leonid Brezhnev, Soviet leader from 1964 to 1982, and U.S. president Richard Nixon, signing a nuclear arms limitation treaty in 1973 at the White House (Associated Press/STF)

party leaders. The congress did revive two important political terms from the Stalin era: The party leader (first secretary) again became its general secretary, and its top policy-making body (the Presidium) again became the Politburo. It says a great deal about Brezhnev's approach to governing that reviving those two terms was one of the few things the congress actually did.

When Brezhnev and his colleagues assumed power, they understood that one Khrushchev policy they had to retain was the effort to raise the overall standard of living. The economy became one of their most urgent concerns. While heavy industry and the military continued to hold primacy of place, other sectors received attention and additional resources. In agriculture they eased restrictions on private plots and livestock and expanded the markets where peasants could sell their wares. The government also increased investments in agriculture, giving the collective farms more machinery and better infrastructure; raised prices paid to the collective farms for deliveries to the state; and provided peasants with both a minimum wage and retirement pensions. As a result grain production rose significantly. So did the production of fruit, vegetables, milk, and meat, much of which came from the collective farmers' private plots and livestock. Overall the Soviet diet improved in both quantity and quality.

The government also dramatically increased the production and availability of other consumer goods. By the early 1980s the vast majority of Soviet households owned refrigerators and television sets, and more than half had washing machines. They could afford to buy these and other products because real wages rose 50 percent between 1965 and 1977. Soviet citizens also enjoyed a broad range of social welfare benefits, including job security, free (though badly flawed) medical care, cheap (but cramped) housing, and a respectable system of primary and secondary education for most children. The Soviet education system, while highly politicized with Marxist dogma, excelled in mathematics, science, and technical subjects. Higher education, with the same strengths and weaknesses, was available at 70 universities and 800 technical institutes, with about 5 million full- and part-time students.

In foreign affairs stability and security meant a two-track approach in dealing with the United States. The first track was a massive military buildup to redress the nuclear imbalance highlighted by the Cuban Missile Crisis. By the end of the decade that imbalance had been overcome, with the Soviets having deployed enough ICBMs and submarine-launched ballistic missiles (SLBMs) to achieve overall nuclear parity with the United States. By the late 1970s the Soviets led the United

States in the number of deployed ICBMs and SLBMs, although overall American technological superiority negated the Soviet numerical advantage. A parallel buildup of conventional arms increased what already was a Soviet advantage in that area, especially in Europe, where NATO and Warsaw Pact forces faced each other.

Moscow's second foreign policy track is known as détente, or relaxation of tensions, with the United States and its NATO allies. The central pillar of détente was an effort to limit the deployment of nuclear weapons, a goal strongly desired by both sides in light of the expense and danger of an open-ended nuclear arms race. The vehicle was the Strategic Arms Limitation Talks (SALT), which began in 1969 and in 1972 produced the SALT I agreement. It included two treaties: one limiting the deployment of antiballistic missiles (ABMs) to a minimal level and the other establishing a five-year interim ceiling on strategic nuclear missiles (ICBMs and SLBMs).

Détente also included expanded Soviet-American trade relations that facilitated large Soviet purchases of American wheat, along with a series of agreements with the countries of Western Europe. In 1974 Moscow and Washington reached an agreement on a framework for SALT II, which was projected to take effect when SALT I expired and included more comprehensive limits on offensive strategic nuclear weapons than its predecessor. Détente reached its peak, both literally and figuratively, in July 1975 when a Soviet *Soyuz* spacecraft docked in space more than 100 miles above the earth with an American *Apollo* vehicle.

A month later the Soviet Union and the United States joined with more than 30 other nations in signing the Helsinki Accords. This agreement finalized the post–World War II border changes in Europe, a longtime Soviet goal. The signatories also agreed to respect a list of basic human rights, a promise the Soviet leadership did not take seriously but that soon embarrassed it when a small group of courageous Soviet citizens did. Thereafter détente eroded, largely because the Soviet Union continued its conventional arms buildup and aggressively supported Communist insurgencies in the Third World. By the end of the decade détente was dead. Among the casualties of its demise was SALT II, signed in mid-1979 by Brezhnev and U.S president Jimmy Carter but never ratified by the U.S. Senate.

The Era of Stagnation

Whatever the accomplishments of the long-lived Brezhnev leadership, its refusal or inability to implement major reforms had severe consequences.

Since the Stalin era the military had received a disproportionate share of the country's overall resources, not only in terms of quantity but also quality. Khrushchev's attempts to moderate this situation for the benefit of the civilian economy contributed to his downfall. Under Brezhnev the military almost always got what it wanted. Defense spending increased by about 4 percent per year between 1964 and 1976; thereafter the rate fell to 2 percent, still a significant rate of growth.

The burden on the economy as a whole was staggering. Between a quarter and a third of the Soviet Union's gross national product was devoted to military needs. About half of the country's industrial enterprises and between one-half and three-quarters of its scientific and technical personnel in one way or another served the military. That enabled the Soviet Union to produce high-quality aircraft, ballistic missiles, rifles, tanks, and other weapons but only by compromising the quality of civilian goods.

Nor was anything done to correct the flaws of central planning. Central planning had been an effective, although not an efficient, method of promoting industrial development during the 1930s. However, it was an ineffective and inefficient tool for managing an advanced and complex industrial economy. For example, planners could set quotas for goods in terms of measurable categories such as quantity, size, and weight, but there was no way to assure quality. To meet their quotas factories produced shoddy goods such as shirts without buttons, trucks or tractors that were carelessly assembled, sheets of metal too heavy for many industrial uses, and so on.

Without a market governed by supply and demand, factories met their quotas by producing goods that consumers did not want or, because of poor quality, were unwilling to buy. In a market economy such factories would soon go out of business. In Brezhnev's Soviet Union they carried on. What mattered was not making a profit but meeting the quota. Year after year the economy rang up large output numbers padded by useless goods. Furthermore, the central planning system, unlike a market system, lacked any automatic mechanism to encourage technological innovation, which is one reason the electronics and computer revolution that generated so much growth in the West and Japan failed to do the same in the Soviet Union.

The few and very tentative efforts to introduce market mechanisms into Soviet planning in the 1960s and 1970s all ran afoul of opposition from the central planning bureaucracy and the general conservatism of the Communist Party leadership. Nor were things better in agriculture. Collective farming, with its inherent lack of incentives, remained the basis of Soviet agriculture. No amount of investments, and they were enormous, could make that system work efficiently so it could feed the Soviet Union properly. Poor weather often made things worse. Grain production peaked in 1978, but even in that year the Soviet Union had to import grain to meet its needs. A series of poor harvests in the years that followed turned the Soviet Union, a major world exporter of grain under the czars, into the world's leading grain importer.

Meanwhile, the cheap natural resources used to fuel industrialization became more expensive as deposits west of the Ural Mountains were depleted and the Soviets had to turn to resources from Siberia. Falling birthrates among Russians and other Slavic peoples deprived the Soviet economy of the vast cheap labor pool that had helped the country industrialize.

After 1970 overall economic growth began to slow, and by 1975–80 the rate of growth was only half of what it had been 10 years earlier. The Soviet standard of living stagnated and fell further behind that of citizens in capitalist Europe, the United States, and Japan. Even worse, because of modern communications not only the elite but also ordinary Soviet citizens had a sense of how poorly they lived compared with people elsewhere in the industrialized world. Unlike in the past, they could tune in to foreign radio broadcasts or use tape recorders smuggled into the country from abroad to receive and transmit information the government did not want them to have.

Against this background a number of other problems emerged. To get the goods they wanted, Soviet citizens turned to a burgeoning black market, which grew to such enormous proportions that it was dubbed the "second economy." Since everything that took place in the second economy was illegal, it became a source of corruption that pervaded Soviet society, especially when officials at every level were paid to look the other way.

The shortages and frustrations that affected ordinary Soviet citizens did not bother the higher-ranking members of the Communist Party, who shopped in special stores, lived in the best apartments, and enjoyed services such as high-quality medical care unavailable to ordinary people. But ordinary people, including the 30 percent of working-class families still crowded into multifamily communal apartments, were aware of these inequalities. They were also demoralized by them, as inequality was supposed to be a characteristic of capitalism, not communism. That in turn led to widespread cynicism summed up by the saying, "We have communism, but not for everybody." The demoralization was reflected in a broad range of social pathologies, including a soaring rate of alcoholism—per capita consumption of alcohol, already high, grew by 50 percent between 1965 and 1979—and spreading drug use by the early 1980s.

The Dissident Movement

Whatever their opinions or complaints, most Soviet citizens kept their views to themselves or shared them only within a personal circle of family and friends. Although Stalin's terror was gone, they still lived in a totalitarian state that did not tolerate open expression of dissent. Yet a few Soviet citizens dared to express their dissent openly, despite the risk of reprisals that included prison sentences under harsh conditions. Because the authorities now at least ostensibly had to follow the law, albeit laws that overwhelmingly favored the state, some well-placed or famous Soviet citizens could get away with openly criticizing the regime, at least for a time. That post-Stalin situation gave birth to a range of protest known as the dissident movement. Two men in particular, each a Nobel laureate, symbolized the dissident movement. One was Andrei Sakharov, the country's leading physicist and the chief designer of the first Soviet hydrogen bomb. The other was novelist Aleksandr Solzhenitsyn.

While both men were strong critics of the Soviet regime, they disagreed about how it should be changed. Sakharov was a modern-day Westernizer who wanted to see the regime reformed along Western democratic lines. As early as 1968, in "Thoughts on Progress, Peaceful Coexistence, and Intellectual Freedom," he called for freedom of thought and a multiparty system in the Soviet Union. He also warned that without these changes the Soviet Union would decline and become a second-rate power. Sakharov was awarded the Nobel Peace Prize in 1975 but was prevented by the authorities from accepting it. For several years his international status protected him from reprisal, but in 1980 he was exiled to Gorky, a city several hundred miles from Moscow and closed to foreigners.

Solzhenitsyn was a modern-day Slavophile who had as little use for Western democracy as he did for Soviet communism. He wanted to see the Soviet system abolished and Russia return to its pre-revolutionary Slavic roots. He expressed his total rejection and hatred of the regime in the novels *The First Circle* (1968) and *The Cancer Ward* (1969), both of which had to be published abroad, and in the *The Gulag Archipelago* (1973–75), a groundbreaking three-volume history of Stalin's labor camp system. In 1974, fearing to arrest the 1970 Nobel laureate, the authorities seized Solzhenitsyn, put him on an airplane, and sent him into exile abroad.

The dissident movement never reached a wide audience in the Soviet Union, and by the early 1980s many of its most prominent members were in prison or exile. Ideas critical of the Soviet regime had their broadest appeal among some of the non-Russian minority nationalities, especially in Lithuania, Latvia, Estonia, and to a lesser extent in Ukraine, but to little effect. Non-Russian dissident leaders often suffered harsh repression, as Soviet authorities regarded their activities as an especially dangerous threat.

Some dissidents organized around their religious beliefs. The most successful of these groups were Jews who wanted to emigrate to Israel. They were fortunate to have a limited goal that did not challenge any aspect of the Communist Party's power and to have outside support, especially in the United States. During the 1970s more than 200,000 Jews received permission to emigrate. However, those who applied and were not permitted to leave were usually fired from their jobs and harassed by the authorities. Some of them were imprisoned or exiled to Siberia.

The Old Guard Fades Away

In December 1979 the Brezhnev leadership made its last major decision when it sent the Soviet army into neighboring Afghanistan to keep a tottering Communist regime in power. The decision was disastrous. Instead of establishing order, 100,000 Soviet troops fighting in rugged mountain terrain were unable to defeat anti-government Muslim guerrillas, who were supplied by the United States and Pakistan with arms and ammunition, including antiaircraft missiles. Many demoralized Soviet troops began using drugs while in Afghanistan, and they brought their drug addiction and the multiple problems it causes home with them.

Meanwhile, the aging Soviet leadership—the average age of Politburo members was about 70—was increasingly infirm and unable to govern effectively. Kosygin died in 1980, Suslov in early 1982, and Brezhnev himself in November 1982. Brezhnev was succeeded as general secretary by 68-year-old Yuri Andropov, the former head of the KGB, who had the reputation as a corruption fighter and reformer. Andropov began to prepare the ground for reform, but his health declined quickly and he died of kidney disease in February 1984. He was succeeded by Konstantin Chernenko, a conservative functionary who was also in poor health. Chernenko survived in office barely 13 months before dying in March 1985. The Soviet public watched in dismay as their frail leaders, too old and sick to govern, quietly followed each other to the grave. It seemed to many as if they were apt symbols for a moribund society unable to cope with its many problems.

On March 11, 1985, the Politburo chose Mikhail Gorbachev as general secretary. The youngest member of the Politburo, Gorbachev was 54, vigorous and intelligent, and firmly committed to reform. More important, he was open to new ideas and became increasingly so as he realized that traditional solutions would not solve his country's problems.

Gorbachev's election marked the long-delayed transfer of power from one generation to another. Within a year many older officials at the party's top levels went or were pushed into retirement and were replaced by Gorbachev appointees. What transpired next defied predictions and left the citizens of the Soviet Union and observers throughout the world in shock.

Gorbachev, Reform, and Chernobyl

Mikhail Gorbachev had a conventional background for a Soviet leader. Like Khrushchev, Brezhnev, and most other top-ranking party officials since Stalin, he was an ethnic Russian. Born in 1931 in a collective farm village in the Stavropol region of the north Caucasus, Gorbachev excelled as a student and worker on his collective farm and after high school studied law at Moscow State University. He then forged a highly successful career as a Communist Party official, rising through the ranks quickly until he became the Stavropol regional first secretary in 1970. Promoted to the Central Committee in 1971, Gorbachev was called to Moscow in 1978 to serve on the party's powerful Secretariat. He reached the Politburo as a candidate member (without voting rights) in 1979 and became a full member (with voting rights) in 1980. That made Gorbachev one of the 15 most powerful men in the Soviet Union. He moved closer to the number-one position when serving as Yuri Andropov's right-hand man between 1982 and 1984 but lacked the political backing to succeed his mentor. Gorbachev bided his time for another year while the sickly Konstantin Chernenko did his feeble best to lead the country. After Chernenko's death in 1985, after considerable backroom maneuvering, Gorbachev's Politburo colleagues unanimously elected him general secretary.

Gorbachev came to power as well informed about the Soviet Union's problems as any of his colleagues, and convinced that much had to be

Mikhail Gorbachev, Soviet leader from 1985 to 1991, and U.S. president Ronald Reagan relax during their first summit meeting, which took place in Geneva, Switzerland, in 1985. (Associated Press)

changed. As he told his wife just before he became general secretary, "We can't go on living this way" (quoted in Brown 1997: 81). Earlier he had shared similar views with the two men who became his most important advisers: Aleksandr Yakovlev, who has been called the architect of Gorbachev's reform program, known as perestroika; and Eduard Shevardnadze, who served as Soviet foreign minister from mid-1985 to late 1990. At the same time, it is clear that neither Gorbachev nor other advocates of reform fully understood how deep those problems ran and how they were connected. That is one reason why Gorbachev started out with what in retrospect were very limited reforms. The other, which dates back to the Khrushchev era, was fear of reform that pervaded the party leadership. This meant that before he could do very much Gorbachev had to solidify his political base by replacing Brezhnev holdovers at every level of the party, from the Politburo on down.

The parallel processes of learning the true scope of the country's problems and solidifying his political base lasted from March 1985 well into 1986. Then a catastrophic accident provided deadly proof of how urgently change was needed. On April 25, 1986, an explosion destroyed one of the reactors at the Chernobyl nuclear power plant in

THE MAKING OF A RADICAL REFORMER

Nothing in Gorbachev's conventional career path indicated that he would become the radical reformer he turned out to be. Had there been, he would never have been elected general secretary. Yet with the benefit of hindsight one can see certain elements in his background that help explain his openness to new ideas. None of them explains why Gorbachev was willing to turn to radical reforms to solve the Soviet Union's problems, but they may explain how he had the potential to do so.

Although Gorbachev was born into the new Soviet rural elite—his maternal grandfather was a Communist Party member when he was born and his father joined while serving in the army during World War II—both of his grandfathers were arrested during Stalin's purges. Although both men survived the ordeal, Gorbachev knew that family members on both sides had suffered during the Stalin era. He also knew that the official upbeat history of collectivization was totally false, a heretical viewpoint he shared in confidence with a university friend during the early 1950s.

Gorbachev began his career in the party when Nikita Khrushchev was launching his de-Stalinization program and was heavily influenced by that era's reformist spirit. Like Khrushchev, as a local and regional party boss Gorbachev was known for getting out among the people rather than ruling from his office like most party officials. He knew how the Soviet people lived. He also experimented as much as possible with methods that might improve collective farm efficiency, including allowing peasants to sell a greater portion of what they produced at market prices. Gorbachev was also aware of how people lived in the West, having made two unescorted trips to Western Europe with his wife, Raisa, herself a serious and politically aware advocate of reform.

the Ukraine, sending huge quantities of radioactive poisons into the atmosphere. Those poisons threatened not only Soviet citizens living near the plant but were carried westward by air currents across the Ukraine and Belarus and beyond into Western Europe.

News of the disaster appeared first in the West, demonstrating the extent to which the Soviet Union, lacking a free press or any legal alter-

The Chernobyl nuclear reactor, days after it was destroyed by an explosion on April 26, 1986 (Associated Press)

native to the state-controlled media, was still covering up its problems. While Gorbachev's government was saying nothing to the public and doing nothing to evacuate the people closest to the explosion, truly heroic local firefighters, many of whom died later of radiation sickness, contained the damage and prevented an even greater disaster. Chernobyl was, as Shevardnadze would say later, the event that "tore the blindfold from our eyes" (Shevardnadze 1991: 175–176). It pushed Gorbachev and his supporters along an uncharted path to policies far more radical than anything they had in mind in March 1985.

Perestroika and Its Perils

Gorbachev began using the term *perestroika,* which means "restructuring," shortly after becoming general secretary. The term was initially applied to the economy, but before long Gorbachev realized that to fix the economy he had to deal with other areas of Soviet life as well. The meaning of the term expanded, and soon perestroika included three policies that went well beyond economic reform: glasnost, *democratizatsia,* and *novoe myshlenia.*

223

Glasnost, or "openness," referred to a reduction in censorship, a freer flow of information, and genuine public debate. As Gorbachev stressed, it was impossible to respond to problems and formulate effective reforms without ending the obsessive secrecy and cover-ups that were so much a part of Soviet life. This essential and useful tool proved to be a two-edged sword, as a little bit of glasnost soon led to demands for a great deal more, and it was not long before glasnost went far beyond what Gorbachev had intended and became a phenomenon he could not control.

Demokratizatsiia, or "democratization," meant opening up the Soviet political system by permitting some choice of candidates in party and state elections. It did not mean democracy as understood in the West. It was a tool to engage the public as a whole in the reform effort, as well as a method Gorbachev needed to circumvent the opposition to reform he encountered within the party. But like glasnost, *democratizatsia,* once started, proved to be something Gorbachev could not control.

Finally, *novoe myshlenie,* or "new thinking," meant a new approach to foreign affairs that would allow the Soviet Union to establish genuinely peaceful relations with the capitalist West. Of the three components of perestroika, it was the one that Gorbachev, ably aided by Shevardnadze, was best able to manage.

By the summer of 1986 perestroika as Gorbachev conceived it had evolved from Andropov-style reforms to a comprehensive program that would significantly affect, in Gorbachev's words, "not only the economy but all other sides of social life: social relations, the political system, the spiritual and ideological sphere, the style and work methods of our Party and of all our cadres. Restructuring is a capacious world. I would equate restructuring with revolution . . . a genuine revolution in the hearts and minds of the people" (quoted in Lapidus 1989: 122). And that in the end was the problem. After 1986 as glasnost made thousands of previously banned books available and allowed Soviet citizens to see films made in their own country dealing with controversial issues, it simultaneously raised questions about the fundamental nature of the Soviet system that Gorbachev did not want discussed. It was fine with him for the public to criticize Stalin, but he did not want that criticism to extend, as it inexorably did, to Lenin and the Bolshevik Revolution. Criticism and questioning also soon extended to Gorbachev's economic policies, which undermined the old and inefficient Soviet central planning system but put nothing workable in its place. By 1987 those policies had produced accelerating economic decline and increased hardship rather than the promised better life.

THE SOVIET FEDERAL FACADE AND ITS LEGACY

Like the Russian Empire it succeeded, the Soviet Union was a multinational state with more than 100 distinct nationalities. Beginning in the early 1920s the country was officially a federal state—the Union of Soviet Socialist Republics—made up of what were called union republics, each ostensibly the homeland of a national group that in theory enjoyed significant local autonomy. From the mid-1950s there were 15 union republics; thus 15 of the country's 22 largest nationalities had their own republics. The largest union republic was the Russian Soviet Federated Socialist Republic (RSFSR), with half the country's population and three-quarters of its area. Below the union republics were several dozen autonomous republics, regions, and areas, each officially designated as a homeland for a minority nationality. The RSFSR contained most of these ethnic units.

In practical terms the Soviet federal structure was a facade for a centralized totalitarian dictatorship, but it did serve a propaganda purpose and thereby helped the regime control its far-flung and diverse populations. Ironically, this fake federal structure began to take on real importance in the Gorbachev era. Several union republics became centers of nationalist feeling that by 1990 threatened to destabilize the entire Soviet state. When the Soviet Union imploded in 1991, once meaningless internal borders of the 15 union republics suddenly became national borders with real significance. Some of those borders, which were never intended to be genuine national boundaries, have caused international disputes and violence to this day.

By 1988 Gorbachev had pushed into retirement the last Brezhnev-era conservatives who opposed all reform. By then, however, many former supporters within the Communist Party, officials who believed in moderate reform, had begun to oppose him. They were convinced, not without reason, that perestroika was running out of control and becoming a threat to the entire Soviet system. That threat took various forms, but none was more ominous than the growing national consciousness and assertiveness among some non-Russian minority groups. In the Caucasus region and in central Asia, nationalism fueled interethnic conflicts that sometimes flared into deadly violence, as happened in the Caucasus between Christian Armenians and Muslim Azerbaijanians and in central Asia between various Muslim ethnic groups.

Of even greater concern to Gorbachev and his colleagues was national consciousness directed against Russia that led to demands for autonomy or, eventually, independence. This phenomenon emerged in the Baltic region in the Latvian, Lithuanian, and Estonian union republics as early as 1987. By 1989 it had spread to the Ukraine, where it found fertile ground among the Soviet Union's second-largest ethnic group. The Soviet dictatorship had covered up its problems so thoroughly, even from itself, that these nationalist sentiments came as a complete surprise to Gorbachev, who before 1985, like fellow party bosses had believed the Communist myth that non-Russians were happy inside the Russian-dominated Soviet fold.

It was under these circumstances that during 1988 Gorbachev, with great difficulty, managed to push through a set of far-reaching and dramatic political reforms. They were designed to strengthen his political support among the population at large and bypass opposition from the Communist Party leadership. Gorbachev's reform abolished the old rubber-stamp Soviet parliament and replaced it with a new 2,250-member parliamentary body known as the Congress of People's Deputies (CPD). The CPD constituted a radical political change because its members would be elected under a system that permitted a choice of candidates, something unprecedented in Soviet history. Nor did candidates have to be members of the Communist Party, although one-third of the seats were reserved for ranking party loyalists.

The March 1989 balloting for the CPD constituted the first reasonably free national election in Soviet history. (The November 1917 election to the ill-fated Constituent Assembly in fact took place before the Bolsheviks had consolidated their control of the country.) Among the outsiders to win seats was Andrei Sakharov. Another was Boris Yeltsin, a member of Gorbachev's leadership team until being dismissed in the fall of 1987 for criticizing what he called the slow pace of reform. Yeltsin, formerly the party boss of Moscow, was elected from a district in that city with an impressive 89 percent of the vote.

Yeltsin's election to the Congress of People's Deputies marked the beginning of a remarkable political comeback that soon would have national implications. By 1989 Gorbachev's only successes were in the realm of foreign policy. In December 1987 he negotiated a nuclear arms control agreement that eliminated all intermediate nuclear missiles from Europe. In 1988, in a dramatic speech at the United Nations in New York, Gorbachev repudiated the Soviet commitment dating from Lenin to spread communism across the world. And in 1989, as the Communist regimes established by Stalin in Eastern Europe began to collapse, Gorbachev demonstrated his commitment to his new foreign policy by doing nothing to stop that process, which in a matter of eight months dramatically undid Stalin's work with almost no violence. The end of the Soviet empire in Eastern Europe, along with important Gorbachev initiatives such as the Soviet withdrawal from Afghanistan, marked the last gasp of the Cold War, which was officially declared ended on a number of occasions, including once by U.S. president George H. W. Bush during 1990.

The End of the Line

The Soviet Union did not long outlive the Cold War. Economic conditions continued to deteriorate in 1990 and 1991, while anti-Russian nationalist sentiment swelled in Latvia, Lithuania, Estonia, the Ukraine, and other non-Russian republics. Gorbachev could no longer control political events. Despite his new position as president of the Soviet Union, a post with extensive powers he had convinced the Congress of People's Deputies to establish and then elect him to in early 1990, he lost control of the situation.

In 1991 Gorbachev suffered a major setback when he was unable to prevent the Russian Republic (the RSFSR) from carrying out an election to choose a president of its own, who presumably would manage local affairs while Gorbachev ran national affairs. The successful candidate, with 57 percent of the vote, was Boris Yeltsin. Since most of the Soviet Union's ethnic Russian population lived in the RSFSR, in June 1991 Yeltsin in effect became the first leader to be elected directly by the Russian people in their 1,100-year history. The contrast with President Gorbachev, who had been elected to his post not by the people but by the CPD, was unmistakable. Yeltsin made that contrast even more striking at his inauguration in early July by spurning the Communist Party, from which he had resigned almost a year earlier, and instead accepting the blessing of the Russian Orthodox Church.

During late 1990 and into 1991 Gorbachev tried a number of desperate gambits, suddenly shifting away from reform to lessen conservative criticism and then with equal suddenness moving back to his original path. Nothing helped. On August 19, 1991, conservatives he had appointed to key positions the year before staged a coup, removing him as the country's president "for health reasons." The coup was poorly planned and fizzled within three days in the face of popular resistance.

Boris Yeltsin reading a statement condemning the coup against Mikhail Gorbachev while standing on a tank on August 19, 1991 (Associated Press)

With Gorbachev under house arrest at his vacation home on the Black Sea, leadership of that resistance fell to Boris Yeltsin. He further gave the resistance a potent symbol in the first hours of the coup by rallying people from atop a tank in front of the Soviet parliament building in the center of Moscow. Gorbachev soon was back in Moscow and restored to office, but to little effect. The union republics began declaring independence, a bandwagon Yeltsin quickly jumped on and then began to lead as head of the Russian Republic.

All that remained was to give the Soviet Union an orderly burial. On December 8 Yeltsin and the presidents of Ukraine (no longer "the" Ukraine) and Belarus (no longer "Belorussia") agreed to abolish the Soviet Union and replace it with a loose association called the Commonwealth of Independent States (CIS), whose real purpose was vague and undefined. On December 21, 11 of the former Soviet union republics—all had declared their independence—reaffirmed the creation of the flimsy CIS. On December 25 Gorbachev resigned as president of what had become a nonexistent Soviet Union. That same day the Russian parliament—it had been elected in 1990—voted to change the name of the RSFSR officially to the Russian Federation. The Soviet Union officially ceased to exist on midnight, December 31, 1991. As a new year dawned January 1, 1992, so did a new era in the history of Russia and its long-suffering people.

9

POST-SOVIET RUSSIA: YELTSIN AND PUTIN (1991-2008)

The Russian Federation officially came into existence on January 1, 1992. Despite the loss of the other former Soviet union republics, it was an immense country, still the world's largest by far, with problems that corresponded to its size. Russia's population was confused, demoralized, and in poor physical health. Its economy, an unworkable hodgepodge of crumbling socialist institutions and free-market anarchy, was in a state of precipitous decline. Its political system was an equally unworkable combination of decayed Soviet-era institutions and fledgling and fragile democratic practices. Corruption and organized crime were out of control, and Communists who opposed both the collapse of the Soviet Union and democratic and free-market reforms were still entrenched in key positions of power.

None of the other former Communist countries, at least those committed to democracy, faced problems of such scope and interrelated complexity, and it was imperative to solve them quickly. An Armenian Communist leader posed a reasonable question in December 1991 when he asked his Russian colleagues, "How are you Russians going to live? We don't envy you" (Remnik 1997: 4). Yet amazingly the Russian people showed a measure of optimism, hope, and even good cheer as they looked forward to a brighter future, what Yeltsin a year earlier had called "the spiritual, national, and economic rebirth of Russia" (Murray 1995: 144).

President Yeltsin and Czar Boris

Much of that optimism was based on confidence in Boris Yeltsin, an imposing bear of a man of peasant stock from a small village in the Urals near the city of Sverdlovsk (which in late 1991 reverted to its pre-revolutionary name Yekaterinburg). Yeltsin was a construction engineer

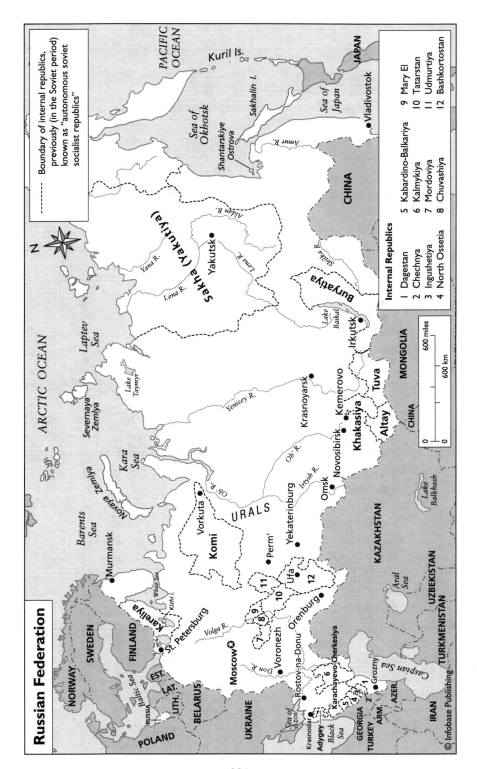

Russian Federation

Boundary of internal republics, previously (in the Soviet period) known as "autonomous soviet socialist republics"

Internal Republics

1 Dagestan
2 Chechnya
3 Ingushetiya
4 North Ossetia
5 Kabardino-Balkariya
6 Kalmykiya
7 Mordoviya
8 Chuvashiya
9 Mary El
10 Tatarstan
11 Udmurtiya
12 Bashkortostan

ARCTIC OCEAN

PACIFIC OCEAN

Kuril Is.

Sea of Okhotsk

Sakhalin I.

Shantarskiye Ostrova

Sea of Japan

JAPAN

Vladivostok

Amur R.

CHINA

Laptev Sea

Yana R.

Lena R.

Aldan R.

Sakha (Yakutiya)

Yakutsk

Lena R.

Shilka R.

Buryatiya

Lake Baikal

Irkutsk

Tuva

MONGOLIA

CHINA

Barents Sea

Kara Sea

Novaya Zemlya

Severnaya Zemlya

Lake Taymyr

Yenisey R.

Krasnoyarsk

Kemerovo

Khakasiya

Altay

Ob' R.

Novosibirsk

Omsk

Irtysh R.

KAZAKHSTAN

Lake Balkhash

Murmansk

White Sea

Vorkuta

URALS

Komi

Perm'

Yekaterinburg

Ufa

11

10

12

9

8

Orenburg

Aral Sea

UZBEKISTAN

TURKMENISTAN

Kizhi I.

Kareliya

St. Petersburg

Volga R.

7

Voronezh

Don R.

Moscow

Rostov-na-Donu

Sea of Azov

Karachayevo-Cherkesiya

6

Krasnodar

Adygey

Black Sea

5 4 3

2

1

Grozny

Caspian Sea

GEORGIA

ARM.

AZER.

TURKEY

IRAN

NORWAY

SWEDEN

FINLAND

Baltic Sea

EST.

LAT.

LITH.

RUSSIA

BELARUS

POLAND

UKRAINE

N

0   600 miles
0   600 km

© Infobase Publishing

231

before switching to politics, working his way up the local Communist Party ladder to the position of first secretary of the Sverdlovsk region. Called to Moscow by Gorbachev in 1985 to head the city's party organization, Yeltsin was fired in late 1987 for criticizing what he called the slow pace of Gorbachev's reforms. Beginning in 1989 he staged a political comeback that within two years took him to the presidency of the RSFSR. He was the hero of the hour during the August coup against Gorbachev. That distinction and his populist political style gave him considerable popularity among the Russian people. When the Soviet Union was dissolved four months later, in part because of his own efforts, as the democratically elected president of the defunct RSFSR Yeltsin became the first president of the newly independent Russian Federation.

Given the enormity of the task, it is difficult to imagine who the right man for the job might have been. But it was not Boris Yeltsin. To be sure, he had a populist side and had been freely elected to office, but all of his experience in governance was as a Communist Party boss. He had never been abroad and had little understanding of democracy or free markets. While he had rejected communism and had no desire to be a dictator, the paternalistic Yeltsin knew only how to govern by decree. If he had no use for Lenin, he likewise did not appreciate George Washington; instead he seemed to see himself as a benign version of Peter the Great. He did not flinch when referred to as "Czar Boris" and in fact at times used that moniker himself. Yeltsin also had personal shortcomings. Capable of impressive bursts of creative energy, he was given to depression and excessive drinking as well. It was the latter two characteristics that increasingly predominated during Yeltsin's eight difficult years in office, to the point where he became virtually incapacitated.

Yeltsin understood the urgency of the situation he faced, especially the need for reforms that would put the Russian economy on a free-market footing and reverse the process of decline that had already caused widespread hardship. He surrounded himself with a group of youthful advisers who argued that the government had to smash what was left of the old Soviet centralized economy and promote the development of a free-market economy based on private property as quickly as possible. This would accomplish two things: make a Communist revival impossible and get the country through economic hard times before the Russian people turned against the proposed reforms. The president and his advisers honestly believed this could be done, and Yeltsin conveyed that message to the people with the following promise: "Everyone will find life harder for approximately six months, then prices will fall and goods will begin to fill the market. By the autumn of 1992 the economy will have stabilized" (quoted in Suny 1998: 490).

It was not to be. Yeltsin launched Russia's hoped-for rapid transition to a market economy with a decree on January 1, 1992, that ended state control of prices on almost all goods and services. Only a small group of products and services deemed necessities were excluded, among them bread, milk, medicine, public transport, and—in a grim but telling commentary on the condition of far too many Russians—vodka. Another decree legalized private trading. The program received the unfortunate name, from a public relations point of view, of "shock therapy." More unfortunate than the name were the results, which many commentators noted consisted of a great deal more shock than therapy. With production of almost everything falling, Russians faced runaway inflation that reached 2,500 percent by the end of the year. This impoverished millions living on fixed incomes and destroyed the savings of millions of others, while again others suffered from the appearance and rapid growth of unemployment.

One problem was that most Russian enterprises were still in state hands and totally unsuited to operating under free-market conditions. The proposed solution was privatization: transferring tens of thousands

Heavy automobile traffic in modern Moscow (Losevsky Pavel, 2007. Used under license from ShutterStock, Inc.)

233

of state enterprises to private hands. That process went very slowly until the fall of 1992, when each Russian citizen was issued a voucher valued at 10,000 rubles to invest in businesses that were being privatized. This program was designed to create a large class of property owners, what Yeltsin called "millions of owners, not a small group of millionaires" (quoted in Sakwa 1993: 231). Unfortunately, it did the opposite.

Inflation drastically eroded the value of the vouchers before they were issued; in any case most Russians, who had grown up in a socialist system, did not understand how to make proper use of them. Many people sold or traded their vouchers for a fraction of their value, including some who exchanged them for a bottle or two of cheap vodka. While voucher privatization did put most retail trade businesses in private hands, the real beneficiaries of the program were well-placed insiders, often former Communist Party officials or hustlers who had operated successfully in Russia's second economy during the Gorbachev era. Ordinary Russians justifiably called the whole process "grabitization."

Economic hardship fueled opposition to Yeltsin both among the public at large and in Russia's parliament, whose members had been elected in 1990. Those who opposed Yeltsin in the parliament ranged from moderate centrists, including some former allies, to unrepentant Communists and newly emerged neo-fascists. This odd coupling of political groups was promoted by a confluence of individual political ambitions. Tensions began to build in the spring of 1992 and culminated in an attempted coup against Yeltsin by parliamentary leaders in October 1993, a showdown marked by the worst street violence in Moscow since the Bolshevik Revolution. Yeltsin prevailed because the military remained loyal to him, the decisive action occurring when army tanks shelled the parliament building and forced his opponents to surrender. But the violence tainted him and permanently hurt his popularity and standing with the population at large. Official reports put the toll at 150 dead and more than 600 wounded; the actual figures were probably higher.

Yeltsin used his victory to overhaul Russia's political system. He issued a decree that Russia's voters would elect a new two-house parliament in December. A second presidential decree called for a referendum on a new constitution that greatly increased presidential powers at the expense of parliament. When the voting took place on December 12, about 58 percent of voters approved the new constitution, as Yeltsin wanted. However, they did not support political parties backing his free-market reforms. A misnamed group called the Liberal Democratic Party—it had a neo-fascist, anti-Semitic agenda—led all parties with 23 percent of the popular vote in the balloting for the lower house of parliament. A party called the Communist Party of the Russian Federation (CPRF), in effect the successor to the defunct CPSU, combined with a close ally, the Agrarian Party, to garner 20 percent of the vote. The major reformist parties together managed to win just over a third of the popular vote, although one of them, Russia's Choice, ended up as the party with the most Duma seats because of victories in single-member districts.

Despite his December 1993 electoral setback, Yeltsin managed to launch a second round of privatization in 1995 known as money privatization. Under the new system many large enterprises were sold at auction

RUSSIA'S PARLIAMENT

The Federal Assembly, the parliament decreed by Yeltsin prior to the December 1993 election and then enshrined in Russia's new constitution, is a two-house body. The lower house, the Duma, has 450 seats. In the 1993 election and in subsequent elections until 2005, half of the Duma's members were elected according to proportional representation, with each political party surpassing the cutoff of 5 percent of the vote in national balloting, receiving a corresponding percentage of those 225 Duma seats. The remaining half of the Duma was chosen by majority vote in 225 single-member districts. In 2005 President Vladimir Putin won passage of a law that abolished the single-member districts and made all seats subject to proportional representation. Most experts agreed that this change would make it more difficult for independent candidates to win election to the Duma, and thereby would weaken opposition parties. This became even more the case in 2007 when the minimum a party needs to win Duma seats was raised from 5 to 7 percent of the popular vote.

The upper house, or Federation Council, has two members from each of Russia's territorial divisions, which numbered 85 as of 2007. The first Federal Council was chosen in 1993 by regional voters, but under the system in place since 1995 representation is indirect. Each regional legislature chooses one representative, and each regional executive chooses another. Previously local republic presidents and regional governors held the Federal Council's executive branch seats, but in August 2000 a new law passed on Putin's initiative barred these officials from serving in that body and instead required them to appoint representatives. The practical effect was to decrease the power of these regional leaders vis-à-vis Russia's president.

to the highest bidder. Unfortunately, the auction process was corrupt, as was so much else in Russia at the time. This allowed unscrupulous insiders or those with connections to win control of valuable enterprises at a tiny fraction of their true value. Money privatization helped give birth to a small group of fabulously wealthy businessmen who became known as the "oligarchs." They then extended their grip on Russia's most valuable assets, including large chunks of the country's natural resources, through the so-called loans for shares scheme. The government received loans from so-called bankers using shares of valuable state-controlled enterprises as collateral. When the government failed to repay the loans, ownership of those enterprises passed to the banks and the oligarchs who controlled them. The entire privatization episode became a scandal of staggering proportions that compromised both Russia's economic development and its attempted transition to democracy.

At the same time, Russia was inundated by a wave of criminality, including the growth of organized crime. According to reasonable estimates by the mid-1990s there were 5,000 organized criminal gangs in Russia, 10 times more than at the beginning of the decade. Organized crime controlled half of Russia's banks and perhaps a third of the overall economy. Assassinations of government officials and businesspeople, often on city streets in broad daylight, became commonplace. Ordinary Russians increasingly spoke of the *mafiya* menace, while President Yeltsin grimly called organized crime a "superpower" and the country's number-one problem.

By 1994 Russia's gross domestic product had dropped by almost 40 percent compared to the already diminished levels of 1991. Yeltsin's popularity fell along with it. Then in December 1994 he made the worst mistake to date when he sent the Russian army to reassert control over Chechnya, a predominantly Muslim region in the north Caucasus near the Caspian Sea. The corrupt local Chechen leadership was certainly a problem for Yeltsin. It was asserting Chechnya's right to independence, which could set a dangerous precedent for other non-Russian territories in the north Caucasus and elsewhere in Russia, and it was allowing the region to be a base for organized criminal activities. Chechnya's criminality and violence were driving the local ethnic Russian population from the region. Yet Yeltsin had more immediate reasons for resorting to military force in Chechnya: the need for a major success to mute criticism of his leadership, especially from Russian nationalist circles, and to restore his popularity.

Yeltsin's closest advisers promised him a quick victory. They delivered a bloody fiasco instead. The operation was poorly planned;

Russian troops sent into Chechnya were inexperienced and unprepared; and the Chechens, who had a long history of resistance to Russian rule, proved to be skilled guerrilla fighters. Not until March 1995 did Russian troops take the Chechen capital Grozny (the word means "terrible" in Russian), and even after that they faced Chechen guerrilla bands they could not defeat. The Chechens soon extended the fighting beyond their territory with several bloody raids into neighboring north Caucasus regions before storming back into Grozny and

Nevsky Prospect in modern St. Petersburg (Anisimov Kirill Stanislavovitch)

237

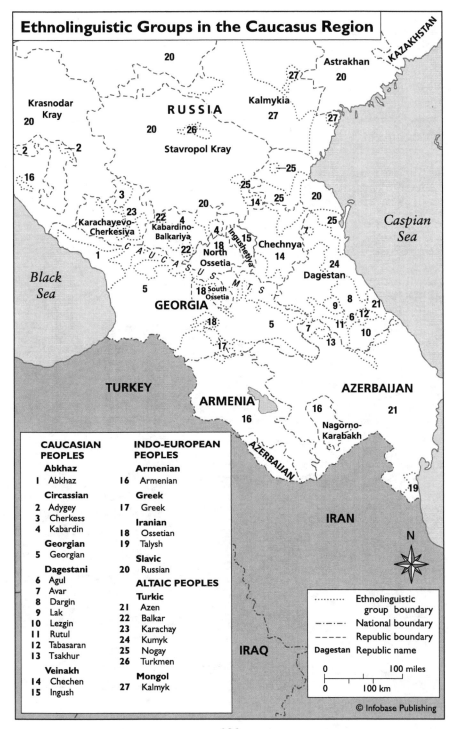

Ethnolinguistic Groups in the Caucasus Region

KAZAKHSTAN

20

27   Astrakhan
20

Krasnodar
Kray   Kalmykia
20   27   27

R U S S I A
20   26

Stavropol Kray

2   2
16
25
3   20   25   20
23 22 4   14   25
Karachayevo- Kabardino-   4   7
Cherkesiya   Balkariya   4 15 Chechnya
1   22 18 North 14
North   24
18 Ossetia   Dagestan
5   18 South   8 21
Ossetia   9   6 12
GEORGIA   11   10
18   7   13
17   5

Black
Sea

Caspian
Sea

TURKEY   AZERBAIJAN

ARMENIA   16   21
16
Nagorno-
Karabakh

AZERBAIJAN

19

CAUCASIAN PEOPLES	INDO-EUROPEAN PEOPLES
Abkhaz	**Armenian**
1 Abkhaz	16 Armenian
Circassian	**Greek**
2 Adygey	17 Greek
3 Cherkess	**Iranian**
4 Kabardin	18 Ossetian
Georgian	19 Talysh
5 Georgian	**Slavic**
Dagestani	20 Russian
6 Agul	**ALTAIC PEOPLES**
7 Avar	**Turkic**
8 Dargin	21 Azen
9 Lak	22 Balkar
10 Lezgin	23 Karachay
11 Rutul	24 Kumyk
12 Tabasaran	25 Nogay
13 Tsakhur	26 Turkmen
Veinakh	**Mongol**
14 Chechen	27 Kalmyk
15 Ingush	

IRAN

IRAQ

N

.... Ethnolinguistic
          group boundary
—·—·— National boundary
— — — Republic boundary
Dagestan Republic name

0   100 miles
0   100 km

© Infobase Publishing

seizing the city from demoralized Russian troops in the spring of 1996. At that point, having shed so much Russian blood and spent so much treasure, Yeltsin was compelled to negotiate a humiliating settlement under which Russian troops withdrew from the region; the issue of Chechnya's final status was left unresolved.

Yeltsin's dilemmas were reflected by parliamentary elections in 1995, in which the CPRF (Communists) emerged as the leading political party, well ahead of both the Liberal Democrats and a group called Our Home Is Russia, the strongest pro-Yeltsin party. By January 1996 Yeltsin's approval rating according to national polls had dropped to 5 percent. He managed to win reelection to a second term later that year only because of financial backing from oligarchs, who feared a CPRF victory would threaten their ill-gotten gains and because government media outlets combined with those controlled by several oligarchs to create a drumbeat of pro-Yeltsin propaganda.

The second term was a sad saga of continued national and presidential decline. One of the few positive moments occurred on July 17, 1998, when Russia finally held a formal funeral for Nicholas II and his family, murdered by the Bolsheviks 80 years before to the day. Yeltsin, in poor health and increasingly given to excessive drinking, pulled himself together for the occasion to deliver a moving speech in which he called for national reconciliation. A month later, pressured by falling oil prices, the ruble collapsed; Russia in effect was bankrupt. By then President Yeltsin was adding to the general instability by periodically dismissing the country's prime minister for unspecified reasons. When he finally appointed the unknown Vladimir Putin in August 1999, Russia had its fifth prime minister in 17 months.

Then on December 31 1999, Yeltsin suddenly resigned, appointing Putin in his place as acting president. Old and sick, broken by burdens he had not expected to bear, Boris Yeltsin faded into retirement, leaving Russia's presidency and a listing ship of state in the hands of a young, untested protégé whose abilities, and to an extent whose views, were a mystery to the country he was expected to lead.

Boris Yeltsin died on April 23, 2007. His funeral was attended by President Vladimir Putin and much of Russia's political elite as well as by dignitaries from many countries, including former U.S. presidents Bill Clinton and George H. W. Bush. The traditional Orthodox service took place in the Cathedral of Christ the Savior, a 19th-century Moscow landmark destroyed by Stalin in 1931 but rebuilt during Yeltsin's presidency. Yeltsin was buried in the Novodevichy Cemetery, since the early 20th century the final resting place of many famous Russian cultural figures.

"I WANT TO ASK YOUR FORGIVENESS"

When Boris Yeltsin resigned as Russia's president on December 31, 1999, his short speech provided a metaphor not only for his difficult eight-year term in office but also for much of Russia's turbulent 1,100-year history. He began by heralding the arrival of the year 2000—"the magic date in our history," the beginning of "a new century and a new millennium"—that had once seemed "so remote" but finally had arrived. He then turned to his own term in office, delivering a farewell that was at once typically dramatic, uncharacteristically apologetic, as well as deeply moving:

> I want to ask your forgiveness. I want to ask your forgiveness because many of our dreams did not come true, because some things that seemed so simple to us have turned out to be tormentingly difficult. I ask your forgiveness for not living up to some of the hopes of the people who believed that we would be able in one fell swoop, in one leap, [to] jump from the dreary, stagnant totalitarian past into a bright, affluent, and civilized future. I myself believed in this. . . .
>
> But it didn't work out—in one leap. I have proved too naïve in some things; in some cases problems proved to be too complex. . . . But I want you to know—I never said it but today it is important for me to say it to you. The pain of each of you has echoed in me, in my heart, in my sleepless nights, in my agonizing over what should be done to make people's lives if only a little easier and better. I have never had a more important task.
>
> I am leaving. I have done all I could. . . .
>
> I have always been confident of the extraordinary wisdom of the Russian people. . . . As I bid you farewell I would like to say to each and every one of you, be happy. You deserve happiness and tranquility.
>
> A Happy New Year. I congratulate you on a new century, my dear fellow Russians. (Press Service of the Russian Federation 1999: n.p.)

The Presidency of Vladimir V. Putin

Vladimir Putin's rise to power was even more rapid than Yeltsin's decline. Born in 1952, a career KGB officer before the Soviet Union's collapse, he ranked no higher as recently as 1996 than deputy mayor of St. Petersburg. Putin then moved to Moscow and worked for Yeltsin, who

240

in 1998 appointed him head of the FSB, the defunct KGB's main successor agency (it had been broken up into several agencies). The next year Yeltsin gave Putin a second important job as head of the county's national security council, then in August 1999 appointed him prime minister. When Yeltsin resigned four months later, Putin became acting president. Aided by the Yeltsin political machine, Putin was elected president in March 2000 in his own right from a field of 11 candidates with 52.9 percent of the vote.

If the Yeltsin presidency was a roller-coaster ride of crises and inconsistencies, the Putin presidency became a relatively steady drive toward political consolidation of power in Moscow and economic growth for the country as a whole. In January 2000, even before his official election as president and five months before his formal inauguration, Putin made it clear that he drew many of his core political beliefs from time-honored Russian traditions. Russia, he said, was unlikely to become a "second edition" of the United States or Great Britain. Instead: "Our state and its institutions have always played an exceptionally important role in the life of the country. For Russians, a strong state is not an anomaly that should be got rid of. Quite the contrary, they see it as a source and guarantor of order and the initiator and main driving force of any change" (quoted in Herspring 2003: 260–261). As for which branch of the state should play the leading role, a month later Putin made this equally clear to a group of Siberian law students: "Thus we had tsarism, then Communism, and now the president has appeared, the institution of the presidency" (*New York Times*: March 9, 2000).

Putin's first moves to strengthen Russia's central government took place when he was still prime minister. After a string of horrific terrorist attacks against targets from the north Caucasus to Moscow that killed hundreds of people during September 1999, the Russian government in October again sent the army into Chechnya.

Vladimir Putin, former Russian president, now prime minister (Vova Pomortzeff, 2007. Used under license from ShutterStock, Inc.)

This time, however, the army was prepared for war. Despite encountering determined opposition, Russian forces took Grozny in February 2000 and drove Chechen fighters into the mountains to the south, from where they continued to fight a guerrilla war. Notwithstanding Chechen guerrilla activities and terrorist raids outside Chechnya itself, during the next several years Moscow tightened its control over the increasingly war-weary local population. Not incidentally, by launching the war Putin boosted his popularity, and parties supporting his agenda did surprisingly well in the December 1999 parliamentary elections. However, the CPRF again finished first in proportional representational balloting.

Putin's inauguration in May 2000 was a historic event: the first democratic transfer of power in Russia's 1,100-year history. That, however, did not make Russia a democracy. As soon as he took office Putin moved decisively to strengthen both Russia's central government in general and the presidency in particular. By presidential decree Putin in the spring of 2000 established seven federal districts, each headed by a presidential appointee, to oversee Russia's 89 regions. A law passed in the summer of 2000 and taking effect in 2002 deprived regional governors and republic presidents of their seats in the Federation Council; henceforth they had to nominate a representative, an appointment subject to the approval of regional or republic assemblies. Meanwhile, the government used threats and police power to wrest control of important media outlets from oligarchs opposed to Putin's policies. In June 2003, allegedly because of unpaid debts, it seized control of TVS, Russia's last independent television network.

Government control or influence over both the broadcast and print media was a major factor in the December 2003 parliamentary elections. United Russia, a party controlled by the Kremlin, won 306 of the Duma's 450 seats. Many of the remaining seats were won by parties favorably disposed to Putin. In an ironic twist, given Russia's Soviet experience, the only genuinely independent party in the Duma was the CPRF. By the presidential election of March 2004, no Russian politician was in a position to challenge Putin seriously. While foreign observers technically declared the 2004 campaigning balloting "free and fair," government domination of the media meant there never was any doubt as to who would win, and Putin was duly elected with 70 percent of the vote. His nearest rival, the CPRF candidate, won less than 14 percent of the vote.

A December 2004 law ended the election of regional governors and republic presidents. Under the new system Russia's president appoints these officials subject to approval by local legislatures. In 2005, a year after his reelection to a second term, Putin pushed a bill through parliament eliminating single-seat districts in the Duma in favor of proportional representational balloting for all seats, a step that clearly hurt the chances of opposition candidates to win election to the Duma. A subsequent amendment to that law raised the threshold for representation in the Duma from 5 to 7 percent, further raising the odds against independent parties winning parliamentary seats.

On the economic front Putin followed two contradictory paths. One involved free-market economic reforms. Thus in 2001 a new tax law lowered the income tax rate for all taxpayers to a flat 13 percent. Two other laws, respectively, legalized the sale of commercial and residential land (2 percent of Russia's territory) and agricultural land, with the proviso that foreigners could only lease but not buy agricultural land. Foreign companies were encouraged to invest in Russian industry, and many did, from Coca-Cola and General Electric to Toyota and Daimler Chrysler.

At the same time the Putin government began a concerted campaign to assert state control over Russia's oil industry, the economy's main growth engine and Russia's most important source of export income. That campaign peaked between 2003 and 2005 with the dismantling of Yukos, Russia's largest private oil company, and the conviction and imprisonment of its owner, oligarch Mikhail Khodorkovsky. The assets of Yukos ended up in the hands of Rosneft, a state-owned oil company. State control also grew in other selected industries. Most notably, in 2006 the state-owned arms conglomerate Rosoboroneksport bought controlling interest in Russia's largest domestic car manufacturer and a leading local producer of titanium.

After the collapse of 1998 the Russian economy as a whole enjoyed a period of steady and substantial growth that was still going strong as of 2008. Of course, that growth had little to do with government policy and almost everything to do with soaring world prices for oil and natural gas; Russia is the world's second-largest oil exporter and the largest exporter of natural gas. Yet that growth, even as it contributed to the growth of the middle class, did nothing to mitigate the glaring economic inequalities that emerged during the 1990s, both between different social classes and between various geographic regions. By 2008 Russia's middle class probably constituted a fifth of the population; the percentage of the population living below the poverty line was slightly less. Aside from a tiny wealthy elite, the rest of the population was wedged economically between these two groups, able to afford the necessities of life but struggling to get by.

Pipelines for transporting oil. The oil industry is the key factor promoting Russian economic growth. (Yury Zakharov, 2007. Used under license from ShutterStock, Inc.)

Putin's foreign policy focused on restoring Russia's standing as a great power. In the late 1980s Gorbachev had repudiated seven decades of Soviet foreign policy and moved to establish genuinely peaceful relations with the United States and other Western powers. Yeltsin continued that policy for a time, but in large part due to nationalist pressures at home by the mid-1990s Russian foreign policy, while not reverting to Soviet objectives, became noticeably more confrontational. That trend intensified under Putin, although not before Russia's new president took a few steps welcomed in Washington. In 2000, just before his inauguration, Putin succeeded where Yeltsin had failed in winning Duma ratification of the START II nuclear arms treaty. And in the wake of the destruction of New York City's World Trade Center and the attack on the Pentagon by al-Qaeda in September 2001, Russia later that year cooperated with the United States in destroying the Taliban regime in Afghanistan, which had sheltered that Islamic terrorist organization.

However, cooperation with the United States in dealing with the Taliban proved fleeting, subsumed by the Kremlin's imperative of promoting Russia's great-power status. One important objective was to limit and if possible eliminate American influence in countries once part of the former Soviet Union, from Ukraine and Belarus in the west to the Caucasus in the south to central Asia in the east. Beyond that Putin used energy exports to boost Moscow's influence in Europe and Asia.

Other initiatives were far more disturbing, at least to the United States and other Western powers. Although Putin had no interest in messianic Soviet international objectives, he relentlessly promoted Russia's great-power status by reviving or updating Soviet-era policies that had created or inflamed so many crises during the Cold War. As it did during the Cold War, Moscow supported aggressive regimes and movements that were destabilizing the Middle East. This included arms sales to and diplomatic support for Syria and Iran, both of which were deeply involved in promoting world terrorism. Among the nonstate recipients of large supplies of Soviet arms was the Lebanese Shi'ite organization Hezbollah, an Iranian-controlled terrorist group responsible for killing 241 American marines in a suicide bombing in Beirut in 1983. Those arms reached Hezbollah via Syria, and in 2006 Hezbollah used them in a five-week war against Israel, which it was determined to destroy. That war seriously undermined efforts to establish a stable government in Lebanon.

Russia also offered diplomatic support to Hamas, a fundamentalist Palestinian movement that like Hezbollah was committed to Israel's destruction. Another Russian arms customer was Sudan, whose fundamentalist Islamic regime received warplanes in 2004 as it engaged in mass murder and ethnic cleansing in its western Darfur region.

These activities inevitably created tensions with the United States and other countries attempting to promote peace and stability in the Middle East, but that downside did not deter Putin. His most ominous move was to continue Russia's profitable and dangerous agreement, dating from the Yeltsin era, to build a nuclear power plant for Iran, whose radical fundamentalist Islamic regime was working to develop nuclear weapons in violation of international agreements and several UN Security Council resolutions. A $1 billion arms agreement in December 2005 provided Iran with advanced missiles to protect its nuclear facilities from possible American air strikes. By 2007 it was clear that Russia was planning much larger arms sales to Iran, including the sale of advanced fighter-bombers and tanker aircraft that would increase the range of those warplanes by permitting in-flight refueling. Putin also consistently opposed international sanctions against Iran that might have impaired its nuclear weapons program or punished Tehran for its support of Islamic terrorism. Making matters worse, during late 2007 and early 2008 Russia delivered to Iran the enriched uranium fuel necessary to run its new nuclear power plant. As a result, notwithstanding Putin's suppression of Islamist forces in Chechnya, by 2008 Russia was a major impediment rather than a help in combating Islamic fundamentalism and promoting stability in the Middle East.

The only good news about Moscow's foreign policy was that Putin's Russia showed no interest in undermining and destroying Western capitalist societies. Far from it. Russia was developing its own form of capitalism and wanted to be considered a leading Western industrialized nation. But Russia was not part of the West either. It was an occasional partner and oftentimes rival pursuing what one observer called a "friend-foe" strategy that frequently was anti-Western and especially anti-American (Shevtsova 2003: 312).

In May 2007 Vladimir Putin, barred by the Russian constitution from seeking a third consecutive term, began his last full year in office. Speculation about a successor focused on the president's views and those of his fellow Kremlin power brokers. There was far less interest in Russian public opinion. Late in the year, Putin announced his support for the relatively obscure Dmitry A. Medvedev, a 42-year-old lawyer, to succeed him as president. Medvedev's qualifications for the job consisted of being a loyal supporter, having managed Putin's election campaign in 2000, worked as his chief of staff, and, most recently, occupied the position of first deputy prime minister in charge of social programs. Medvedev promptly announced that if elected he would designate Putin as prime minister, an arrangement that conveniently would put the protégé in the president's office while leaving the former president, who undoubtedly would control the so-called power ministries of defense, security, and foreign affairs, in power. Putin then spent his last months as president making sure that no genuine opposition candidate managed to even secure a place on the ballot. The result was that in March 2008 Medvedev was overwhelmingly chosen president in a meaningless election; when he was inaugurated in May, ex-president Putin promptly became prime minister. The new prime minister could take satisfaction that he had achieved what not even Ivan the Terrible, Peter the Great, Lenin, or Stalin had managed: He had designated and installed his own successor. That political state of affairs, along with steady economic growth and Russia's growing international influence as a rival to the West, constituted the core of Vladimir Putin's presidential legacy.

10

CONCLUSION:
THE RUSSIAN RIDDLE

In a speech to parliament as he began his second term as Russia's
president in May 2004, Vladimir Putin outlined his objectives for
the coming years: "Our goals are absolutely clear: high living standards
in the country, with life safe, comfortable and free, a mature democracy
and a developed civil society, the strengthening of Russia's position in
the world" (quoted in McFaul 2004: 313). As that term ended, Putin
could reasonably claim progress in fulfilling at least part of his ambitious agenda. Yet Russia remains a deeply troubled land, scarred by a
long history of suffering and turmoil and especially by the dreadful
20th-century legacy of three generations of Soviet rule.

Russia's troubles take many forms and are expressed in various
symptoms. None is more telling than the population decline, which
has reached crisis proportions. A host of social problems during the late
Soviet era caused the Russian birth rate to fall steeply. It dropped below
the replacement level (about 2.1 live births per woman), and continued
to drop after 1992, hitting a low of 1.17. It has revived slightly since
2000, inching up to 1.37 in 2007. At the same time the death rate rose,
and stayed high. Between 1999 and 2002 deaths outnumbered births by
at least 900,000 per year. During the late Soviet era there was a decline
in health care and an increase in alcoholism; both have remained part
of the Russian social landscape. Along with violence and crime, these
factors took an especially severe toll among men, whose average life
expectancy fell during the 1980s and 1990s by more than five years
to 58, before rebounding a bit to the current 60. Life expectancy for
women also fell, though only slightly, and currently stands at 72.

The result was that despite a net immigration over the course of
more than a decade—as the return of over 5 million ethnic Russians
from non-Russian parts of the former Soviet empire between 1989

247

and 2002 more than offset those who emigrated to other countries—
Russia's population fell from almost 149 million in 1992 to about 142
million in 2007.

Projections for the future vary, in part because of variables such as the
impact of AIDS, another scourge taking an increasing toll of the Russian
people with each passing year. Unless something drastic happens, that
decline will become an implosion. One reasonable estimate, and it is
on the optimistic side, is that Russia will have a population of only 100
million in 2050. Pessimistic estimates are worse. And because within
the Russian Federation non-Russian ethnic groups have higher birthrates than Russians, a growing percentage of the country's population
will be non-Russian and Muslim. In 2006 President Putin announced
a government initiative to reverse the population trends by providing
substantial financial benefits to women who have children, especially
those who have more than one child. In a country where 70 percent of
Russian women of childbearing age have either one child or none at all,
it remains to be seen what effect, if any, this program will have.

Another problem visible everywhere is environmental degradation.
With rare exceptions the Soviet regime pursued economic growth with-
out regard for the ecological damage its policies and projects caused.
Dams and wastes from industry and agriculture have turned the Volga,

Russian dolls known as matrioshkas, *which fit inside one another, representing Russian/Soviet leaders from Putin back to Lenin* (vixique, 2007. Used under license from ShutterStock, Inc.)

the river Russians traditionally call their "Dear Little Mother," into a polluted and stagnant waterway. Industrial pollution in many regions, from the Kola Peninsula in the far northwest to a large area around the steel-producing city of Magnitogorsk in the Urals, have poisoned not only animals and plants but also sickened people who live there. Even stretches of remote Siberia suffer from the effects of industrial pollution, which is often carried great distances by winds before falling back to earth in the form of acid rain. Perhaps worst of all, many waterways across Russia, both inland and coastal, have been polluted by nuclear wastes, whose impact will be felt for centuries, if not longer. It all adds up to what two experts aptly called "death by ecocide" (Feshbach and Friendly 1992: 1).

There is no doubt the Russian economy has grown impressively since the turn of the century. Since hitting bottom in 1998, Russia's economy has grown for eight consecutive years. Between 2003 and 2005 the rate of growth declined slightly, but the trend was reversed in 2006, when the economy grew by an estimated 6.7 percent. Equally encouraging was the growth in investment, the most important factor in future growth. The inflation rate in 2006 of 9 percent would be considered high in many countries. but it was the lowest Russia had experienced in 15 years. Russia's positive foreign trade balance, growth in private consumption, and other economic indicators all were impressive and encouraging.

An overriding concern, however, is the extent to which the Russian economy is dependent on energy exports, and especially on world oil prices. Another concern is that too many Russian citizens are not benefiting from their country's growth and development. A middle class is developing, but wealth is concentrated at the top of the social pyramid. The gap between the very rich and the poor is widening. As of 2007 Russia had 25 billionaires and 88,000 millionaires. Their playground was Moscow, a city increasingly studded with upscale shopping malls, expensive apartment buildings, and pricey restaurants and nightclubs. Symbolically Moscow was one of the main stops for the Millionaire Fair, a traveling exhibit selling products such as bejeweled $150,000 cellphones, gold-plated computer mouses, luxurious yachts, million-dollar sports cars, and even island villas that once belonged to Hollywood movie stars. In 2005 the Millionaire Fair did $600 million worth of business in Moscow. Some of the buyers were the elite of Russia's oil industry or magnates from other business fields, but as one sports car salesman noted, "A lot of rich people here don't say how they made their money" (New York Times, November 1, 2006, C10). All this was taking place in a country with a per capita GDP comparable to that of Portugal.

Meanwhile, many parts of the country and tens of millions of people everywhere struggle just to get by. Thousands of villages, no longer viable as collective farms and older industries decline, are losing their populations and turning into ghost towns. In cities across the country pensioners watch helplessly as inflation erodes their meager stipends. Crumbling infrastructure and lax enforcement of safety codes place many people in dangerous conditions daily, a grim reality driven home by an epidemic of fire-related deaths. In 2006 more than 17,000 Russians died in fires, five times the number in the United States, a country with double the population. Nor were matters improving: In early 2007 a coal mine explosion in Siberia killed more than 100, and a fire in a state-run Moscow nursing home, the worst such incident of the post-Soviet era, took the lives of more than 60 patients and staff.

The government's failure to protect people cannot be blamed on a shortage of personnel. Another Soviet legacy that still burdens Russia is the size of the government bureaucracy, which in 2005 numbered more than 1.4 million employees (excluding military and security personnel), a larger figure than during the Soviet era. Not surprisingly, upper-level officials such as ministers do very well despite modest salaries, with perks such as cars and drivers, free medical care, state-rented dachas, and state subsidies for mortgages worth tens of thousands of dollars per year. Hundreds of thousands of lower-level officials must get by on much less, which helps explain why bribery is such a problem. A reasonable estimate is that corruption eats up 10 percent of Russia's gross domestic product, with much of that loss in the form of bribes paid by businesspeople to government officials.

Yet the problem extends much further. Police and other security personnel are easily bribed and expect to be. Moscow traffic police, for example, stop motorists for the smallest violation in the expectation they will be paid off on the spot. Worse, on several occasions terrorists have used bribery to help them commit acts of mass murder. In 2004 two female Chechen suicide bombers without reservations bribed their way on board two separate airline flights, both of which ended with midair explosions that killed 90 people. Shortly afterward Chechen terrorists reached a school in the North Ossetian town of Beslan by bribing police at checkpoints. The terrorists then took more than 1,200 hostages, and more than 300 people, including 186 children, died before that horrific incident was over. No wonder that shortly after the Beslan slaughter President Putin admitted, "We have allowed corruption to

A Kremlin tower and traffic: the old and the new in Moscow (4780322454, 2007. Used under license from ShutterStock, Inc.)

undermine our judicial and law enforcement system" (*Los Angeles Times*, November 8, 2004).

Putin's solution to this and other problems, as his country's most powerful politician, has been to strengthen Russia's central government, especially the presidency. In the process he has undermined, and arguably reversed, the effort to turn Russia into a Western-style parliamentary democracy. By 2005 the political situation was such that Freedom House, a respected independent think tank, downgraded Russia in its annual rankings from "partially free," a rating it had received since the 1990s, to "not free," its lowest rating. In doing so Freedom House criticized not only the elections but the Putin regime's suppression of dissent through government control of key media outlets and intimidation of the remaining independent news media. The assassination of the highly respected investigative journalist Anna Politkovskaya in October 2006 by an unidentified gunman was a particularly disturbing event. Freedom House was not entirely negative, noting that freedom of assembly is usually respected, thousands of nongovernment organizations exist, and property rights have been strengthened. Still, it bluntly stated, "Russians cannot change their government democratically" (Freedom House 2006: n.p.).

The Russian Riddle

A month after the outbreak of World War II, Winston Churchill was asked what he thought the Soviet Union would do in response to the threat Nazi Germany so clearly posed to every nation in Europe. Two months earlier, in August 1939, the Soviets had shocked the world by signing a nonaggression pact with Nazi Germany, supposedly its ideological archenemy. Churchill replied that he could only venture a guess as to what Moscow would do next. Russia, he said, "is a riddle, wrapped in a mystery, inside an enigma."

Almost seven decades later, that characterization still applies, perhaps more than ever. Russia remains a riddle, wrapped in seemingly intractable problems no less than mystery, hidden inside a dark tunnel of misfortune as well as inside an enigma. In October 1939 Churchill also ventured that "perhaps there is a key" to Russian behavior, and suggested "Russian national interest" (Churchill 1939). He hoped that the Soviet Union, judging by how he understood its national interest, would align itself with Britain and France against Nazi Germany. Of course, this Joseph Stalin did not do until Hitler betrayed him and launched Germany's devastating onslaught against the Soviet Union in June 1941.

Today it would seem that in the wake of the catastrophes that visited the country during the 20th century—World War I, the Bolshevik Revolution, the murderous terror of the Stalin years, World War II, and decades more of Communist rule—Russia's overriding national interest, in the words of Alexander Solzhenitsyn, is to "preserve our people" (OrthodoxyToday.org/Solzhenitsyn 2005). The Kremlin leadership under Vladimir Putin has paid some attention to that imperative but not nearly enough as it pursues an agenda focused on restoring Russia's international standing as a great power. The key question, the contemporary version of the Russian riddle, is whether that orientation will change. If it does, that may answer the most fundamental Russian riddle: whether the Russian people for the first time in their history will be able to enjoy the fruits of their considerable talents and exhausting labors.

APPENDIX 1

BASIC FACTS ABOUT RUSSIA

Official Name
Russian Federation

Government
Russia is a federal republic, divided into 85 administrative units of various types as of early 2008. However, that number will be reduced slightly if some of the smaller units continue to be combined with each other or absorbed by other units. The national executive branch is headed by a president with extensive powers. The legislative branch consists of a bicameral parliament called the Federal Assembly. The lower house, the Duma, has 450 members elected according to proportional representation. To win representation a political party must win at least 7 percent of the popular vote. As of 2008 the most important political parties are the Kremlin-controlled United Russia (by far the most powerful), the Communist Party of the Russian Federation (CPRF), the neo-fascist Liberal Democratic Party, and Motherland, which is allied with United Russia. The upper house, the Federation Council, has two members from each of the country's administrative subdivisions. The judicial branch consists of three high courts. The Supreme Court is the top court of the regular court system; the High Court of Arbitration stands atop a system of arbitration courts; and the Constitutional Court stands as a single body to hear cases dealing with federal laws, the actions of the president and parliament, and related matters. All justices are appointed for life by the Federation Council, after recommendation by the president.

Political Divisions
As of early 2008 there are 47 regions (Russian, *oblast*), 21 republics, six autonomous regions (Russian, *okrug*), 8 territories (Russian, *krai*), two federal cities (Moscow and St. Petersburg), and one autonomous region.

Geography

Area

Russia has an area of 6,592,849 square miles. It is by far the largest country in the world and about 1.8 times the size of the United States. Siberia alone is larger than Canada, the second-largest country in the world.

Boundaries

Russia has the world's longest frontiers (about 12,000 miles) and borders on 14 countries, more than any other in the world. To the west are Finland, Estonia, Latvia, Belarus, and Ukraine. The Kaliningrad region, which is separated from the rest of the country by Lithuania and Belarus, borders on Lithuania to the northeast and Poland to the south. Russia's immediate southern neighbors are Georgia, Azerbaijan, Kazakhstan, Mongolia, and China. North Korea lies southwest of Russia's far eastern territory on the coast of the Sea of Japan. Russia's longest borders are with Kazakhstan (about 4,000 miles), China (about 2,160 miles), and Mongolia (about 2,090 miles). Its shortest border, about 11.4 miles, is with North Korea.

Topography

Most of Russia is a broad plain that stretches across northern Eurasia. Moving west to east, the plain is broken by the low Ural Mountains where Europe and Asia meet. Farther east the land rises to form a plateau and then the mountains of eastern Siberia. To the south, between the Black and Caspian seas, the land rises sharply to form the Caucasus Mountains, whose northern slopes are within Russian territory. Russia has four major vegetation zones. North to south they are the tundra, the largest forest belt in the world, the grassy steppe, and a desert region.

The major rivers of European Russia are the Dnieper, the Don, and the mighty Volga, Europe's longest (2,194 miles). All flow southward, the Dnieper into the Black Sea, the Don into the Sea of Azov, a northern appendage of the Black Sea, and the Volga into the Caspian Sea. Even mightier rivers—the Ob-Irtysh (3,362 miles), Lena (2,700), and Yenisey (2,543)—flow northward through Siberia to the Arctic Ocean. Siberia also has Lake Baikal, the world's deepest lake, which holds more water than any other lake and as much as all North America's Great Lakes combined.

Climate

Russia lies at the same latitudes as Canada and Alaska and far from the moderating Atlantic Ocean Gulf Stream. Most of Russia therefore has a severe continental climate. Winters are long and bitterly cold; summers are short and warm. Much of European Russia has a humid continental climate, but more rain falls on the northern forest region with its poor soil than on the fertile southern steppe. Rainfall decreases on the steppe as one moves eastward. The most moderate climate is found along the Black Sea coast.

Elevation
Russia's highest point, the highest in Europe, is Mt. Elbrus, 18,510 feet above sea level. Its lowest point, along the Caspian Sea coast, is about 91 feet below sea level.

Demographics

Population
The single most important demographic fact about Russia is the continued population decline, which has reduced the country's total population from just under 149 million in 1992 to just above 141 million in mid-2007. The current birthrate is 10.9 per thousand; the death rate is 16 per thousand. Russians make up 79.8 percent of the population, which has about 100 distinct national or ethnic groups. Among the largest minority groups, Tatars account for 3.8 percent of the population and Ukrainians about 2 percent.

Major Cities
Moscow is Russia's capital as well as its largest and richest city, with a population of 8.2 million inside its city limits and a total of 10.8 million within its metropolitan area. St. Petersburg has a population of 4.6 million and 5.35 million in its metropolitan area. Russia's third-largest city, with a population of about 1.4 million, is Nizhny Novgorod, about 250 miles east of Moscow. Novosibirsk, population 1.35 million, is the largest city in Siberia, and Yekaterinburg, population 1.26 million, is the largest city in the Urals. Other cities in the European part of the country with a population of a million or more are Samara, Kazan, Rostov-on-Don, Ufa, and Volgograd. East of the Urals, Chelyabinsk and Omsk each have just over 1 million people.

Language
The great majority of the population speaks Russian. There are dozens of minority languages, each spoken by small numbers of people.

Religion
Before the Bolshevik Revolution most Russians belonged to the Russian Orthodox Church, but one legacy of the Soviet era is that only about 20

percent of the population are practicing Orthodox worshippers. Other Christians account for about 2 percent of the population. Between 10 and 15 percent of the population is Muslim, and that percentage is increasing because of the low ethnic Russian birthrate. Russia's Jewish community continues to decline due to emigration and today probably numbers perhaps 700,000.

Economy

Gross Domestic Product

Russia's gross domestic product is about $1.7 trillion when measured according to the purchasing power parity (PPP) system, the method increasingly favored by economists. This makes it the world's 11th-largest economy according to the CIA. It is a different story when one looks at Russia's per capita income, which is about $12,100 dollars (PPP). That places Russia at 81st in the world, with a per capita income about 27 percent that of the United States, which ranks 11th in the world in per capita income. In 2006 agriculture accounted for just over 5 percent of Russia's economy. Industry accounted for more than 36 percent and services for just over 58 percent. It took Russia eight years of economic growth to recover from the decline of the 1990s that culminated in the economic collapse of 1998.

Currency

Russia's currency is the ruble.

Agricultural Products

Russia's most important products are grains, sugar beets, sunflower seeds, vegetables, fruits, beef, and milk.

Minerals

Russia has a treasure trove of mineral resources, including the world's largest reserves of natural gas and the ninth-largest reserves of oil. It also has vast coal deposits and large deposits of diamonds, gold, aluminum, copper, and nickel. In addition, there are important deposits of rare metals with significant industrial and military uses such as tungsten, manganese, cobalt, platinum, chromium, and vanadium. Its huge forests are a major source of wood.

Industry

Russia's most important industry is its energy sector, in particular the production of oil and natural gas. Russian industry is a world leader in the production of high-tech weapons, including missiles, aircraft, tanks, artillery, and radar. It also produces machinery, scientific instruments, construction equipment, and other products such as consumer durables and textiles.

Trade

Russia is the world's second-largest oil exporter, and these exports have driven Russia's economic growth since 1999. Russia also is the world's largest exporter of natural gas. In addition it exports wood and wood products, metals, and chemicals. It is the world's second-largest exporter of weapons, ranking only behind the United States. Russia exported more than $8 billion worth of weapons in 2006, with China, India, Iran, and Venezuela among its major customers. Arms exports are handled by a government monopoly called Rosoboronexport, which in early 2007 reported it had $30 billion in future orders on its books.

Appendix 2

CHRONOLOGY

Russia before the Russians

c. 1000–700 B.C.E.	Cimmerians control what later becomes the Russian part of the Eurasian plain
c. 700–200	Scythians control the region
late sixth century	Darius of Persia invades Scythian territory
200 B.C.E.–200 C.E.	Sarmatians control the region
200	Goths displace the Sarmatians
370	Huns displace the Goths
mid-sixth century	Avars take control of the steppe north of the Black Sea; Slavic tribes already live in the region
seventh century	Khazar state established; eventually rules from the Volga to the Dnieper
seventh and eighth centuries	Khazars hold off invading Arab armies and block expansion of Islam into region, leaving eastern Europe open to Christianity
eighth–ninth century	Khazar ruling class adopts Judaism; Khazar state remains the leading power on the steppe until defeated in mid-10th century

Kievan Rus

ninth century	Slavs well established on the Eurasian plain as agriculturalists and traders with more than 300 towns
c. 862	Varangians, warriors and traders from Scandinavia, take power in Novgorod, establishing the Rurikid dynasty
c. 880	Oleg, Rurik's successor, takes control of Kiev, which becomes capital of loose federation of fortified cities ruled by princes

911	Oleg wins favorable trading treaty with Byzantine Empire allowing Russian merchants to trade in Constantinople
944	Prince Igor secures another trade treaty with Byzantines
966	Prince Svyatoslav defeats the Khazars
988	Prince Vladimir (r. 978–1015) converts to Greek Orthodox Christianity; Kievan Rus becomes a Christian state
1019–1054	Reign of Yaroslav the Wise. He issues the *Russkaya Prava,* Russia's first law code, and builds Kiev's Cathedral of St. Sophia.
1113–1125	Reign of Vladimir Monomakh, who issues his *Testament* to his successors; Kiev is urban center with 50,000 people
12th century	Novgorod is a flourishing trading center, with extensive ties to Europe. With its strong *veche,* it is now a republic
	The *Primary Russian Chronicle* and *The Tale of the Host of Igor* are written
1147	First mention of Moscow in Russian chronicles
1169	Prince Andrei Bogolyubsky, ruler of Rostov-Suzdal principality, leads coalition of princes that sacks Kiev, as Kievan state is weakened by disunity and civil war
1223	Battle of Kalka River: Mongols defeat Russian-Polovtsy forces
1237	Mongols begin conquest of Kievan Rus
	Mongols destroy Ryazan
1240	Mongols sack and destroy Kiev
1240–1480	Mongols complete conquest of Kievan Rus; establish Golden Horde state on the steppe; control Russia and extract heavy tribute.
1242	Aleksandr Nevsky defeats Teutonic Knights on the ice of Lake Peipus

Muscovite Russia

13th–16th centuries	Lithuania and Poland expand into East Slav territory;

	Gradual division of East Slavs into Russians (Great Russians), Ukrainians (Little Russians), and Belarusians (White Russians)
1301	Moscow (Muscovy) becomes a separate principality with its own ruling house
1303–1325	Reign of Prince Yury, made grand prince by the Golden Horde khan; Territorial expansion of Muscovy begins
1325–1341	Reign of Ivan I (*Kalita,* or "moneybags") who recovers title of grand prince for Moscow, where it stays; Russian Orthodox Church moves its headquarters to Moscow
1359–1389	Reign of Dmitry Donskoi
c. 1360–1430	Life of Andrei Rublev
1380	Battle of Kulikovo Field: Donskoi wins first ever Russian victory over Mongols
1389–1425	Reign of Vasily I, who commissions Rublev to paint frescoes at the Assumption Cathedral in Vladimir
1425–1462	Reign of Vasily II, who defeats and weakens Novgorod in 1456
1462–1505	Reign of Ivan III, the "Great"
1472	Ivan marries niece of last Byzantine emperor, enhancing the prestige of Moscow's grand princes. In the 1480s Ivan sometimes refers to himself as "czar"; Increased use of Byzantine symbols and ceremonies at Moscow court
1478	Ivan annexes Novgorod, abolishes its *veche,* and brings its famous bell to Moscow
1480	Ivan declares independence from the Golden Horde, then faces down a Mongol army near the Oka River
1493	Ivan takes the title "Sovereign [*gosudar*] of All Russia"
1497	Ivan issues a new law code, the *Sudebnik,* reinforcing the growing and increasingly autocratic power of Moscow's grand princes
1500–1503	Successful war against Lithuania wins territory for Moscow

1505–1508	Construction of Ivan's Great Bell Tower, the tallest structure in Moscow until the late 19th century
1505–1533	Reign of Vasily III
1510	Moscow annexes the principality of Pskov
	Letter to Vasily from leading Orthodox churchman calling Moscow the "Third Rome"
1514	Moscow annexes city of Smolensk
1533–1584	Reign of Ivan IV, the "Terrible"
1547	Ivan's coronation: he formally takes the title "Czar of All the Russias";
	Fire almost destroys Moscow
1549 or 1550	First meeting of the *zemsky sobor*
1550	Ivan issues new law code, the *Sudebnik* of 1550
1552	Ivan's troops conquer Kazan
1552–1560	Ivan builds St. Basil's Cathedral
1558–1582	Livonian War, which is costly and unsuccessful
1564–1572	Era of Ivan's *oprichnina* (reign of terror)
1581	First "forbidden year" restricting movement of peasants;
	Ivan kills his eldest son and heir to the throne
1598–1605	Reign of Boris Godunov
1605–1613	Time of Troubles
1606–1607	Rebellion of peasants and others led by Ivan Bolotnikov
1613	*Zemsky sobor* chooses Michael Romanov as czar, beginning the Romanov dynasty that will rule until 1917
1613–1645	Reign of Michael Romanov
1645–1676	Reign of Alexis
1649	Alexis issues new law code, which finalizes and confirms the serfdom of Russia's peasants
1670–1671	Rebellion of Stepan Razin

Imperial Russia

1682–1725	Reign of Peter I, the "Great"
1696	Russia takes Azov from the Ottoman Empire
1697–1698	Peter's grand embassy tour of Europe
1700	Peter adopts the Julian calendar

1701	Russia's first secular school, the School of Mathematics and Navigation in St. Petersburg, founded
1701–1704	Seven ironworks built in Urals, effectively marking the beginning of Russia's industrialization. By 1725 Russia has about 200 large industrial enterprises
1700–1721	Northern War with Sweden
1703	St. Petersburg founded on territory along the Baltic coast seized from Sweden
1707–1708	Cossack revolt led by Kondraty Bulavin
1709	Peter defeats Charles XII of Sweden at Poltava
1711	Peter defeated by Turks in battle along Pruth River; Russia loses Azov
1711–1765	Life of Mikhail Lomonosov
1714	Major Russian naval victory over Sweden
1718	Poll tax instituted, tightening serfdom's controls; a careful census follows; Alexis, heir to the throne, dies from torture during Peter's investigation of alleged plot
1721	Treaty of Nystadt, confirming Russian annexation of Swedish territory along the Baltic coast; Peter establishes Holy Synod
1722	Peter establishes Table of Ranks
1722–1723	War with Persia
1741–1761	Reign of Elizabeth
1754–1762	Construction of the Winter Palace by Italian architect Bartolomeo Rastrelli
1755	Founding of Moscow University at urging of Lomonosov
1756–1763	Seven Years' War
1761–1762	Reign of Peter III; he is murdered in a coup
1762	Peter frees nobility from compulsory state service and takes Russia out of the Seven Years' War, saving Prussia
1762–1796	Reign of Catherine II, the "Great"
1766	Catherine issues her *Nakaz* calling for reform of Russia's law code
1768–1774	War with Turkey; ends with Treaty of Kuchuk Kainardji, giving Russia major territorial gains north of the Black Sea

1783	Annexation of the Crimea
1772–1795	Partition of Poland, in three stages (1772, 1793, 1795)
1773–1774	Pugachev rebellion
1775	Reform of provincial governments
1785	Catherine issues Charter of the Nobility, codifying and solidifying noble privileges
1787–1791	War with Turkey confirms and adds to Russian territorial gains
1790	Aleksandr Radishchev publishes *A Journey from St. Petersburg to Moscow*; shortly thereafter he is exiled to Siberia
1792	Odessa founded; Nikolai Novikov arrested
1792–1856	Life of Nikolai Lobachevsky
1796–1801	Reign of Paul I, which ends when he is murdered in a coup
1799–1837	Life of Aleksandr Pushkin
1801–1825	Reign of Alexander I
1803	Decree on "free agriculturalists" allows landlords to free serfs
1804–1813	War with Persia
1805–1807	War with France under Napoléon Bonaparte; ends with the Peace of Tilsit
1806–1809	War with Turkey
1809–1852	Life of Nikolai Gogol
1812–1815	War with France after Napoléon invades Russia in June 1812
1812	Alexander dismisses Mikhail Speransky
1814	Russian army enters Paris
1814–1841	Life of Mikhail Lermontov
1815	Alexander forms Holy Alliance with Prussia and Austria
1816–1819	Serfdom abolished in Baltic provinces, but peasants freed without land
1818–1883	Life of Ivan Turgenev
1820–1880	Golden age of Russian literature
1821–1881	Life of Fyodor Dostoyevsky
1825	Decembrist Revolt after Alexander's death
1825–1855	Reign of Nicholas I
1826	Third Section established

1827–1829	War with Turkey ends with Russian victory and Treaty of Adrianople
1828–1910	Life of Leo Tolstoy
1830–1831	Polish rebellion
1834–1907	Life of Dmitry Mendeleyev
1840s	Emergence of Slavophiles and Westerners
1841–1893	Life of Peter Tchaikovsky
1844–1930	Life of Ilya Repin
1845	New criminal code with 54 pages of political crimes
1849–1936	Life of Ivan Pavlov
1851	Railroad connecting St. Petersburg and Moscow opened
1853–1856	Crimean War; Nicholas I dies in 1855; War ends with Russian defeat and territorial losses
1855–1881	Reign of Alexander II
1860–1900	Life of Isaac Levitan
1860–1904	Life of Anton Chekhov
1861	Emancipation Edict frees serfs; Beginning of Great Reforms
1863	Education reform restores autonomy to universities
1864	Zemstvos established, reforming local government; reform of judiciary makes it independent branch
1865–1911	Life of Valentin Serov
1866	State peasants freed; Assassination attempt against Alexander II
1868–1936	Life of Maksim Gorky
1870	Reform of town government
1870–1953	Life of Ivan Bunin
1872–1929	Life of Sergei Diaghilev
1873–1938	Life of Fyodor Chaliapin
1873–1943	Life of Sergei Rachmaninoff
1874	Reform of military service—the last Great Reform
1874–1875	Going to the People movement

1877–1878	War with Turkey ends with Treaty of San Stefano; its terms are revised to Russia's detriment by the Congress of Berlin
1879	Formation of People's Will
1880–1921	Life of Aleksandr Blok
1880–1934	Life of Andrei Bely
1881	Alexander II assassinated by members of People's Will
1881–1894	Reign of Alexander III
1881	Political police reorganized as the Okhrana; new law subjects much of Russia to the equivalent of martial law; Deadly wave of pogroms against Jews
1881–1931	Life of Anna Pavlova
1882–1971	Life of Igor Stravinsky
1888–1966	Life of Anna Akhmatova
1889	New law creates land captains to control peasantry
1890	New law reduces peasant influence in the zemstvos and tightens government control over those bodies
c. 1890–1917	Silver age of Russian culture
1891–1892	Severe famine
1891–1938	Life of Osip Mandelstam
1892–1903	Sergei Witte serves as finance minister, promoting railroads and industrialization
1894–1917	Reign of Nicholas II
1902	Lenin publishes What Is to Be Done?
1903	Second Social Democratic Party Congress; Bolshevik-Menshevik split; Nicholas II dismisses Witte; Wave of strikes sweeps southern Russia
1904–1905	Russo-Japanese war; ends in Russian defeat
1905	Bloody Sunday, Revolution of 1905; St. Petersburg Soviet formed; October Manifesto issued by Nicholas; St. Petersburg Soviet arrested and Moscow uprising crushed
1906	Fundamental Laws issued; First Duma meets;

	Prime Minister Peter Stolypin begins "wager on the strong" agricultural reforms
1906–1910	SRs assassinate more than 4,000 government officials
1907–1966	Life of Sergei Korolev
1914	World War I begins
1915	Nicholas takes command of the army
1916	Rasputin assassinated
1917	Disorder breaks out in Petrograd

Soviet Russia

1917	March Revolution: Disorder and riots lead to the formation of a Provisional Government and the Petrograd Soviet of Workers' and Soldiers' deputies; Nicholas II abdicates: end of Romanov Dynasty; November Revolution: Bolsheviks seize power in Petrograd; Constituent Assembly elections won by SRs; Cheka founded
1918	Bolsheviks disperse Constituent Assembly by force; Civil War begins; Nicholas II and his family executed by Bolsheviks; Bolsheviks begin Red Terror and implement policies that later are given the name War Communism
1919–1920	Decisive battles of the Civil War
1921	Kronstadt Rebellion; 10th Party Congress introduces the New Economic Policy (NEP) and bans all "factions" within the Communist Party
1921–1989	Life of Andrei Sakharov
1922	Cheka abolished but reemerges as the GPU (later OGPU); Stalin appointed general secretary of Communist Party; Trial and execution of SR leaders; Lenin suffers two strokes and writes his "Testament"
1923	Lenin writes his "Postscript," urging Stalin be demoted; New constitution written for the Union of Soviet Socialist Republics (USSR); Lenin incapacitated by third stroke

1924	Lenin dies; his former lieutenants struggle for power
1924–1928	"Industrialization Debate"
1925	Trotsky loses post as commissar of war; Stalin's power grows
1927	Stalin crushes short-lived Trotsky alliance with Zinoviev and Kamenev
1929	Stalin consolidates power; Trotsky deported to Mexico;
	First Five-Year Plan, calling for rapid industrialization along socialist lines;
	Collectivization begins as part of full-scale industrialization drive, accompanied by dekulakization
1929–1937	First two five-year plans produce rapid industrial development and a socialist, centrally planned economy
1930	Temporary halt to collectivization in the face of massive peasant resistance
1931–1932	Catastrophic famine in the Ukraine and other grain-growing regions; 5 million die in the Ukraine alone
1934	Chief Administration of Camps—Gulag—set up;
	17th Party Congress
1934–1938	Stalin's great purge (or Great Terror); major show trials take place between 1936 and 1938; peak years of the terror are 1937–1938
1939	Nazi-Soviet Pact
1939–1945	World War II
1941	Germany attacks the Soviet Union along 2,000-mile front
1942–1943	Battle of Stalingrad turns tide of battle in Soviet Union's favor
1945	World War II ends
1945–1947	Soviet expansion in Eastern Europe causes tensions that lead to the Cold War
1946	*Zhdanovshchina* begins
1953	Stalin dies;
	Malenkov becomes prime minister; Khrushchev becomes party's first secretary;

	Beria arrested and later executed;
	First small group of Gulag prisoners released
1954	Beginning of Virgin Lands project
1955	Khrushchev emerges as top Soviet leader;
	Geneva summit meeting
1956	Khrushchev's Secret Speech at 20th Party Congress; start of de-Stalinization;
	Upheaval in Poland; Hungarian uprising against Soviet rule;
	Release of Gulag prisoners accelerates
1957	Khrushchev defeats "anti-Party" group, confirming his position as Soviet leader;
	Khrushchev's economic decentralization plan instituted;
	Sputnik launched
1958	Boris Pasternak wins Nobel Prize in literature for *Dr. Zhivago*
1961	Yury Gagarin first man to orbit earth;
	Yevgeny Yevtushenko publishes "Babi Yar";
	Berlin Wall is built
1962	Riots and repression in Novocherkassk;
	Yevtushenko publishes "The Heirs of Stalin";
	Cuban Missile Crisis;
	Aleksandr Solzhenitsyn publishes *One Day in the Life of Ivan Denisovich*
	Manezh modern art exhibition
1963	"Hot line" installed connecting the Kremlin and White House;
	Partial nuclear test-ban treaty
1964	Khrushchev removed from office;
	Brezhnev new Soviet leader; several Khrushchev reforms reversed
1965	Andrei Sinyavsky and Yuli Daniel arrested
1966	23rd Party Congress
1968	Andrei Sakharov publishes "Thoughts on Progress, Peaceful Coexistence, and Intellectual Freedom"
1969	SALT talks begin
1970	Solzhenitsyn wins Nobel Prize in Literature
1972	SALT I treaty signed

1973	Solzhenitsyn publishes first volume of *The Gulag Archipelago*
1974	SALT II framework signed
1975	Helsinki Accords; Soviet and American spacecraft dock in space; Sakharov wins Nobel Peace Prize
1979	Soviet Union invades Afghanistan
1982	Brezhnev dies; Andropov becomes party general secretary
1984	Andropov dies; Chernenko becomes general secretary
1985	Chernenko dies; Mikhail Gorbachev chosen general secretary; Era of perestroika begins
1986	Chernobyl nuclear reactor explodes; Many previously banned books and films become available because of glasnost
1987	Boris Yeltsin demoted for criticizing pace of reform; demands for autonomy in some non-Russian regions; nuclear arms control treaty eliminates all medium-range missiles from Europe
1988	Communist Party approves creation of the Congress of People's Deputies; Gorbachev speech at UN repudiates Leninist commitment to spread communism worldwide
1989	Elections to Congress of Peoples Deputies; Yeltsin and Sakharov among those elected; communism collapses in Eastern Europe
1990–1991	Economic conditions deteriorate as demands for autonomy by non-Russian minority nationalities grow
1991	Yeltsin elected president of the RSFSR, becoming first leader ever elected directly by the Russian people; coup against Gorbachev fails; Yeltsin and presidents of Ukraine and Belarus agree to dismantle the Soviet Union and create CIS; confirmed by 11 Soviet republic heads two weeks later; Gorbachev resigns as president; Soviet Union ceases to exist at midnight December 31

The Russian Federation

1992	Yeltsin ends state control of prices on most goods and services, beginning shock therapy; voucher privatization begins
1993	Attempted coup against Yeltsin fails; voters elect new parliament: neo-fascists, Communists (CPRF) do well. Voters also approve new constitution providing for powerful president
1994	Russian economy has declined by 40 percent since 1991; Yeltsin orders Russian army into Chechnya
1995	Yeltsin launches second round of privatization; CPRF wins proportional representation ballot in parliamentary elections
1996	Russians withdraw troops from Chechnya; Yeltsin reelected to second term
1998	Russia holds funeral for Nicholas II and family; Yeltsin calls for reconciliation; Russian ruble collapses; Russia in effect is bankrupt
1999	Russian economy begins to revive due to rise in oil price; Vladimir Putin becomes prime minister; Russian troops again invade Chechnya; Yeltsin resigns as president; Putin becomes acting president
2000	Duma ratifies START II; Russian forces retake Grozny; guerrilla war continues with Chechnya; Putin elected president, marking first democratic transfer of power in Russia's history; Putin establishes seven federal districts to oversee Russia's regions
2001	New tax law lowers income tax rates to 13 percent
2002	Regional governors excluded from Federation Council
2003	TVS, Russia's last independent television network, falls under government control; parliamentary elections won by Kremlin-controlled party called United Russia

2004	Putin overwhelmingly reelected to a second term with almost no real opposition; new law ends election of regional governors and republic presidents; Chechen terrorists seize 1,200 hostages in school in Beslan; more than 300 die; Putin admits disastrous effects of corruption
2005	New law abolishes single-seat districts in Duma, hurting independent parties; Khordorkovsky arrested, Yukos seized by government; Russia reaches billion-dollar arms agreement with Iran and continues work on Iranian nuclear reactor; Solzhenitsyn stresses Russia's need to "preserve the people"
2006	Russian population continues to fall; Russian economy continues to grow for eighth consecutive year; inflation drops to 9 percent
2007	Russia has 25 billionaires and 88,000 millionaires, as gap between wealthy and others grows; mine explosion kills more than 100 people; nursing home fire kills more than 60; Russia's population drops below 142 million
2008	Dmitry Medvedev elected president; Putin becomes prime minister; Russia invades Georgia, a former Soviet republic south of the Caucasus Mountains, in effect taking control of Abkhazia and South Ossetia, two regions of that country

APPENDIX 3

BIBLIOGRAPHY

Avrich, Paul. *Russian Rebels, 1600–1800*. New York: Norton, 1972.

Billington, James H. *The Icon and the Axe: An Interpretive History of Russian Culture*. New York: Vintage, 1970.

Brovkin, Vladimir. *Russia after Lenin: Politics, Culture, Society*. New York and London: Routledge, 1998.

Brown, Archie. *The Gorbachev Factor*. New York and Oxford: Oxford University Press, 1997.

Brown, Archie, Michael Kaser, and Gerald S. Smith, eds. *The Cambridge Encyclopedia of Russia and the Former Soviet Union*. Cambridge: Cambridge University Press, 1994.

Chamberlin, William Henry. *The Russian Revolution, 1918–1921: From the Civil War to the Consolidation of Power*. New York: Grosset and Dunlap, 1965.

Churchill Papers. "CHAR 9/138/46, 1 October 1939." Available online. URL: www.chu.cam.ac.uk/archives/gallery/Russia/CHAR_09_138_46. php. Accessed on April 16, 2007.

Cohen, Stephen N., ed. *An End to Silence: Uncensored Opinion in the Soviet Union*. New York: Norton, 1982.

Crankshaw, Edward. *The Shadow of the Winter Palace: The Drift to Revolution, 1825–1917*. New York: Penguin, 1976.

Cross, Anthony, ed. *Russia Under Western Eyes*. London: Elek Books, 1971.

Dallin, David, and Boris Nicolaevsky. *Forced Labor in Soviet Russia*. New Haven, Conn.: Yale University Press, 1945.

Dostoyevsky, Fyodor. *The Brothers Karamazov*. Translated by David McDuff. London and New York: Penguin, 1993.

Dmytryshyn, Basil, ed. *Medieval Russia: A Sourcebook, 900–1700*. Hinsdale, Ill.: Dryden Press, 1973.

Editors of *Horizon Magazine*. *The Horizon History of Russia*. New York: American Heritage, 1970.

————. *The Horizon Book of Arts of Russia.* New York: American Heritage, 1970.

Fennell, J. L. I., ed. and trans. *The Correspondence between Prince Kurbsky and Ivan IV of Russia (1564–1579).* New York: Cambridge University Press, 1955.

Feshbach, Murry, and Alfred Friendly Jr. *Ecocide in the USSR: Health and Nature Under Siege.* New York: Basic Books, 1992.

Florinsky, Michael T. *Russia: A History and Interpretation.* Vol. 1. New York: Macmillan, 1953.

————. *Russia: A History and Interpretation.* Vol. 2. New York: Macmillan, 1955.

Freedom House. *Freedom in the World—Russia (2006)* Available online. URL: www.freedomhouse.org. Accessed on April 18, 2007.

————. *Russia.* Available online. URL: www.freedomhouse.org. Accessed on April 18, 2007.

Gilbert, Martin. *Atlas of Russian History.* New York: Dorset Press, 1984.

Golder, F. A., ed. *Documents of Russian History, 1914–1917.* New York: Century, 1927.

Hare, Richard. *Pioneers of Russian Social Thought.* 2nd ed., revised. New York: Vintage, 1964.

Heller, Mikhail, and Aleksandr M. Nikrich. *Utopia in Power: The History of the Soviet Union from 1917 to the Present.* Translated by Phyllis B. Carlos. New York: Summit Books, 1986.

Herspring, Dale R. "Conclusion: Putin and the Future of Russia." In Dale R. Herspring, editor. *Putin's Russia: Past Imperfect, Future Uncertain.* Lanham, Md.: Rowman and Littlefield, 2003.

Kochan, Lionel, and Richard Abraham. *The Making of Modern Russia.* 2nd ed. New York: Penguin, 1983.

Kort, Michael. *The Columbia Guide to the Cold War.* New York: Columbia University Press, 1998.

————. *The Soviet Colossus: History and Aftermath.* Armonk, N.Y.: M.E. Sharpe, 2006.

Kravchenko, Victor. *I Chose Justice.* New York: Scribner, 1950.

Lapidus, Gail W. "State and Society: Toward the Emergence of Civil Society in the Soviet Union." In Seweryn Bailer, ed. *Inside Gorbachev's Russia: Politics, Society, Nationality.* Boulder, Colo., and London: Westview Press, 1989.

Lenin, V. I. *What Is to Be Done? The Burning Questions of Our Movement.* New York: International Publishers, 1943.

Lincoln W. Bruce. *Between Heaven and Hell: The Story of a Thousand Years of Artistic Life in Russia.* New York: Viking, 1998.

Lozanoga, A. N. *Pesni i Skazaniya o Razina i Pugacheve* (Songs and Tales of Razia and Pugachev). Moscow: Academiya, 1935.

Marks, Steven G. *How Russia Shaped the Modern World: From Art to Anti-Semitism, Ballet to Bolshevism.* Princeton, N.J.: Princeton University Press, 2003.

Massie, Robert K. *Peter the Great: His Life and World.* New York: Ballantine Books, 1980.

Massie, Suzanne. *Land of the Firebird: The Beauty of Old Russia.* New York: Simon and Schuster, 1980.

McCauley, Martin. *Who's Who in Russia since 1900.* London and New York: Routledge, 1997.

McConnell, Allen. *Tsar Alexander I: Paternalistic Reformer.* New York: Thomas Y. Crowell, 1970.

McFaul, Michael. "Reengaging Russia: A New Agenda," *Current History* (October 2004): 307–313.

Medvedev, Roy. *Khrushchev: A Biography.* Garden City, N.Y.: Anchor Books, 1984.

Miller, Wright. *The Russians as People.* New York: E.P. Dutton, 1961.

Mosse, W. E. *Alexander II and the Modernization of Russia.* Rev. ed. New York: Collier Books, 1962.

Murray, Donald. *Democracy of Despots.* Boulder, Colo.: Westview Press, 1995.

OthodoxyToday.org. "Interview with Alexander Solzhenitsyn." June 5, 2005. OthodoxyToday.org. Available online. URL: www.orthodoxyto-day.org. Accessed on April 15, 2007.

Pipes, Richard. *The Russian Revolution.* New York: Knopf, 1990.

Press Service of the President of the Russian Federation.

Pushkin, Alexander. *The Poems and Plays of Alexander Pushkin.* Edited by Avrahm Yarmolinsky. New York: Modern Library, 1964.

Putnam, Peter, ed. *Seven Britons in Imperial Russia, 1698–1812.* Princeton, N.J.: Princeton University Press, 1952.

Remnik, David. *Resurrection: The Struggle for a New Russia.* New York: Random House, 1997.

Riasanovsky, Nicholas. *A History of Russia.* 2nd ed. New York: Oxford University Press, 1969.

———. *Nicholas I and Official Nationality in Russia, 1825–1855.* Berkeley: University of California Press, 1967.

Sakwa, Richard. *Politics and Russian Society.* London and New York: Routledge, 1993.

Service, Robert. *A History of Twentieth-Century Russia.* Cambridge, Mass.: Harvard University Press, 1997.

Seton-Watson, Hugh. *The Russian Empire, 1801–1917.* London: Oxford University Press, 1967.

Shevardnadze, Eduard. *The Future Belongs to Freedom.* London: Sinclair-Stevenson, 1991.

Shevstova, Lydia. "Russia's Ersatz Democracy." *Current History* (October 2006): 307–314.

Shukman, Harold, ed. *The Blackwell Encyclopedia of the Russian Revolution.* New York and Oxford: Blackwell, 1988.

Slonim Marc. *The Epic of Russian Literature: From Its Origins through Tolstoy.* New York: Oxford University Press, 1964.

———. *From Chekhov to the Revolution: Russian Literature, 1900–1917.* New York: Oxford University Press, 1953.

Solzhenitsyn, Aleksandr I. *The Gulag Archipelago, 1918–1956: An Experiment in Literary Investigation I-II.* New York: Harper and Row, 1973.

Spector, Ivar, and Marion Spector, eds. *Readings in Russian History and Culture.* Palo Alto, Calif.: Pacific Books, 1965.

Suny, Ronald Grigor. *The Soviet Experiment: Russia, the USSR, and the Successor States.* New York and Oxford: Oxford University Press, 1998.

Szamuely, Tibor. *The Russian Tradition.* New York: McGraw-Hill, 1974.

Taubman, William. *Khrushchev: The Man and His Era.* New York: Norton, 2003.

United States Central Intelligence Agency. *The World Factbook.* 2007. Available online. URL: www.cia.gov/cia/publications/factbook. Accessed on August 3, 2007.

Utechin, S. V. *A Concise Encyclopedia of the USSR.* New York: Dutton, 1964.

Vernadsky, George. *A History of Russia.* New Haven, Conn., and London: Yale University Press, 1961.

Werth, Nicolas. "A State against Its People: Violence, Repression, and Terror in the Soviet Union." In Stephane Courtois et al., editors. *The Black Book of Communism: Crimes, Terror, Repression.* Cambridge, Mass.: Harvard University Press, 1999.

Wolfe, Bertram. *Three Who Made a Revolution.* New York: Delta, 1964.

Yakovlev, Alexander N. *A Century of Violence in Soviet Russia.* Translated by Anthony Austin. New Haven, Conn., and London: Yale University Press, 2002.

Yarmolinsky, Avrahm, ed. *Two Centuries of Russian Verse, An Anthology: From Lomonosov to Voznesensky.* Translated by Babette Deutsch. New York: Random House, 1966.

Yeltsin, Boris N. "Address of the President of the Russian Federation," December 31, 1999. Press Service of the Russian Federation.

Yevtushenko, Yevgeny, ed. *20th Century Russian Poetry: Silver and Steel: An Anthology.* New York: Doubleday, 1994.

Zenkovsky, Serge A., ed. and trans. *Medieval Russia's Epics, Chronicles, and Tales.* Revised and enlarged edition. New York: E.P. Dutton, 1974.

APPENDIX 4

SUGGESTED READING

Overviews of Russian History

Berlin, Isaiah. *Russian Thinkers.* Edited by Henry Hardy and Aileen Kelly. New York: Viking Press, 1978.

Blackwell, William L. *The Industrialization of Russia.* New York: Crowell, 1970.

Blum, Jerome. *Lord and Peasant in Russia.* New York: Atheneum, 1965.

Brooks, Jeffrey. *Thank You, Comrade Stalin: Soviet Public Culture from Revolution to Cold War.* Princeton, N.J.: Princeton University Press, 2000.

Daniels, Robert V. *The End of the Communist Revolution.* London and New York: Routledge, 1993.

Graham, Loren R. *Science in Russia and the Soviet Union: A Short History.* New York: Cambridge University Press, 1994.

Laqueur, Walter. *The Dream That Failed: Reflections on the Soviet Union.* New York: Oxford University Press, 1994.

Lincoln, W. Bruce. *The Romanovs: Autocrats of All the Russias.* New York: Dial Press, 1981.

McNeal, Robert A. *The Bolshevik Tradition: Lenin, Stalin, Khrushchev, Brezhnev,* 2nd ed. Englewood Cliffs, N.J.: Prentice Hall, 1975.

Medvedev, Zhores. *Soviet Agriculture.* New York and London: Norton, 1987.

Merridale, Catherine. *Night of Stone: Death and Memory in Twentieth-Century Russia.* New York: Viking Penguin, 2001.

Nove, Alec. *An Economic History of the USSR, 1917–1991,* 3rd ed. New York: Penguin, 1992.

Pipes, Richard. *Russia Under the Old Regime.* New York: Scribner, 1974.

Raeff, Marc. *Understanding Imperial Russia.* Translated by Arthur Goldhammer. New York: Columbia University Press, 1984.

Ragsdale, Hugh. *The Russian Tragedy: The Burden of History.* Armonk, N.Y.: M.E. Sharpe, 1996.

Reshetar, John S., Jr. *A Concise History of the Communist Party of the Soviet Union*. Rev. and exp. ed. New York: Praeger, 1964.

Robinson, Geroid Tanquary. *Rural Russia Under the Old Regime*. Berkeley: University of California Press, 1967.

Sakwa, Richard, ed. *The Rise and Fall of the Soviet Union, 1917–1991*. London and New York: Routledge, 1999.

Schapiro, Leonard. *The Communist Party of the Soviet Union*. New York: Vintage, 1964.

Sinyavsky, Andrei. *Soviet Civilization: A Cultural History*. New York: Arcade, 1988.

Szamuely, Tibor. *The Russian Tradition*. New York: McGraw-Hill, 1974.

Volkogonov, Dmitri. *Autopsy for an Empire: The Seven Leaders Who Built the Soviet Union*. Edited and translated by Harold Shukman. New York: Free Press, 1998.

Von Laue, Theodore H. *Why Lenin? Why Stalin? Why Gorbachev?* New York: HarperCollins, 1993.

Werth, Nicholas. "A State against Its People: Violence, Repression, and Terror in the Soviet Unon." In Stéphane Courtois et al. *The Black Book of Communism: Crimes, Terror, Repression*. Translated by Jonathan Murphy and Mark Kramer. Cambridge, Mass.: Harvard University Press, 1999.

Kievan Russ to Muscovite Russia

Cheriavsky, Michael. *Tsar and People*. New Haven, Conn.: Yale University Press, 1961.

Fennel, J. L. I. *The Crisis of Medieval Russia, 1200–1304*. London: Longman, 1981.

Grey, Ian. *Ivan III and the Unification of Russia*. New York: Collier, 1967.

———. *Ivan the Terrible*. Philadelphia: Lippincott, 1964.

Vernadsky, George. *Kievan Russia*. London and New York: Cambridge University Press, 1948.

The Eras of Peter the Great and Catherine the Great

De Madariaga, I. *Russia in the Age of Catherine the Great*. New Haven, Conn.: Yale University Press, 1981.

Dukes, P. *Catherine the Great and the Russian Nobility*. Cambridge: Cambridge University Press, 1967.

Jones, R. E. *The Emancipation of the Russian Nobility*. Princeton, N.J.: Princeton University Press, 1973.

Klyuchevsky, Vasili. *Peter the Great*. Translated by Liniana Archibald. New York: Vintage, 1958.

Oliva, L. Jay. *Russia in the Era of Peter the Great*. Englewood Cliffs, N.J.: Prentice Hall, 1969.

Raeff, Marc. *The Origins of the Russian Intelligentsia in the Eighteenth Century Nobility*. New York: Harcourt Brace, 1966.

Rogger, Hans. *National Consciousness in Eighteenth-Century Russia*. Cambridge, Mass.: Harvard University Press, 1960.

Rounding, Virginia. *Catherine the Great: Love, Sex, and Power*. New York: St. Martins Press, 2007.

Sumner, B. H. *Peter the Great and the Emergence of Russia*. New York: Collier, 1962.

The Nineteenth Century Crisis:
The Mystic and the Knout

Blackwell, William L. *The Beginnings of Russian Industrialization, 1800–1860*. Princeton, N.J.: Princeton University Press, 1968.

Carr, Edward Hallett. *The Romantic Exiles: A Nineteenth Century Portrait Gallery*. Boston: Beacon Press, 1961.

Curtiss, John Shelton. *Russia's Crimean War*. Durham, N.C.: Duke University Press, 1979.

Lincoln, W. Bruce. *In the Vanguard of Reform: Russia's Enlightened Bureaucrats*. De Kalb: Northern Illinois University Press, 1982.

———. *The Great Reforms*. De Kalb: Northern Illinois University Press, 1990.

———. *Nicholas I: Emperor and Autocrat of All the Russias*. London and Bloomington: Indiana University Press, 1978.

Malia, Martin. *Alexander Herzen and the Birth of Russian Socialism*. New York: Grosset and Dunlap, 1961.

Mazour, Anatole G. *The First Russian Revolution, 1825*. Stanford, Calif.: Stanford University Press, 1961.

Monas, Sidney. *The Third Section*. Cambridge, Mass.: Harvard University Press, 1961.

Pinter, Walter M. *Russian Economic Policy Under Nicholas I*. Ithaca, N.Y.: Cornell University Press, 1967.

Reform, Reaction, and Revolution, 1861–1917

Ascher, Abraham. *The Revolution of 1905*, 2 vols. Stanford, Calif.: Stanford University Press, 1988, 1992.

Berdyaev, Nicholas. *The Origin of Russian Communism.* Ann Arbor: University of Michigan Press, 1960.

Charques, Richard. *The Twilight of Imperial Russia.* New York: Oxford University Press, 1958.

Florinsky, Michael. *The End of the Russian Empire.* New York: Collier Books, 1961.

Getzler, Israel. *Martov: A Political Biography of a Russian Social Democrat.* Cambridge: Cambridge University Press, 1967.

Harcave, Sidney. *First Blood: The Russian Revolution of 1905.* New York: Macmillan, 1964.

Harding, Neil. *Leninism.* Durham, N.C.: Duke University Press, 1996.

Hosking, Geoffrey. *The Russian Constitutional Experiment: Government and Duma, 1907–1914.* New York: Cambridge University Press, 1973.

Kochan, Lionel. *Russia in Revolution 1890–1918.* London: Granada, 1970.

Kolakowski, Leszek. *Main Currents of Marxism, Vol. 2: The Golden Age.* Translated by F. S. Fella. Oxford: Oxford University Press, 1978.

Le Blanc, Paul. *Lenin and the Revolutionary Party.* Atlantic Highlands, N.J.: Humanities Press International, 1990.

Liebman, Marcel. *Leninism Under Lenin.* Translated by Brian Pearce. London: Merlin Press, 1980.

Meyer, Alfred G. *Leninism.* Cambridge, Mass.: Harvard University Press, 1955.

Pomper, Philip. *The Russian Revolutionary Intelligentsia.* New York: Crowell, 1970.

Schapiro, Leonard. *Russian Studies.* Edited by Ellen Dahrendorf. London: Collins Harvill, 1986.

Service, Robert. *Lenin: A Political Life, Vol. 1: The Strengths of Contradiction.* Bloomington: Indiana University Press, 1985.

Shukman, Harold. *Lenin and the Russian Revolution.* New York: Capricorn Books, 1966.

Ulam, Adam. *The Bolsheviks.* New York: Collier, 1965.

Venturi, Franco. *Roots of Revolution.* Translated by Francis Haskell. New York: Grosset and Dunlap, 1966.

Von Laue, Theodore H. *Sergei Witte and the Industrialization of Russia.* New York: Atheneum, 1969.

Soviet Russia, 1917–1953:
Utopian Dreams and Dystopian Realities

Applebaum, Anne. *Gulag: A History.* New York: Doubleday, 2003.

Bacon, Edwin. *The Gulag at War: Stalin's Forced Labour System in the Light of the Archives.* New York: New York University Press, 1994.

Brovkin, Vladimir N. *The Mensheviks after October: Socialist Opposition and the Rise of the Bolshevik Dictatorship.* Ithaca, N.Y.: Cornell University Press, 1987.

————. *The Bolsheviks in Russian Society: The Revolution and the Civil Wars.* New Haven, Conn.: Yale University Press, 1997.

Chamberlin, William Henry. *The Russian Revolution,* 2 vols. New York: Grosset and Dunlap, 1963.

Cohen, Stephen. *Bukharin and the Bolshevik Revolution: A Political Biography.* New York: Knopf, 1980.

Conquest, Robert. *The Great Terror: A Reassessment.* New York: Oxford University Press, 1990.

————. *Harvest of Sorrow: Soviet Collectivization and the Terror-Famine.* New York: Oxford University Press, 1986.

Daniels, Robert V. *The Conscience of the Revolution.* Cambridge, Mass.: Harvard University Press, 1965.

Deutscher, Isaac. *The Prophet Armed. Trotsky: 1879–1921, Vol. 1.* New York: Vintage, 1965.

————. *The Prophet Unarmed. Trotsky: 1921–1929, Vol. 2.* New York: Vintage, 1965.

Figes, Orlando. *A People's Tragedy: The Russian Revolution, 1891–1924.* New York: Penguin, 1998.

Gerson, Leonard. *The Secret Police in Lenin's Russia.* Philadelphia: Temple University Press, 1976.

Glantz, David M., and Jonathan House. *When Titans Clashed: How the Red Army Stopped Hitler.* Lawrence: University Press of Kansas, 1995.

Gorlizki, Yoram, and Oleg Khlevniuk. *Cold Peace: Stalin and the Soviet Ruling Circle, 1945–1953.* Oxford and New York: Oxford University Press, 2004.

Gregory, Paul, and Valery Lazarev, eds. *The Economics of Forced Labor: The Soviet Gulag.* Stanford, Calif.: Hoover Institution Press, 2004.

Holloway, David. *The Soviet Union and the Arms Race.* New Haven, Conn.: Yale University Press, 1984.

————. *Stalin and the Bomb: The Soviet Union and Atomic Energy.* New Haven, Conn.: Yale University Press, 1994.

Ivanova, Galina Mikhailovna. *Labor Camp Socialism: The Gulag in the Soviet Totalitarian System.* Translated by Carol A. Flath. Armonk, N.Y.: M.E. Sharpe, 2000.

Jakobson, Michael. *Origins of the Gulag: The Soviet Prison Camp System, 1917–1934.* Lexington: University Press of Kentucky, 1993.

Janson, Marc, and Nikita Petrov. *Stalin's Loyal Executioner: People's Commissar Nikolai Ezhov.* Stanford, Calif.: Hoover Institution Press, 2002.

Jasny, Naum. *Soviet Industrialization 1928–1952.* Chicago: University of Chicago Press, 1961.

Kenez, Peter. *The Birth of the Propaganda State: Soviet Methods of Mass Mobilization, 1917–1929.* Cambridge: Cambridge University Press, 1985.

Khlevniuk, Oleg V. *The History of the Gulag: From Collectivization to the Great Terror.* New Haven, Conn., and London: Yale University Press, 2004.

Kotkin, Stephen. *Magnetic Mountain: Stalinism as a Civilization.* Berkeley: University of California Press, 1995.

Laqueur, Walter. *Stalin: The Glasnost Revelations.* New York: Scribner, 1990.

Lewin, Moshe. *Lenin's Last Struggle.* Translated by A. M. Sheridan Smith. New York: Pantheon, 1968.

Mastny, Vojtech. *The Cold War and Soviet Insecurity: The Stalin Years.* New York: Oxford University Press, 1996.

———. *Russia's Road to Cold War: Diplomacy, Warfare, and the Politics of Communism, 1941–1945.* New York: Columbia University Press, 1979.

McNeal, Robert A. *Stalin: Man and Ruler.* New York: New York University Press, 1988.

Medvedev, Roy A. *Let History Judge.* Translated by Colleen Taylor. New York: Vintage, 1971.

Pipes, Richard. *Russia Under the Bolshevik Regime.* New York: Knopf, 1993.

Pipes, Richard, ed. *The Unknown Lenin: From the Secret Archive.* New Haven, Conn.: Yale University Press, 1996.

Merridale, Catherine. *Ivan's War: Life and Death in the Red Army, 1939–1945.* New York: Henry Holt, 2006.

Montefiore, Simon Sebag. *Stalin: The Court of the Red Tsar.* New York: Knopf, 2004.

Nekrich, Aleksandr. *The Punished Peoples: The Deportation and Fate of Soviet Minorities at the End of the Second World War.* New York: Norton, 1978.

Overy, Richard. *Russia's War: A History of the Soviet War Effort, 1941–1945.* New York: Penguin, 1998.

Rabinowitch, Alexander. *The Bolsheviks Come to Power.* New York: Norton, 1976.

Schapiro, Leonard. *The Origin of the Communist Autocracy.* New York: Praeger, 1965.

————. *The Russian Revolutions of 1917: The Origins of Modern Communism.* New York: Basic Books, 1984.

Service, Robert. *The Bolshevik Party in Revolution.* New York: Barnes and Noble, 1979.

————. *Lenin: A Political Life, Vol. 2: Worlds in Collision.* Bloomington: Indiana University Press, 1991.

————. *Lenin: A Political Life, Vol. 3: The Iron Ring.* Bloomington: Indiana University Press, 1995.

————. *Stalin: A Biography.* Cambridge, Mass.: Belknap Press of Harvard University Press, 2005.

Solzhenitsyn, Aleksandr. *The Gulag Archipelago.* 3 vols. Translated by Thomas P. Whitney. New York: Harper and Row, 1973, 1975, 1978.

Stone, David R. *Hammer and Rifle: The Militarization of the Soviet Union, 1926–1933.* Lawrence: University Press of Kansas, 2000.

Theen, Rolf H. W. *Lenin.* Princeton, N.J.: Princeton University Press, 1973.

Thompson, John M. *Revolutionary Russia, 1917.* New York: Scribner, 1981.

Tolstoy, Nikolai. *Stalin's Secret War.* Translated by George Saunders. New York: Holt, Rinehart and Winston, 1981.

Trotsky, Leon. *Stalin: An Appraisal of the Man and His Era.* Edited and translated by Charles Malamuth. New York: Grosset and Dunlap, 1941.

Tucker, Robert C. *Stalin as Revolutionary.* New York: Norton, 1990.

————. *Stalin in Power: The Revolution from Above, 1928–1941.* New York: Norton, 1977.

Tucker, Robert C., ed. *Stalinism: Essays in Historical Interpretation.* New York: Norton, 1976.

Ulam, Adam. *Stalin.* New York: Viking, 1973.

Volkogonov, Dmitri. *Lenin: A New Biography.* Edited and translated by Harold Shukman. New York: Free Press, 1994.

————. *Stalin: Triumph and Tragedy.* Edited and translated by Harold Shukman. Rocklin, Calif.: Prima, 1992.

Werth, Alexander. *Russia at War, 1941–1945.* New York: Dutton, 1964.

Soviet Russia, 1953–1991: Reform, Decline, and Collapse

Adelman, Deborah. *The "Children of Perestroika" Come of Age: Young People of Moscow Talk about Life in the New Russia.* Armonk, N.Y., and London: M.E. Sharpe, 1994.

Breslauer, George W. *Khrushchev and Brezhnev as Leaders.* London: George Allen and Unwin, 1982.

Burlatsky, Fedor. *Khrushchev and the First Russian Spring: The Era of Khrushchev through the Eyes of His Advisor.* Translated by Daphne Skillen. New York: Scribner, 1988.

Cohen, Stephen, et al., eds. *The Soviet Union since Stalin.* Bloomington: Indiana University Press, 1980.

d'Encausse, Hélène. *Confiscated Power.* Translated by George Holoch. New York: Harper and Row, 1982.

Desai, Padma. *Perestroika in Perspective: The Design and Dilemmas of Soviet Reform.* Princeton, N.J.: Princeton University Press, 1989.

Dornberg, John. *Brezhnev: The Masks of Power.* New York: Basic Books, 1974.

Fitzer, Donald. *The Khrushchev Era: De-Stalinization and the Limits of Reform in the USSR, 1953–1964.* London: Macmillan, 1993.

Goldman, Marshall. *What Went Wrong with Perestroika.* New York and London: Norton, 1992.

Hosking, Geoffrey. *The Awakening of the Soviet Union.* Cambridge, Mass.: Harvard University Press, 1990.

Kaiser, Robert. *Why Gorbachev Happened: His Triumphs, His Failure, and His Fall.* New York: Simon and Schuster, 1992.

Lewin, Moshe. *The Gorbachev Phenomenon: A Historical Interpretation.* Berkeley and Los Angeles: University of California Press, 1988.

Linden, Carl A. *Khrushchev and the Soviet Leadership.* Baltimore: Johns Hopkins University Press, 1990.

Medvedev, Roy A., and Zhores A. Medvedev. *Khrushchev: The Years in Power.* Translated by Andrew R. Durkin. New York: Columbia University Press, 1975.

Remnick, David. *Lenin's Tomb: The Last Days of the Soviet Empire.* New York: Random House, 1993.

Rubinstein, Joshua. *Soviet Dissidents.* Boston: Beacon Press, 1980.

Satter, David. *Age of Delusion.* New York: Knopf, 1996.

Smith, Hedrick. *The Russians.* New York: Ballantine Books, 1976.

Tompson, William J. *Khrushchev: A Political Life.* New York: St. Martin's Press, 1995.

Voslensky, Michael. *Nomenklatura: The Soviet Ruling Class.* Translated by Erich Mosbacher. Garden City, N.Y.: Doubleday, 1984.

Post–Soviet Russia

Gustafson, Thane. *Capitalism Russian-Style.* New York: Cambridge University Press, 1999.

Lowenhardt, John. *The Reincarnation of Russia: Struggling with the Legacy of Communism, 1990–1994.* Durham, N.C.: Duke University Press, 1994.

McFaul, Michael. *Russia's Unfinished Revolution: Political Change from Gorbachev to Putin.* Ithaca, N.Y., and London: Cornell University Press, 2001.

Meier, Andrew. *Black Earth: A Journey through Russia after the Fall.* New York: Norton, 2003.

Satter, David. *Darkness at Dawn: The Rise of the Russian Criminal State.* New Haven, Conn., and London: Yale University Press, 2003.

Service, Robert. *Russia: Experiment with People.* Cambridge, Mass.: Harvard University Press, 2002.

Shevtsova, Lilia. *Yeltsin's Russia: Myths and Realities.* Washington, D.C.: Carnegie Endowment for International Peace, 1999.

———. *Putin's Russia.* Washington, D.C.: Carnegie Endowment for International Peace, 2003.

Simes, Dmitri K. *After the Collapse: Russia Seeks Its Place as a Great Power.* New York: Simon and Schuster, 1999.

Strayer, Robert. *Why Did the Soviet Union Collapse: Understanding Historical Change.* Armonk, N.Y.: M.E. Sharpe, 1998.

Yeltsin, Boris. *Against the Grain: An Autobiography.* Translated by Michael Glenny. New York: Summit Books, 1990.

INDEX

Note: **Boldface** page numbers indicate primary discussion of a topic. Page numbers in *italic* indicate illustrations. The letters *c, m,* and *t* indicate chronology, maps, and tables, respectively.